The Russian Intelligentsia

The Russian Intelligentsia

Edited by RICHARD PIPES

1961

COLUMBIA UNIVERSITY PRESS, NEW YORK

This group of essays originated in the American Academy
of Arts and Sciences and was first published in the
summer 1960 issue of its journal *Dædalus*.

RICHARD PIPES

Foreword

HIGH ON THE LIST of surprises the twentieth century has brought us
stands the unexpected growth in numbers and importance of two
social and cultural groups, the bureaucracy and the intelligentsia.
In the classical period of liberal and socialist thought these groups
were not generally considered of critical importance for the course
of human progress. Attention then was focused on the institution
of property, and the future was seen either in terms of the growth
and spread of that institution or in terms of its abolition. For that
reason social thought in the nineteenth century was to a large extent
dominated by the problem of the relationship between the propertied
and nonpropertied classes, and the habit of viewing social events in
this light still prevails in many parts of the world to this day, even
though the conditions which gave rise to it are rapidly disappearing.

In our century the place of property is taken by knowledge,
because our political and economic well-being depend to an ever
increasing degree on science, technology, and administrative tech-
nique. Large-scale organization, characteristic of modern activity,
further reduces the importance of private ownership. More and
more, it is not the possession of material property, decisive in landed
and commercial economies, but the possession of scientific insight,
technical skill, and experience that determines one's place in society.
In this connection there arise two groups, the bureaucrats and intellectuals, who as repositories of knowledge acquire a position of
leadership in society. The relations between them—sometimes
friendly and accommodating, more often bitterly hostile—constitute
one of the most critical problems of our time.

The following group of essays deals with one aspect of this
problem, namely, the condition and prospects of a body of intellectuals known in Russia, pre-Revolutionary and Soviet, as the intelligentsia. In Russia the question of the social function and historic

mission of the intellectuals always had and still has a particular urgency, first of all, because the early and rapid Westernization of the country produced an extraordinarily large, virile, and self-conscious body of intellectuals, and, second, because there modernization has been carried out with greater intensity and single-mindedness than anywhere else in the world. The intellectuals' reactions to modern changes, their successes and failures in accommodating themselves to the new order, their relations with the other groups of the population, and in particular the technical and administrative bureaucracy—all these are matters of interest not only to the Russian specialist but also to others, because they emerge in one form or another in every modern or "modernizing" country.

I think I speak for all the contributors to this volume when I say that we entertain no illusions of having solved, exhausted, or even fully outlined the problem to which we are addressing ourselves. There are two main reasons why this should be so. In the first place, the problem itself, real though it is, cannot be formulated in a precise and universally acceptable manner. What is the "Russian intelligentsia," or, for that matter, an "intellectual" or *intelligent* anywhere? As the passage quoted by Leopold Labedz at the beginning of his essay suggests, these terms can mean all sorts of things to all sorts of people. Some use the term intelligentsia to refer to anyone engaged in nonphysical labor, whether he be a lyric poet or a veterinarian (such, for example, is the official Soviet definition); others apply it to a person with a liberal education regardless of the nature of his employment; yet others confine it to persons critically disposed to the existing economic and political order, and ready to sacrifice themselves in order to change it fundamentally in accord with some higher (but secular) ideal. Ultimately, the criterion turns out to be a subjective one, and to define the term "intelligentsia" with any degree of accuracy it would be necessary to have free access to all the groups which could possibly come within the meaning of the term. But this, for obvious reasons, is not possible. The lack of direct access to the Russian intelligentsia of today constitutes the second great difficulty facing the authors of this volume. It has compelled us to rely far more than we would have wished on fragmentary evidence, on inference, and on historical and sociological analogy.

The nature of the problem and of the evidence has helped to shape the format of this volume. Rather than seek a comprehensive treatment of the intelligentsia in Russia, it has seemed preferable to concentrate on several crucial aspects of the problem. To begin with, there is the question of the character of the pre-Revolutionary intelligentsia, in particular, its attitude toward civic responsibility. The first of these topics is treated by Martin Malia, the second, from different standpoints, by Leonard Schapiro and Boris Elkin.

The middle part of this volume is devoted to the Soviet intelligentsia. My own paper endeavors to find in Russian history and in the experience of intellectuals in other modern societies clues to developments within the Soviet Union. Mr. Labedz seeks to define the term "intelligentsia," as it is officially used in the Soviet Union, by analyzing the social groups included in this category by Soviet statisticians. The other essays in this section deal with particular social or professional groups in which one may expect to find attitudes broadly defined as intellectual. David Burg describes, on the basis of extensive personal experience and a close study of Soviet printed sources, the social and political attitudes of students at higher educational institutions in the Soviet Union. Leopold H. Haimson traces the conflict between generations of intellectuals, in particular, that between the present-day younger generation and the one that came of age in the heyday of Stalinism. Max Hayward takes a look at professional Soviet writers. Finally, David Joravsky and Gustav Wetter discuss the relationship between the natural scientists and official ideology in the Soviet Union in the first two decades of the Communist regime, and since the death of Stalin, respectively.

The third and last part tries, by means of two essays dealing with intellectuals in two other non-democratic countries, to give the discussion a certain amount of comparative depth. This section consists of essays dealing with intellectuals in contemporary Spain by Julián Marías, and with intellectuals in Communist China (with some allusions to their Russian counterparts) by Benjamin Schwartz. Appended to this volume are translations of two important Soviet documents which touch directly on matters raised in several of the essays. One is a letter sent to Boris Pasternak by the editorial office of the journal *Novyi Mir*, explaining the reasons for its rejection of *Dr. Zhivago*, and spelling out its dissatisfaction with Pasternak's treatment of the intelligentsia. The other represents the record of a conference held in October 1958 on the critical subject of the philosophic implications of modern science.

It is hoped that from these diverse papers the readers will obtain a somewhat clearer picture of a problem which, although perhaps especially acute in the Soviet Union, in some measure affects everyone concerned with the survival of liberal values and critical attitudes.

Contents

The Russian Intelligentsia

MARTIN MALIA

What Is the Intelligentsia?

To BLASÉ WESTERNERS one of the most engaging qualities of the
Russian intellectuals of the old regime is the moral passion with
which they attacked the great questions of the human condition, and
their pursuit to a ruthlessly logical conclusion—in life no less than in
thought—of the heady answers such exalted inquiry invariably brings.
It is this quality which the two giants of the tradition, Tolstoy and
Dostoevsky, in spite of so much that separates them, have in common and which gives Russian literature of the last century its unique
character and power. In lesser figures this same moral quest is often
expressed just as intensely but with a naïve, utilitarian bluntness that
is conveyed by such classic titles of their works as *Who Is To
Blame?*, *What Is To Be Done?*, *Who Are The Friends of The People?* Like Marx, whom some of them eventually followed to a shattering outcome of their searchings, they wished "not just to understand the world, but to change it."

Still, they had first to understand, and their moral utilitarianism
was ultimately founded on an exacerbated faculty of introspection.
Their initial question was always, "Who are we?"—as individuals, as
Russians, as thinking men in a barbarous society. A more pragmatic
way of putting the same question was, "What is the intelligentsia?"
The number of works so entitled is legion, with almost as many different, ardent answers. The subject of this essay, then, is one of the
classic questions of modern Russian life, yet about which it is always possible to say something new, since it is as rich as that life
itself.

The term intelligentsia was introduced into the Russian language
in the 1860's by a minor novelist named Boborykin, and became current almost immediately. This fact is of more than anecdotal significance, for it suggests that the group so designated did not acquire

1

full awareness of its identity until that time. Yet almost all authorities would agree that the origins of the group itself went back to the "circles" of the 1830's and 1840's, which introduced into Russia the ideological turn of mind in the form of German philosophical idealism. Still, the fact that there was a term for the group under Alexander II, whereas there was none under Nicholas I, indicates a watershed in its development that coincides with the beginning of the Great Reforms after 1855.

It was Turgenev who, in his greatest novel, gave the classical terminology to describe these two stages: the aristocratic "fathers" and the plebeian "sons." Very roughly, the intellectual difference between the two was the difference between idealists and materialists; nevertheless, both were what Napoleon once contemptuously dubbed "ideologues." A third stage came after the assassination of Alexander II in 1881 with the advent of a more heterogeneous body sometimes baptized the "grandsons," or the various Populist, Marxist, liberal, and neo-Kantian groups of the turn of the century, who revived in different ways the legacy of their predecessors, but who remained just as thoroughly ideological.

It is this primacy of the ideological that is fundamental to the group as a whole; the intelligentsia, therefore, should not be taken to mean just the revolutionary opposition. Indeed, the word ever since its creation has had at least two overlapping uses: either all men who think independently—of whom Pisarev's "critically thinking realists," or "nihilists," were only the most extreme and famous manifestation; or, more narrowly, the intellectuals of the opposition, whether revolutionary or not. "Fathers," "sons," and "grandsons," therefore, are all unmistakably intelligentsia, and might for convenience's sake be designated "classical intelligentsia."

There are two other groups, however, which are candidates for inclusion under the same rubric. Some writers on the subject would consider as intelligentsia all oppositional figures since the end of the eighteenth century, including Radishchev and Novikov under Catherine II and the Decembrists under Alexander I. Yet here we find nothing approaching a consensus, and this in itself indicates that although these figures had certain characteristics in common with their successors, they were not quite the real thing. Because of this equivocal status, therefore, they are best considered as no more than a "proto-intelligentsia," and though some account must be taken of them here, they will not be central to the story.

Finally, it is clear that after 1917 the term intelligentsia suffered a drastic change. Although Marxism makes no provision for such a class, the Soviet regime has officially proclaimed what it calls the intelligentsia as one of the three pillars of the socialist order, together with the proletariat and the toiling peasantry. The term, however, no longer has any connotations of "critical" thought, because all questions have now been answered; still less does it have the connotation of opposition. In Soviet usage intelligentsia means simply all those who "toil" with their minds instead of with their hands, that is, the technological, liberal-professional, managerial, administrative, or merely white-collar personnel of the state. Only the Party presents a partial exception to this definition, for, as we shall see, it has preserved something of the intelligentsia's spirit, if not of its personnel. Otherwise, the Soviet intelligentsia is so different from its predecessor as to deserve a separate name—such as Trotsky's "bureaucracy" or Djilas' "new class"—and just as certainly, a different mode of analysis.

This discussion, therefore, will be limited to what has been called the "classical" and "proto-"intelligentsias. In addition, it should be said that, since the subject is complex, much simplification is inevitable. In the remarks that follow, the emphasis will be on the more radical and revolutionary elements of the intelligentsia, who, if they were by no means the whole of the movement in the nineteenth century, are a likely choice for special consideration in a general survey for the practical reason that they eventually had the greatest impact on history.

The word intelligentsia itself most probably is no more than the Latin *intelligentia*—discernment, understanding, intelligence—pronounced with a Russian accent.* Yet such bold use of a term for an abstract mental faculty to designate a specific group of people obviously implies a very exalted notion of that group's importance, and its members—*intelligenty*, "the intelligent or intellectual ones"—are clearly more than intellectuals in the ordinary sense. Whether merely "critically thinking" or actively oppositional, their name indicates that they thought of themselves as the embodied "intelligence," "understanding," or "consciousness" of the nation. In other words, they clearly felt an exceptional sense of apartness from the society in which they lived. To use an old qualificative of German idealism which the intelligentsia in its more lucid moments understood only too well, and which in a diluted sociological meaning now enjoys a great vogue in America, they were clearly "alienated" intellectuals of some sort.

* See Note at the end of this essay.

Alienated intellectuals, of course, exist everywhere, even in such sound societies as Britain and the United States. In Britain they fulminate in anger against the injustice that keeps them "outsiders." In America, where they seem to have more money, they formerly emigrated to Paris and its Left Bank and got "lost"; at present, and somewhat more democratically, they hitch-hike to California and become "beat." In each of these cases, however, the most that results is picturesque behavior and a few novels, which in college classrooms inspire the next generation's quest for identity and its consequent revolt against parents, authority, and convention. Still the peace of society is never fundamentally disturbed, even when in times of exceptional stress matters go to the point of voting for Henry Wallace or forming a small Communist party.

The alienation of the Russian intellectual was far deeper, however, and its social impact infinitely more devastating. In any society, individuals who take thought seriously experience an alienation which arises from a tension between the ideal and the real, or between what the individual wishes to become and what society permits him to be. In Russia this phenomenon was pushed to its ultimate development. It led to the formation of what can only be termed a separate social category, indeed, a "class." Lest this term seem too strong, it should be pointed out that not only did the intelligentsia assume a distinctive name, but other, more indubitably "real" classes accepted this name and the apartness it connoted as justified. To be sure, the other classes and the government did not concede the intelligentsia's pretention to be the incarnate consciousness of Russia, but they took account of its existence as a fact and, with time, as a force.

Indeed, so real was this force that for decades the intelligentsia was able to exert a political pressure on the autocracy greater than that exercised by more palpable classes such as the gentry or the bourgeoisie. Moreover, when the collapse of the old order came, one faction of the intelligentsia was able to exploit the furies of peasant and worker anarchy to the extent of assuming absolute power over all classes more "real" than it, before being dissolved in the conditions created by its own success. No class in Russian history has had a more momentous impact on the destinies of that nation or indeed of the modern world. In defining it, therefore, we would do well to bend our categories to its characteristics, rather than to attempt to reduce it to the familiar and the known with minor adjustments for "alienation."

This does not mean that the Russian intelligentsia is absolutely *sui generis* in modern history. Both in its headily ideological temper and in its impact on the world it is in many ways comparable to the French *philosophes* of the Enlightenment and to the German romantic thinkers of the years between 1770 and 1840. Indeed, it borrowed most of its fundamental ideas from one or another offshoot of these traditions. Nevertheless, the Russian intelligentsia is sufficiently different from all similar groups of intellectuals to be treated as a distinct social category, and thus to make necessary a thorough-going revision of our usual notions of class in attempting to account for it.

It is precisely the failure to make this revision that explains much of the confusion in discussions of the intelligentsia. No recognized system of social analysis, either those known to the intelligentsia itself or those elaborated since by modern sociology, makes provision for a "class" held together only by the bond of "consciousness," "critical thought," or moral passion. Most writers on the problem, therefore, have concluded that the intelligentsia must be founded on something other than ideology alone. One suggestion, made at the end of the last century by the Populist, Mikhailovsky, is that the *intelligenty* were "conscience-stricken noblemen," but since large numbers of the intelligentsia were clearly not noble, this does not get us very far. Another school of thought, represented most melodramatically by Berdiaev, holds that the *intelligenty* were largely sons of priests and that their cult of absolute reason was a demonic perversion of the absolute faith of Orthodoxy; in fact, however, only a minority of the intelligentsia came from the clergy.

A more sophisticated version of these two approaches consists of an attempt to give the intelligentsia a separate rather than a derivative position in the old-regime system of legal "estates" which existed in Russia down to 1917. In this view (the most widespread among the intelligentsia itself under Alexander II) the intelligentsia were the *raznochintsy*, that is, "people of diverse rank," or "people of no estate in particular." Concretely, this meant those stray individuals who were left over after Peter the Great, who gave the Russian estate system its final form, had exhausted all the more obvious social, economic, or bureaucratic categories. In other words, the notion of *raznochintsy* was, by definition, not very meaningful in the Russian estate system, particularly by the nineteenth century, when the system was beginning to disintegrate. Moreover, the intelligentsia also clearly came from all the other recognized and more meaningful estates: the gentry, the clergy, the merchantry, and even eventually the peasantry. Therefore, it was made up of *raznochintsy* only in the loose sense that it was from all estates in general and from no one estate in particular, and that as its members moved away from their estate of origin they became *déclassé*. One of the primary characteristics of the *intelligenty*, then, was that they could no longer fit into the official estate system.

The Marxist intellectuals were hardly more successful when their turn came to explain "who they were," for where does the intelligentsia belong in the economic definition of class that divides society into feudal aristocracy, bourgeoisie, proletariat, etc.? Still, the problem had to be faced, and since the intelligentsia was more or less a "middle class" between the gentry and the people, Lenin made a valiant stab at defining it as a "bourgeois intelligentsia," although in some way that was not explained he nonetheless considered that his type of intelligentsia really represented the proletariat. It is hard to see how he could have done much better, since in this system of classification the intelligentsia cannot be anything but "middle class," and yet they fit no meaningful economic notion of a "capitalistic bourgeoisie." At the most, they could be only a "petty bourgeoisie," but this class, in Marxist theory, is not the vanguard of the assault against "feudal" autocracy that the intelligentsia clearly represented.

Nor can the intelligentsia be accounted for by refining the socio-economic approach to say that a class is determined by the way its members make their living, and that intellectual work creates a different mentality than is created by manual labor or business. Such a classification can establish the identity of a professional class as opposed to a business or working class. But by no means all members of the Russian professional class were *révolté*; quite a number of them were successful and "integrated" professors, doctors, or lawyers. Yet if this is so, why should other "intellectual workers" of very similar background set themselves apart as an intelligentsia?

It is this confused catalogue of class definitions which is the legacy of the question of the intelligentsia, and it must be faced before it is possible to move in new directions. The intelligentsia's agonies of introspection, however, have not been entirely in vain; there is much that is partially true in their speculations. The intelligentsia came, in fact, from all estates in general and from no one estate in particular, in the loose meaning of *raznochintsy*. It did begin in the gentry, owed much to the clergy, and with time came increasingly to be dominated by commoners of more and more indeterminate origin. Herzen and Bakunin were unmistakably gentry; Chernyshevsky and Dobroliubov came just as clearly from the clergy; Zheliabov or

Tkachev, Lenin, Trotsky, or Stalin, Martov or Chernov, are harder to place in a meaningful spectrum of estates. At the same time, if the intelligentsia was not very "bourgeois" economically, it clearly occupied the middle social position, between the gentry Establishment and the masses, of a bourgeoisie that did not exist, or that at least was inarticulate. Finally, there was something about it of a petty-bourgeois class of "intellectual workers" gravitating around the editorial offices of the "thick journals" in which they labored.

Even the sum of these partial truths does not give the whole truth, however, and we are still faced with the dilemma with which we started. Since efforts to define the intelligentsia as a discrete phenomenon in and for itself inevitably seem to fail, the only remaining solution is to approach it in terms of the "dynamics" of its position in Russian society as a whole. The classical approach to the problem has been through analytical abstraction; let us now examine the concrete historical conditions under which this "class" emerged.

The historian Kliuchevsky has aptly emphasized the extreme simplicity of Russian historical processes as compared to those of Western European countries, a fact which derives largely from the rudimentary nature of the Russian class structure under the old regime. Until well into the nineteenth century there were in effect only two classes in Russia, or at least only two that counted. There was the aristocracy or gentry (*dvorianstvo*), which in spite of its small numbers possessed almost all the wealth, monopolized all privilege, and alone participated in the higher life of the nation. Then there was the peasantry, which was important, not because of any active role in the national life, but because it was so dangerous, at least potentially, since it was both so oppressed and so huge—roughly ninety percent of the population. To be sure, other estates existed as well—the merchants and the clergy—but they were insignificant numerically and counted for even less socially. Under such circumstances the Russian government could be only a very simple and brutal affair: a military autocracy ruling through an irresponsible bureaucracy, officered of course by the gentry, and whose principal function was to maintain order internally and wage war externally.

This system worked admirably throughout the eighteenth century, defeating Swedes, Poles, and Turks and suppressing Pugachev and his peasant hordes. Its success, however, rested on a precarious equilibrium and concealed an acute intrinsic instability. As Pugachev said on his capture in 1774: "I am not the raven but the fledgling, and the real raven is still hovering in the heavens." There was yet

7

another menace to this structure: "critical thought." With great prescience, Joseph de Maistre remarked at the beginning of the nineteenth century, when the fermentation of ideas had barely begun in Russia, that the real danger to order in the country was not the peasants as such but an eventual *"Pougatchev d'université."* It was from the conjunction of these two intuitions that the radical intelligentsia would soon be born: men reared on the general theories of the universities would reach out to greet the hovering democratic storm of a new *Pugachevshchina.* They would have to wait a long time, almost a century, but eventually their dream would come true, if not exactly in the form that all of them had dreamed it.

Nevertheless, de Maistre was more nearly right than Pugachev: the new democratic storm began to gather at the top, rather than at the bottom, of Russian society. The first rumblings were heard in the last years of Catherine II and under Alexander I among the most privileged order, the gentry. Contrary to what is often asserted, the cause of this was not primarily Western "influence"—the gallicization of the gentry, the reading of the *philosophes,* and conversion to the rights of man. The trouble began because under Catherine the gentry for the first time acquired those rights in fact.

Until 1762 the gentry had been bound to serve the state in the same way the peasants were bound to serve their masters: they were in a sense the serfs, although highly privileged serfs, of the autocrat. Since in reality, however, they held all the levers of command in the army and the bureaucracy, they were in time able to extort from the monarchy the grant of unconditional personal liberty. After 1762 they were free to "serve" the state or not to serve, as they chose; they could dispose of themselves and their property entirely as they deemed fit. In consequence, they developed the attitudes of free men, a sense of personal dignity, of pride, even a touchy independence—in a word, all those endowments modern humanism claims for man. It is for this reason that they became Westernized, and took over such ready-made ideological justifications of their new individuality as Montesquieu's "honor," Voltaire's "natural reason," or, in more extreme cases, Rousseau's democratic "rights of man."

Nonetheless, the monarchy remained autocratic, and the gentry's new-found "humanity" was a product of tolerance rather than of imprescriptible right; they lived constantly at the mercy of a capricious return to integral autocracy, such as in fact occurred under Paul. Still worse, if they had any sense of the logic that natural reason commanded, they could not but be disturbed by the contrast between their liberty and the servitude of the majority. With each new generation, raised by French tutors, amidst general principles and ideas, and remote from "life," the sense of moral scandal at the spectacle of autocracy and serfdom grew more acute. How, they asked, can some be free unless all are free, and unless the very principle of servitude that menaces everyone—autocracy—is eradicated? With each generation of freedom, the younger, better educated, more humane members of the gentry generalized from a sense of their own dignity as individuals to the ideal of human dignity for all. Such, by 1790, was the meaning of the protests of Novikov and Radishchev.

This is not to say that a majority of the gentry felt this way. Most of them, particularly after they had inherited the family estate, had the "good sense" to realize that the best way to insure their own independence was to maintain "order," and to keep the peasants in their place, for which it was necessary to preserve the paternal police force of autocracy. There was, however, in each generation a minority of the young and sensitive who put principle before privilege and demanded an end to the existing barbarous state of affairs. It is this primacy of general ideals over immediate interests, and the consequent alienation of the young gentry from their official class, that made of them, by the reign of Alexander I, a prefiguration of the intelligentsia. Held together by no other bonds of cohesion than youth, idealism, and a humane sensitivity, this gentry opposition, goaded to desperation by Alexander's reluctance to reform, at last in 1825 embarked on a military assault against autocracy and serfdom. The Decembrists, as they came to be called, failed, but the shock of their action precipitated the full development of the intelligentsia they had adumbrated.

Perhaps the principal reason for refusing to call the Decembrists *intelligenty* is that, although in their supreme moment they placed ideals before interests, ideas were by no means the whole of their lives. The Decembrists were primarily army officers, men of the world and of action; moreover, in spite of their opinions, they continued to serve the state. Even their revolt was strictly an affair among gentlemen, with no participation by the people, and was designed to take over the existing state from within rather than to destroy it from without. The real intelligentsia came into being only under Nicholas I, when the next generation of young gentry idealists became totally alienated from the state and were left with ideas alone as their whole world.

After the close call for Russia's precariously balanced order that attended his accession, Nicholas, together with the majority of the gentry, was obsessed by the possibility of further betrayal by the educated elite, as well as by the permanent anarchic menace of the masses. Thus, he excluded the now unreliable gentry as much as possible from participation in government, and instead relied on more docile bureaucratic servants. Iron discipline was enforced in the army and the country at large, and captious individualism and "free-thinking" were put down wherever the Emperor's Third Section detected their presence. Matters only grew worse as "red" disorder erupted again, in the Polish lands of the Empire in 1830, and then all over Europe in 1848. The Russian military autocracy quite rightly felt mortally menaced by such developments and defended its existence with all the vigor it could command.

Under such circumstances the more sensitive younger members of the gentry obviously would have no more to do with the state than it would with them. Whereas in 1812 the highest form of idealism had been to serve in the army, after 1825 to serve in Nicholas' national and international "gendarmerie" was a betrayal of all idealism and humanity. The result of this was an exodus of the young gentry from "service" to the universities. Whereas in the generation of Pushkin and the Decembrists, almost all the significant figures of Russian culture had been either army officers or men close to the aristocratic and court circles of the capital—in other words, highly integrated into official society—under Nicholas, and forever after, almost all such figures, the nonpolitical writers no less than the revolutionaries, received their decisive formation in and around the universities and, in varying degrees, were at odds with official society.

The impact of the universities was to transform their noble charges from gentry intellectuals into intellectuals from the gentry, or from dilettante "ideologues" into professional writers, critics, and professors. Just as important, the universities changed them from idealists in the everyday sense into idealists in the metaphysical sense. Following Schelling and Hegel, they came to believe that the essence of the universe was idea, and that the whole of nature and history culminated, indeed acquired meaning and reality, only in the "consciousness" of man, and that they, therefore, were the bearers of the Absolute Idea. Thus, their chief activity and their only sphere of free endeavor was exalted to the level of the first principle of life. In short, the universities made the more serious younger gentry morally *déclassé*, a rootless "internal emigration" with no home but its ideal visions.

At the same time the universities brought together these noblemen with other young men from the lower orders, the clergy, the minor professional and bureaucratic classes, or the famous *raznochintsy*, if that term is taken not in its legal meaning but in the loose sense of all those who came to the university and the higher life of the mind from estates below the gentry. These men had risen only painfully from poverty and social obscurity, making their way precariously by tutoring, translations, or petty journalism, to attain to the dignity of knowledge and that "consciousness" which is liberty. Even more literally than the gentry *intelligenty*, they had no other life than ideas. If worse came to worst, a Bakunin or a Herzen could make it up with father and find refuge on the family estate; a Belinsky, a Chernyshevsky, or a Dobroliubov, if they wished to exist as "human beings," indeed if they wished to exist at all, had no choice but to labor at the tasks of *intelligentia*. This faculty alone conferred on them at the same time dignity, "personality," and the freedom of a livelihood which permitted them to escape from the oppression of their origins yet which did not make them dependent on the state.

These new men came from Belinsky's "cursed Russian reality" and from Dobroliubov's "kingdom of darkness," from provincial, clerical and petty-bourgeois squalor, patriarchal tyranny, and superstition (the epithets must be accumulated in the manner of the day), in a word, from all the human degradation of sub-gentry Russia. It is Dostoevsky who has given perhaps the most unforgettable, if highly caricatured, portraits of this type in his various Raskolnikovs, Verkhovenskys, and Kirilovs. From this "underground" world, "the humiliated and the offended" emerged to the light of the Idea, "consciousness," "humanity," "individuality," and "critical thought." Thereby they took their place beside the only "human beings" who hitherto had existed in Russia—those sons of the gentry who had already cast off the class privileges which had made them free men—and the two groups together embraced the Universal Rational Idea of Man. By the end of the reign of Nicholas the relatively mild frustration of the Decembrists had been generalized into the most sweeping, abstract, and intransigent denial of the real in the name of the ideal.

It is all these things taken together that by the 1840's created what was unmistakably an intelligentsia, at last purged of any other principle of cohesion than intellection and endowed with an exalted sense of difference from and superiority to the barbarous world around it. It is first of all in this abstract but nonetheless real ideological and

11

psychological sense that the intelligentsia constituted a distinct "class" in Russian society.

There were, nonetheless, significant class differences of a more ordinary sort within this fundamental moral unity. Although in the 1840's the intelligentsia included men from all classes, it was in fact dominated by those who came from the gentry. By the 1860's the center of gravity had shifted to the *raznochintsy*. This change, by submerging the group's only privileged element, the gentry, broke the last moorings to official society, and thereby put an end to any possible ambiguity about its separate existence. It is this development which precipitated the group's full awareness of its own identity and thus led, by the 1860's, to the adoption of the distinctive name of intelligentsia. This change, moreover, gave rise to the famous dichotomy of the "fathers" and the "sons."

To rehearse the conventional catalogue of contrasts, the fathers were philosophical idealists and romantics, while the sons were materialists and devotees of empirical science. The fathers were esthetes who believed in art for its own sake as the highest self-realization of the individual; the sons were utilitarians who accepted only a civic, pedagogical art useful for the reform of society. The fathers introduced into Russia the great ideals of humanity, reason, liberty, and democracy; the sons attempted to translate these ideals into reality. Finally, the sons were more bitter and irascible than their better-bred fathers.

The filiation between the two generations, however, was equally unmistakable, for both wished to make "cursed Russian reality" conform to the universal Ideas of Man and Reason, even though the fathers wished to accomplish this primarily by "enlightenment" or education, and the sons preferred direct action. The filiation extends even further, for both believed in the primacy of principles and the ideal vision of Justice over the intractability of everyday life, or what the vulgar call reality. This was true whether they were idealists or materialists, for, as any good empiricist or positivist could have told them, both idealism and materialism are metaphysics. A world in which ideas derive rigorously from matter is no less an ideal construct, unverifiable by scientific examination of sensory data, than a world determined by *a priori* principles. Both views are passionate ideological visions, founded on acts of faith and will, that are all the more "irresponsible" for entertaining the illusion of being founded on scientific rationality. Both fathers and sons, idealists and materialists, were men of ruthlessly logical ideology, and this bond was far stronger than the social and philosophical differences between them.

There was, however, a more concrete common denominator among the intelligentsia as well: the Russian educational system and what it led to. Roughly, down to 1825 all that counted in the country's educational life was the "cadet schools," or the various military and technical academies maintained by the state to train future officers from the gentry. Until 1825 almost everyone who counted—for instance, most of the Decembrists—came from these schools; after 1825 almost no one did.

As of the same date, civilian education was only a very recent phenomenon in Russia. To be sure, there was an Academy of Sciences that went back to 1725, and one university, that of Moscow, had been founded in 1755. But until the nineteenth century neither institution, especially the university, was impressive, and neither, in spite of Lomonosov's exceptional achievements, counted for much in national life. In effect, education as a disinterested venture in Russia began under Alexander I.

After 1803 the Imperial government for the first time set up a network of civilian educational establishments: five new universities were created; high schools (gymnasia) were established in almost all provincial capitals; something was even done for elementary education; finally, diocesan seminaries, which went back to Peter, were reformed and modernized. The government did this in part because Alexander and his advisors (his young friends on the "Official Committee" and Speransky) shared the "humanism" which would later drive the Decembrists to revolt: they sincerely believed that "enlightenment" was necessary to prepare Russia for freedom. The government did this also because it increasingly needed competent nonmilitary personnel to staff an ever more complex bureaucracy. By the 1830's and the 1840's this system was for the first time in full operation. Even Nicholas, though he hardly believed in enlightenment, could not afford to abolish the schools as a practical matter. Indeed, to meet the demands of his perfected bureaucracy, he was forced to improve them.

It was on the rungs of this ladder—seminary, gymnasium, university—that the *raznochintsy* climbed to the light of day; without it they could never have existed. It was the universities, moreover, that brought the *raznochintsy* together with the young gentry into the "circle," or discussion group, of the 1830's and 1840's, and the "student commune," or cooperative living group, of the 1860's and

13

1870's. The most down-to-earth definition one can give of the intelligentsia is to say that they were the "student youth" trained in the various establishments of the "Ministry of National Enlightenment." Indeed, for the unlettered mass of the population, an *intelligent* was anyone with a gynasium or a university training.

The alienation of the intelligentsia may be put in equally concrete terms. In a society that throughout the nineteenth century was over ninety percent illiterate, a gymnasium or a university education was in fact an extraordinary thing, which set its recipients apart in an exalted but also an extremely isolated position. In the 1840's, in any one year there were only 3,000 university students in an empire of some 40 million inhabitants; in the 1860's there were only 4,500, and in the 1870's, just a little over 5,000, out of a population of some 75 million. Quite literally then, the intelligentsia was the embodied "intelligence" of Russia. In the Hegelian language of the 1840's, they personified the penetration of the "darkness" of Russian life by the accumulation of mankind's "consciousness."

In addition to the schools, the only other "institution" which gave cohesion to the intelligentsia was the periodical press. Those intellectuals who took their mission most seriously continued after graduation—or expulsion—to live the life of ideas on the pages of the "thick journals," which served as vehicles for almost all creative culture under the old regime. Before the emergence of political conspiracy in the 1870's, these journals were the intelligentsia's sole means for making the ideal impinge on the real.

Both the schools and the "thick journals," however, were very unsatisfactory institutions for the accomplishment of the intelligentsia's high mission. The schools were subject to continual harassment by a suspicious government, and this often led to isolated protests or general disturbances, from which expulsions inevitably followed. Indeed, it is striking how large a number of *intelligenty*, from Belinsky and Herzen to Lenin, Trotsky, and Stalin, were expelled or arrested students. Then, after expulsion or return from exile, there was the further discouragement of censorship, the suppression of periodicals, and perhaps another arrest if one put too much in print. Again it is noteworthy how many leaders of the intelligentsia, from Chaadaev to Chernyshevsky and Pisarev, experienced a violent end to their journalistic careers. And once the "thick journals" were closed to them, the last recourse of the *intelligenty* was to turn from "critical thought" to revolutionary action. "Socially" or occupationally the intelligentsia was as simple as its own ruthless logic: it was a "class" of expelled students and censored journalists, who in desperation were driven to conspiratorial extremes.

Put less crudely, the dilemma of the intelligentsia was one of an unsatisfactory "circulation of elites." This does not, however, mean that there was a quantitative "overproduction" of intellectuals in Russia; on the contrary, the tiny contingent of the *intelligenty* could easily have been absorbed by the constantly expanding bureaucratic apparatus of the state or the growing range of the liberal professions. Rather there was a qualitative overproduction of "humanism" for the possibilities of mature, individual initiative offered by government service or such professions as law and teaching, both of which were largely under the tutelage of the autocracy. Education meant the development of talent, of ambition, of pride and imagination—in a word, of "individuality." But the state could accommodate only technical competence, not "individuality."

In effect, the experience of the state with its would-be intellectual servants repeated in different form the earlier experience with its military servants, the gentry. By raising each group to an exceptional position in society, the autocracy inadvertently created free men in an order based on unreflecting obedience at the top and servitude at the bottom. Since by its very nature this structure was incapable of accommodating any significant degree of individual initiative, alienation and revolt resulted.

The alienation and revolt of the "student youth," however, was much deeper than that of all save a minority of the gentry. The *raznochintsy* had no concrete privileges to give substance to their "humanity." Moreover, they were cramped in the development of their "personality," not just by the autocracy, but also by the unbending privilege of the majority of the gentry, who steadfastly refused to admit them into the Establishment. Indeed, the alienation of the intelligentsia arose much less from their sense of difference from the masses than from their hostility to the majority of the gentry, whom they considered to be poorly educated in their military schools, uninterested in ideas as such, brutal, boorish, and overbearing. Therefore, the *intelligenty*, rebuffed in their efforts at social betterment, fell back on their Human and Rational essence, and ideology became their sole means of mastery over a hostile world.

Since, however, such self-realization was somewhat abstract for creatures of flesh and blood, many of the intelligentsia eventually turned their gaze from the top to the bottom of society. Aroused by what they considered to be the incomplete and niggardly emancipation of the peasants by Alexander II, they "went to the people" to

15

learn the great human truth of a humiliation far deeper than theirs, a truth beside which their own "rationality" paled into insignificance. Their final ambition was to become the authentic spokesmen of this truth. The quest of the intelligentsia for its own "humanity" ended in the ultimate democratic pathos of "merging with the people," *narodnichestvo,* or Populism.

But how was this handful of turbulent students and ideological journalists able to play so extraordinary a role in Russian life? The answer to this question lies in the idea of Kliuchevsky with which these considerations on the historical development of the intelligentsia began, namely, the extreme simplicity of the Russian social structure under the old regime. In Western Europe, no matter how authoritarian and undemocratic society might have been, there always existed some solid interest groups which could give substance and practical meaning to the generalized protest of the intellectuals. In nineteenth-century Russia the almost total absence of such groups left a great vacuum. It was into this vacuum that the intelligentsia stepped, unfettered in their extremism by the concrete interests of anyone with a potential stake in the existing order. Thus the intelligentsia could speak with absolute purity for man in general, since they had no one to speak for in particular but themselves.

Man in general, however, could also be the people, the great anarchic base and the simplest element of all in Russian society. In spite of the Emancipation of the serfs in 1861 and of the other Great Reforms which followed, Russian society remained essentially an old regime, founded on sharp class inequalities and a lack of significant social mobility. The peasants in particular remained as poorly integrated into the structure as before. Indeed, their first taste of freedom in 1861 simply whetted their appetite for definitive elevation to the status of full "human beings." Thus, it was the ever-present possibility of exploiting the elemental destructiveness of the desperate masses that gave the Russian intelligentsia a leverage against official society which alienated intellectuals elsewhere almost always lacked.

Paradoxically, it was the disintegration of the social system which had brought the intelligentsia into being that at last gave it a chance to act. So long as Russian society remained simple, the intelligentsia failed to make contact with the masses because the very brutality of social relationships made it easy for the autocracy to keep the peasants in hand. In the 1890's, however, under the impact of rapid industrialization, Russian society began to develop the diversity of modern social classes common to the West; business, professional, and other activities in no way dependent on the state became increasingly prevalent. From 1906 on there was even a parliament, and politics became legal for the first time in modern Russian history. Thus, the sole path to self-fulfillment for a free man was no longer pure reason or revolutionary action. It became possible for the less alienated intellectuals to adapt to the real world. Under the impact of these changes the intelligentsia began to have doubts about their self-righteousness and the necessity of their apartness. By 1909, with the self-critique of *Vekhi*, this crisis of identity was thrust into the open. By 1914 bands of die-hard intelligentsia exiles, such as that grouped around Lenin, were becoming increasingly anachronistic.

At the same time this diversification of society created an unprecedented crisis for the government, for it set the masses in motion in ways unpredictable to bureaucrats trained under the old order. The still vital remnants of the radical intelligentsia, however, who for decades had been reflecting on how to foment disorder, were better prepared to cope with the new events. Indeed, this preoccupation with tactics was among the principal contributions of the "grandsons" who emerged on the scene in the 1890's at the outset of industrialization. They added little to the general principles and mentality elaborated by the "fathers" and the "sons," but they were infinitely shrewder, with the wisdom of accumulated experience, about practical revolutionary politics. Then in 1917, when the fortunes of the intelligentsia seemed at their lowest ebb, war knocked apart Russia's expiring old regime. The radical intelligentsia at last got its new *Pugachevshchina*, on which the most hardheaded, tactics-conscious "intelligent ones" rode to power.

With this triumph the extraordinary fortunes of the intelligentsia as a group came to an end, for in the new society which it created the conditions that had called it into being no longer existed. Nonetheless, even though the body of the intelligentsia died, much remained of the spirit. It has often been noted that the ordinary logic of revolutions has not obtained in Soviet Russia and that for over forty years, in spite of temporary retreats, no real Thermidor has come to put an end to the original ideological impetus. This remarkable staying-power has not been founded, however, on the continuity of the nucleus of *intelligenty* who established the regime, since most of them eventually perished at its hands. Nor is this continuity wholly supplied by the equally unconventional yet real "new class" which has come into being with the Party bureaucracy. Rather, the cohesion of the Soviet regime is most clearly founded on the primacy, for all "classes" who have held power in it, of abstract principles over life, and on a ruthless will in bending reality to the tenets of what it claims is a scientific materialism, but which, to the profane, appears as a passionate ideological vision.

How and why all this should be, however, is a problem as vast and as difficult to encompass as that of the intelligentsia itself, and one that can properly be the subject only of a separate study. Nevertheless, there is one remarkable element of continuity between the old "class" of the intelligentsia and the "new class" of the Party which must be emphasized here. The brutal utilitarian use of the ideological by the Soviets is no more than a sectarian version of the spirit of the pre-Revolutionary *intelligenty* carried to a *nec plus ultra* by the experience of power. In spite of its demise as a group, the more radical intelligentsia is with us still as a force. Its ideal vision, whatever one may think of it, has become, in a debased but potent form, the very fabric of Russian reality.

A Note on the Derivation of the Word "Intelligentsia"

No one has any documentable idea of where the word "intelligentsia" came from, but the derivation suggested here seems a plausible one. As has already been indicated, the word *intelligentsiia* emerged in the 1860's, just when the lower-class *raznochintsy* came to dominate the movement. Whereas the first foreign language of the gentry was French, the principal foreign language of the *raznochintsy*, trained as they were in the seminaries and gymnasia, was Latin, the language of clerical learning (even in Greek Orthodox Russia) and of classical humanism. Indeed, Latin was usually their principal language of higher culture —they were obliged to speak it in the seminaries—and their knowledge of modern Western languages was generally poor. For example, in *Fathers and Sons*—and Turgenev was an excellent social reporter—when the young *intelligent* Bazarov, who is of humble, lower-gentry origin, wishes to make an impression by using a foreign phrase, he does so in Latin, whereas the affluent and elegant upper-gentry family, the Kirsanovs, make their *mots* in French. Thus, Latin was something of a symbol for the cultural identity of the *raznochintsy*. Consequently, it is logical to suppose that they took a term from their school jargon to designate the value of intellection that set them apart.

This supposition is reinforced by the word *intelligent*. Nouns ending in "-ent" are very rare in Russian, and all are of foreign origin. At first glance it would seem likely that *intelligent* derives from the French adjective of the same spelling and hence most probably initially came into use among the gentry. However, the use of this adjective as a substantive is extremely rare in French, and never does it imply anything so precise as the Russian *intelligent* or even the vaguer term "intellectual." Furthermore, the gentry knew French too natively to make it likely that they would have used a word from that language in so unusual, and indeed awkward, a way. A far more likely origin grammatically is the Latin adjectival substantive *[vir] intelligens—intelligentis* in the genitive. This origin, moreover, would place the word logically in the period—the 1860's—and the milieu—that of the plebeian seminarians—to which the admittedly scant evidence indicates it in fact belongs.

LEONARD SCHAPIRO

The Pre-Revolutionary Intelligentsia and the Legal Order

CONTEMPT for the science and forms of law and a marked preference for moral principles as a guide to the good life did not, it would seem, originate with the radical intellectuals of the nineteenth century. In 1788, the dramatist Fonvizin, then aged thirty-three, made a journey to France. Writing to Count Panin of his impressions of the University of Montpellier, he noted with unconcealed delight that while the fee for lectures in philosophy was two rubles forty copecks a month, "Jurisprudence, being a science which in the present state of depravity of the human conscience is fit almost for nothing," cost very much less. Some months later he summed up his general view of France. France, he wrote, had taught him that one must distinguish liberty under the law from real liberty. The Russian, while lacking the former, was in many respects more able than the Frenchman to enjoy the latter. In contrast, the Frenchman, while enjoying legal order, on paper, in practice lived in a state of total servitude.[1]

Making a virtue of necessity is not peculiar to the Russian, and by the nineteenth century many thinking Russians were able to discern some grounds for consolation in the almost universal lawlessness which prevailed around them until the reforms of Alexander II. By the more romantic Slavophils it was even regarded as evidence of the superior moral principle which underlay the Russian state. Writing about the middle of the century, Konstantin Aksakov contrasted the historical origins of Russia with those of the countries of Western Europe. The origins of the latter, he writes, were "violence, slavery and enmity." Russia, in contrast, owed her origins as a state to "willing consent, freedom and peace." From this Aksakov deduced that the forms of state order required in each case were entirely different. In the West, relations between government and governed could be

19

founded only on force: in Russia, they rested on mutual faith and confidence. There was therefore no need in Russia for any kind of legal guarantee. Yet, he goes on to say, it will be objected that "either the people or the state power may prove false to the other," and therefore there is need for some guarantee. He immediately rejects this argument, however. "There is no need for any guarantee! Every guarantee is evil. Where it exists, there can be no virtue. It were better that life in which there is no virtue should collapse than that it should be shored up with the aid of evil."[2] (There is a parallel here to much modern Communist thought on the subject of "guarantees," but it would perhaps be unfair to Aksakov to press it too far.)

Konstantin Aksakov was an extreme romantic, whom even his contemporaries were not always able to take quite seriously. But even a sober radical like Herzen, whose love of personal liberty, at any rate, cannot be questioned even if his discernment of the means to achieve it is at times open to doubt, could see grounds for optimism in the universal Russian misrule and lawlessness. His views were fundamentally not unlike those of Aksakov. Writing about the same time, he has the following to say, which may be taken as fairly representative of the views of a good many radicals of the nineteenth century:

> The lack of legal order, which has from the earliest times hung like a cloud over the people, has at the same time been something in the nature of a schooling. The crying injustice of one half of its laws has taught the Russian people to hate the other as well: the Russian submits to the law from force alone. Complete inequality before the courts has killed in him all respect for legality. A Russian, whatever his calling, evades or violates the law whenever he can do so with impunity, and the government does exactly the same. All this is distressing and hard to bear at present, but so far as the future is concerned, it is an enormous advantage. It proves that in Russia there is no ideal, invisible government lurking behind the visible government as some sort of apotheosis of the existing order of things.[3]

But while most early nineteenth-century intellectuals would have subscribed to this vision of anarchy engendered by despair, there were notable exceptions. Such was Chaadaev, whose pessimism for the future of Russia was unrelieved by any ray of hope. In his famous *Philosophical Letters*, written in 1829, he ascribed the past and present ills of Russia squarely to the fact that Russia had developed outside the influences which had done so much to shape the path followed by the countries of Western Europe—Roman Law and the

Renaissance, for example. All the peoples of Europe, save Russia, shared in a certain common heritage of "knowledge and habits" which they absorbed unconsciously from the cradle, "together with the air they breathe." This had created in the Western European a "moral essence even before he enters the world and society," of which the foundations are the ideas of "duty, justice, law and order." The Russian alone was denied this, and had nothing to put in its place. Hence the Russian could neither take pride in the past nor hope in the future.[4]

Chaadaev's pessimism was, of course, the opposite pole of Konstantin Aksakov's naïve optimism, with the added quality that it offended the national pride of most Russians. Pushkin, a close friend of Chaadaev, who (according to tradition, perhaps, rather than to any evidence provided by works of his which have survived) shared Chaadaev's respect for Western constitutional order, gently reproved him. He had done well, Pushkin wrote, to point out that

. . . our social existence, is a sad affair. The absence of public opinion, the indifference to all duty, justice and truth, the cynical contempt for the thoughts and dignity of man are something really desolating. But I am afraid that your historical opinions may do you harm.[5]

The publication of Chaadaev's essays caused an uproar that ended with his being officially declared a lunatic. But his views, if exaggerated, nevertheless contributed something toward the swelling of that small stream of Russian intellectual life which stubbornly clung to traditional constitutional and legal principles as they had developed in Western Europe, seeing in them the only solution to Russian problems. The *Vekhi* group, to which reference is made later, owed much to the rude shock to Slavophil complacency administered by the *Philosophical Letters*. But in the main, Chaadaev and Pushkin represented an already outdated trend in Russian revolutionary thought. Under Western influence this trend had formed a part, albeit a small one, of the constitutional ideas of the Decembrists. When once the abortive rising which these young noble intellectuals in uniform attempted in 1825 had been severely repressed, the voice, though not the hope, of revolt was stilled for over a generation. And when revolutionary activity revived in the 'sixties, constitutional ideas no longer formed any part of its ideological baggage.

The problem of legal order took on new actuality in the 'sixties, when after the accession of Alexander II the whole social order of Russia was transformed by a series of far-reaching reforms. The emancipation of some twenty million serfs in 1861 was the first step in this revolution from above, to be followed by reform of the judicial system and by the establishment of limited but quite real local self-government. The condition of the peasant serfs had for long lain heavily on the conscience of all thinking Russians. The Emancipation Act did little so far as most of them were concerned to ease the intelligentsia's sense of shame and guilt. The provisions laid down in the Act for enabling the peasants to acquire land disappointed the peasants' hopes, even if its meagre concessions were sufficient to arouse opposition from many landowners. As the poet Nekrasov put it, when the great chain broke, one end struck the landowners, and the other the peasants. Almost immediately revolutionary conspiracies, led of course by intellectuals, began to form. The first conflict raised among the intelligentsia by the emancipation was therefore between those who welcomed the reforms as a first step which would ultimately lead Russia along the path of the legal order discernible in Western Europe, and those (the great majority) whose impatience, disappointment, or moral fervor led them to see revolution as the only solution to the achievement of social justice.

For this majority of the intelligentsia, preoccupation with the social problem of land distribution became paramount, and, as will be seen, it obscured or eclipsed all questions of establishing society on the basis of legal order. In contrast, the minority (and it was a very small one) was beset with fear that the mere abolition of serfdom would not of its own accord bring with it abolition of the mentality which had engendered it, and which was itself the result of centuries of arbitrariness on the part of the state and the landlords, of patriarchal administration rather than of law. Among the few who were aware of this danger was B. N. Chicherin, the outstanding liberal jurist and philosopher of the Russian nineteenth century. For several decades Chicherin watched with apprehension the growing forces of socialism, which in his view represented a return to the mentality of serfdom and therefore presented a greater danger to the liberal principles in which he believed than did the autocracy. For the autocracy was now embarked on the road of reform, which would in time lead to the establishment of full civil, if not political, freedom: but the socialists, in his view, with their downright attack on private property, threatened the very principle of civil rights, and therefore all freedom, and could if victorious achieve only despotism.

The kernel of the division between the liberals of the type of Chicherin and those who saw the solution for Russia on quite different lines was the attitude adopted to the traditional peasant commune (the *obshchina* or *mir*).⁶ As time went on this peasant institution for the communal tilling of the land and for the management of local village affairs became the subject of the most heated controversies. It was Herzen who first drew attention to an institution which had hitherto escaped the notice of the intelligentsia. Thereafter its champions were drawn from wide sections of society, whose motives for supporting the commune were very different. To the Slavophil of the type of Aksakov, the commune represented the traditional Russian form of patriarchal life, with all the virtues which anything rooted in Russian antiquity possessed for them. The Populists (the *Narodniki*) saw the commune as the germ of a future socialist society: for them this traditional form of primitive Russian communism could, if encouraged and extended, make it possible for Russia to develop into a full socialist society without going through the industrial phase, which was the path toward socialism embarked on by the socialist parties of Western Europe, and which the Populists were anxious to avoid. Finally, the commune was supported by large sections of the official bureaucracy. They believed, if erroneously, that the commune was a bulwark of conservative support for the emperor. Moreover, it was a convenient institution for the collection of taxes and dues, since responsibility for payment could be laid on the commune as a whole, and not merely on an individual. It also provided a convenient means for preserving the peasant as a kind of ward of the state, subject to separate administration, to separate laws and customs, and to a form of tutelage which the ordinary courts, as reformed after the emancipation, were not equipped to provide. This view of the peasants' needs corresponded with the agelong tradition of serfdom and with the belief, often sincere, that a paternal regime was best for the peasant. It was this attitude above all which for Chicherin represented the survival of the mentality of serfdom.

The attitude toward the commune of those who were mainly responsible for framing the Emancipation Act can perhaps best be described as neutral: they did not intend to abolish it, but on the other hand neither did they intend to shore it up. N. A. Milyutin, the man most responsible for the form which the legislation of 1861 took, later described the intention at the time as follows:

The lawgiver does not impose on the rural class any one form of property preferably to others: it may be individual or communal according to the custom prevailing in each region, and it will be left to the purchasers' own pleasure whether they will transform the lands acquired by the communes into private or individual property.⁷

Certainly it was the intention of the legislators and of the emperor that "the status of the peasant, after the transitional period [required for the payment of compensation for the land acquired by them] was concluded should be the same in law as the status of free landowners."[8] It did not work out that way. Far from letting the commune live or die, as the natural inclination of the peasants dictated, the government shored it up by legislative devices of all kinds. The courts which were set up to replace the personal jurisdiction over the peasants hitherto exercised by their owners did not administer the criminal law of the land, but something which was in theory a form of customary law, supposedly better adapted to the traditional childlike nature of the peasant, but which in practice amounted to, in the words of the late Sir Paul Vinogradoff, "a kind of shifting equity tempered by corruption." A series of decisions in the highest court of appeal, the Senate, soon made it plain that the peasant owner was far from equal in status to the free landowner. The law recognized only the commune as the owner of land. The individual peasant had to look to his remedy within the framework of the "customary" law of his district, and within and against the commune. He could neither enforce civil rights on the basis of the law of contract nor protect his property under the general civil law applicable to those other than peasants.

Thus the emergence of a class of free smallholders with full civil rights and equal before the law, which some at any rate had hoped would be the result of the Emancipation, was made impossible. More serious, from the point of view of those who hoped that the Emancipation would be the first step toward the emergence of a universal legal order, a large class of persons in society was thus isolated and denied full civil rights. No greater obstacle to the development of general habits of law and order could have been imagined. The essentially "administrative revolution" which the shoring up of the commune represented was completed in 1889. The institution of the land captains, by introducing direct bureaucratic intervention and tutelage, undermined self-government in the villages.

The attitude of the intelligentsia to the question of legal order can only be understood against this background of the peasant commune. There were a few, a very few, of whom Chicherin was probably the most consistent, who were convinced that the most important aim for Russia was to develop along the constitutional lines discernible in the countries of Western Europe—toward civil freedom, legal order, and eventually, though this would necessarily take a long time, political freedom and a constitutional order. They rejected out of hand any special Russian solution which did not partake of the same features as those obtaining in the countries of the West—in so far as Russia at present lacked those features, it was necessary for her to acquire them. For Chicherin, the peasant commune was a drag on the development of private property in the villages, which was in his view essential for the development of civil freedom. He believed that the commune should be allowed to disintegrate, as he believed it would if full rein were given to the private property instincts of the more industrious peasants by allowing them freedom to own land as individual bearers of normal civil rights. (Some years before the Emancipation Act Chicherin had already thrown a bombshell among the Slavophil admirers of the commune as a traditional and specific-ally Russian institution in a series of historical essays designed to show that it was neither traditional nor peculiarly Russian, but largely the result of comparatively recent fiscal policy.[9]) Chicherin also wished that all the patriarchal legal *apartheid* under which the peas-ant still lived should be swept away, regarding it as a survival of the serf-owning mentality and inconsistent with legal order.

At the time of the reforms of the 'sixties and until 1868 Chicherin was professor of public law in Moscow University (after that he retired to private scholarship and to active work in the local councils, or *zemstva*). In a series of pungent polemical articles, published in collected form in 1862,[10] he argued the case for legal order in the light of the new hope opened up by the accession of an emperor whose heart was set on reform. In 1858 he caused a storm among the radical intelligentsia by attacking their idol, Herzen's paper *The Bell*, in an open letter in which he argued that the responsible course for those who genuinely desired reform in Russia was to support the new liberal efforts emanating from the throne, and not to encourage revolt and violence. Writing about this letter a few years later he said: "It seemed to me that there was a need of drawing attention to two factors forgotten in our literature—state power and law—which are just as necessary to a society as freedom itself."

The interdependence of freedom and order is the keynote of all Chicherin's writings of this period. Order depends on a strong state. But if a such a state is not to be despotic, its power must be based on legal order, and legal order can only be acquired by the constant practice and observance of the law. Later he returns to the subject:

> The liberation of the peasants and the development of a society stand-ing on its own feet demand the safeguarding of rights and a solid legal

order. . . . Legality does not fall suddenly from the skies. . . . Respect for and confidence in moral force become rooted only after agelong habit. The main task here belongs to the government. By refraining from arbitrariness, by hedging itself in with legal forms, by resolutely adhering to the established legal order, the government points the way, and makes society discern norms and guarantees where before it only saw force and oppression.

Thus Chicherin recognized that the duty was a double one: both society and the state had to show the necessary restraint. He believed, however, that the foundation had been laid in the reforms. What was needed now was moderation and honesty on both sides. The cause of liberalism could now best be served by preserving and nurturing the first fruits: since 19 February 1861 (the date of the Emancipation Act) liberalism and conservatism had become one.

Chicherin offered no short cut to Utopia, no immediate solution for the peasant's hunger for land, and no immediate remedy for the many social injustices which marred Russian life. What he provided was a reasoned argument against a too precipitous attempt to achieve the solution of these social problems without the solid foundation of legal order, and a warning that such an attempt, if made before the consequences of serfdom had been eradicated from the body politic, could only result in a despotism more dangerous than the existing autocracy. If reason alone determined political convictions, Chicherin's influence and that of the few who thought like him might have been greater. But emotion and passion are quite as important in forming opinion as is reason, and there were many emotional reasons which made this liberal approach repellent to the intellectuals.

There was first the fact that this approach was frankly Western European in character. It deliberately turned its back on everything specifically Russian, it offered no sop to Russian pride. It squarely assumed that Russia must go the same way as France or Britain—or else remain sunk in barbarism. Besides, to put all hope for the future in constitutional development on the French or British model was an act of faith which was difficult in the nineteenth century. The July Monarchy was detested among the great majority of enlightened Russians. The critic and writer of memoirs, P. V. Annenkov, records as the general opinion of his contemporaries that the July Monarchy was a betrayal of the old, real, traditional France, a kind of "ghost which had, like a usurper, substituted for the natural physiognomy of the country a repulsively smooth and stupid mask."[11] Somewhat later, Herzen, during the long years of his exile in England, castigated the social injustice he saw behind the façade of Victorian liberalism.

Further, to the majority of the intelligentsia, the long-term liberal constitutional solution for Russia often appeared as a cold and selfish policy, of interest to no one except the small privileged upper class, and of no ultimate benefit to the great majority, the peasants. K. D. Kavelin, a liberal-minded lawyer, who at the same time had strong Slavophil leanings, in 1875 stated the case against constitutionalism:

A constitution can only have some kind of sense when those who put it into effect and safeguard it consist of strongly organized rich classes, enjoying authority. . . . Many among us dream of a constitution. . . . and it is mostly those who hope with its help to seize power for themselves over the government, on the French Napoleonic model, to keep it in the hands of a few families, and exclude the people as a whole. [12]

As a criticism of such a view as Chicherin's, this was unfair. Nevertheless, it represented the genuine moral repugnance which constitutionalism, or indeed the advocacy of legal order in general, evoked among many members of the intelligentsia. Chicherin and those who thought like him were forced to advocate a form of order which in the first instance would have benefited their own class. Had they been better historians, Chicherin's critics might have recalled that civil and political liberty was in the first instance usually asserted by one class for its own benefit, and then only gradually extended to other classes as well—from the barons of Magna Carta to the industrial magnates of nineteenth-century England. But they did not reason in this way and were inclined to be carried away by moral indignation.

The philosophy of moral indignation was perhaps best voiced later in the century by the Populist writer Mikhaylovsky. Writing in 1880 (when the policy of reform had failed and the revolutionary society, the People's Will, with a certain amount of secret support from Mikhaylovsky, was actively planning the death of the emperor), Mikhaylovsky said, "Freedom is a great and tempting thing, but we do not want freedom if, as happened in Europe, it will only increase our agelong debt to the people."

In a general review of the thoughts and aspirations of the radical intelligentsia over the past generation, he goes on to say:

Since we were sceptical in our whole attitude to the principle of freedom, we were ready to refrain from demanding any rights for ourselves: not only privileges—that goes without saying—but even the elementary rights that were in the old days called natural rights. . . . And we did all this for the sake of one possibility into which we put our whole soul: the possibility of immediate transition to a higher order, leaving out the middle stage of European development, the stage of bourgeois government. [13]

These two elements in all nineteenth-century radical thinking—moral indignation, and an intense faith that Russia could progress by some separate path to a higher state than Europe had achieved, without the intermediate European stage of bourgeois capitalism—are most graphically illustrated by a famous controversy in the 'sixties between two very different representatives of the intelligentsia, Turgenev and Herzen. Turgenev, whose acute political insight has perhaps been eclipsed by his genius as a novelist, and distorted by the hostility of the radical intelligentsia, was one of the most consistent advocates of the need for legal order. His acumen in discerning the basic ills of Russian society was already apparent in a memorandum on the peasant question, written in 1842, when at the age of twenty-four, he made application for employment in the Ministry of the Interior. The views expressed there anticipate by some twenty years the analysis later made by such experts as Chicherin.

Turgenev's main argument is that a healthy development of civil order in Russia is impossible unless the entire patriarchal structure of Russia is swept away, with the emancipation of the serfs as the first step. Relations between landowners and peasants must be based on law, not on arbitrariness. However enlightened some landowners may be, benevolent despotism is no substitute for the certainty of a legal order. The peasant must be made to feel that he is a citizen and a full participant in that legal order. The landowner in turn must develop a sense that his relations to the peasants must be based on law, not on will. This is necessarily inconsistent with serfdom, which must be abolished. Turgenev ends with a tribute to Russian traditions and virtues, but remarks,

God forfend that we should fall into blind worship of everything Russian only because it is Russian: God preserve us from limited and, to be frank, ungrateful attacks on the West, and especially on Germany. . . . The most certain sign of strength is to know one's own weaknesses and imperfections. [14]

In contrast, Herzen could never bring himself to accept the view that Russia must either follow the broad lines of development toward law and order upon which Western Europe had embarked, or else remain in her pristine state of barbarism. Russia's salvation, according to him, lay in the Russian peasant, who was uncontaminated by the corruption of modern society, and who in his traditional commune preserved the germ of a future, higher form of society that would avoid the evils accompanying the bourgeois development of the West. The idea of the "separate path" for Russia, the devotion to the peasant commune, the hope of avoiding the evils of bourgeois capitalism—all these basic tenets of Populist philosophy which exercised so enormous an influence on the intelligentsia stem from Herzen. In a series of articles entitled "Ends and Beginnings," which appeared in his paper *The Bell* between July 1862 and January 1863, Herzen again expounded these already familiar ideas. Turgenev, in a series of letters written in the light bantering vein of which he was master, took Herzen to task. The doctrine that any one country could travel by a "separate path" was an illusion. The development of Russia must necessarily follow the broad lines followed by other countries. Since those countries had developed freedom and a legal order in the first instance through the efforts of the middle class, this was the only way in which such a development could take place in Russia. To put faith in some peculiar virtue of the Russian peasant was not only unhistorical but also illusory: the Russian peasant, like peasants the world over, was conservative and bourgeois by nature, without the instincts for socialism which Herzen believed him to possess. (Turgenev, incidentally, had had a good deal more practical experience of life among the peasants than had Herzen.) In short,

Russia is no Venus of Milo, kept in misery and bondage by a wicked stepmother. She is in fact the same kind of young woman as her elder sisters—except, I suppose, that she is a bit broader in the beam.[15]

This correspondence contributed to the rupture between the two lifelong friends which soon followed.[16] The argument may be taken as an apt illustration of the deep emotional gulf between those few courageous enough to embrace the unpopular view that there were no short cuts for Russia if she was to escape from her long tradition of despotism, and the more emotional majority who hoped against hope for some peculiarly Russian miracle.

Such, then, was the background which produced a climate of opinion that regarded the advocacy of law and order as cold, calculating, immoral, selfish, un-Russian, or unpatriotic. It was therefore not surprising that the influence of men like Chicherin was in the end very slight. Such influence was probably most clearly felt in the views of a small intellectual group, which included a number of former Marxists like Struve and Bulgakov, and outstanding thinkers like Frank, Izgoev, and Gershenzon. This group published in 1909 a collection of essays on the Russian intelligentsia under the general title of *Vekhi* (Landmarks).[17] The *Vekhi* group believed in the primacy of moral and religious principles, and the volume they published was essentially a call for the regeneration of the intelligentsia and a plea for the recognition of the need to work *with* the social order, not against it, in an endeavor to transform it along the lines of morality, law, and justice. The failure of the intelligentsia to realize or understand the need for legal order was the subject of one of the essays (by B. A. Kistyakovsky), from which some of those illustrations of the attitude of the nineteenth-century intelligentsia to law and the state discussed above have been drawn. The violent reaction produced by the publication of *Vekhi* showed how far the Russian intelligentsia still was from accepting legal order as a basis for progress. Opposition to the views of the *Vekhi* group was strong, not only among avowed radicals such as the Socialist Revolutionaries, the heirs of the nineteenth-century Populists, but even more so among the *Kadets,* a party with an avowedly liberal program.

In the end it was not the intelligentsia—at least, not in the generally accepted use of this term—but the government bureaucrats who became the real advocates of legal order. It was from this group that two outstanding men emerged, Witte and Stolypin, who sought to attack the problem at its roots—in the peasant commune. Both men realized that without destroying the commune no secure legal order could ever come about in Russia. The failure of their policy (in the case of Witte, he never succeeded even in getting it started) is not a part of the present story. What is significant for our investigation is the fact that their policy had to face the opposition of almost the entire thinking class of the country. The conclusion can best be expressed in the words of Professor K. Zaitsev:

If one disregards a few isolated voices which never exercised any direct influence, one observes with a certain astonishment how political figures of various views, from the most extreme reactionaries to the most passionate revolutionaries, how scholars and writers of all trends of opinion, often urged on by the most different motives, all were committed to the idea of a peculiarly Russian, separate, peasant land law. Populism so called cannot merely be represented as a narrow revolutionary party dogma. . . . It is usually assumed, and quite rightly, that one of the causes of the revolution of 1917 was the gulf between government, intelligentsia and people. But one should not lose account of the fact that populism in its widest sense, the agrarian ideology of the Russian intelligentsia, was nothing but a refined transposition of the legal outlook of the peasants, which to a certain extent was anchored in government decrees and bolstered by government legislation. Government, society and people were therefore at one on this question, the unhappy solution of which led to the collapse of the Russian Empire.[18]

REFERENCES

1 *Polnoe sobranie sochineniy Denisa Ivanovicha Fonvizina* (St. Petersburg, 1893), pp. 198, 216.

2 *Polnoe sobranie sochineniy Konstantina Sergeevicha Aksakova*, Vol. I (edited by I. S. Aksakov; Moscow, 1861), pp. 8-9.

3 Quoted by B. A. Kistyakovsky in *Vekhi: Sbornik statey o russkoy intelligentsii* (2nd edn., Moscow, 1909), p. 130.

4 *Sochineniya i pis'ma P. Ya. Chaadaeva*, Vol. II (edited by M. Gershenzon, Moscow, 1913), pp. 113-114.

5 A. S. Pushkin, *Polnoe sobranie sochineniy v desyati tomakh*, Vol. X (Moscow-Leningrad, 1949), p. 597. For an analysis of Pushkin's political views see S. L. Frank, *Etyudy o Pushkine* (Munich, 1957), pp. 28-57.

6 On the whole question of the importance of the commune and the developments in agrarian legislation generally, and for the evolution of the attitude to legal order in the nineteenth century, see V. Leontovitsch, *Geschichte des Liberalismus in Russland* (Frankfurt-am-Main, 1957), Part II, *passim*. This study is indispensable for the understanding of the intellectual development of the century, but unfortunately is not yet available in English.

7 From a speech in 1863, quoted in Anatole Leroy-Beaulieu, *The Empire of the Tsars and the Russians* (translated from the 3rd edn. by Zenaide A. Ragozin; New York, 1893), Vol. I, p. 485, *note*.

8 V. Leontovitsch, *op. cit.*, p. 149.

9 See B. Chicherin, *Opyty po istorii russkago prava*, Moscow, 1858.

10 B. Chicherin, *Neskol'ko sovremennykh voprosov*. Moscow, 1862.

11 P. V. Annenkov, *Literaturnye vospominaniya* (Leningrad, 1928), p. 299.

12 *Sobranie sochineniy K. D. Kavelina*, Vol. II (St. Petersburg, 1898), pp. 894-895.

13 *Sochineniya N. K. Mikhaylovskago*, Vol. IV (St. Petersburg, 1897), pp. 949, 952.

14 I. S. Turgenev, *Sobranie sochineniy v dvenadtsati tomakh*, Vol. XI (Moscow, 1956), pp. 420-433.

15 A. I. Gertsen, *Polnoe sobranie sochineniy i pisem*. Pod redaktsiey M. K. Lemke. Vol. XV (St. Petersburg, 1920), pp. 242-310, where Turgenev's letters are also reprinted.

16 As to this quarrel, due not only to this particular disagreement, see Henri Granjard, *Ivan Turguénev et les courants politiques et sociaux de son temps* (Paris, 1954), Ch. IX.

17 *Vekhi: Sbornik statey o russkoy intelligentsii*, N. A. Berdyaeva, S. N. Bulgakova, M. O. Gershenzona, A. S. Izgoeva, B. A. Kistyakovskago, P. B. Struve, S. L. Franka. 2nd edn., Moscow, 1909. For a fuller discussion of this group, see the writer's "The *Vekhi* Group and the Mystique of Revolution," *The Slavonic and East European Review*, 1955, *34:* 56-76.

18 Quoted in V. Leontovitsch, *op. cit.*, p. 153.

BORIS ELKIN

The Russian Intelligentsia on the Eve of the Revolution

MANY MISUNDERSTANDINGS have existed—and, it seems, still exist—on the question, what constituted the Russian intelligentsia. In Russia the expression was certainly not regarded as extending to the whole of the educated classes. It is misleading, however, to think of the intelligentsia, as does the author of a recent book, as a group "fanatically devoted to the cause of revolution";[1] this would exclude typical members of the intelligentsia, such as Granovskii or Turgenev in the early period, and Miliukov or Maklakov on the eve of the Revolution of 1917. In fact, revolutionary groups within the Russian intelligentsia formed only a small minority up to 1917.[2] On the other hand, in the last period the educated class as a whole comprised persons of different types of intellect and aspiration. Miliukov, who in his historical works had given much consideration to the origin and development of the Russian intelligentsia, pointed out that purely historically, the terms "educated class" and "intelligentsia" were sometimes used in the same sense, and at others represented different but related notions; their interrelation was that of two concentric circles, of which the intelligentsia was the inner one.[3] Despite some indistinctness and variations of the concept of intelligentsia, in Russia it caused no misunderstanding. There it was understood as applying to that part (the larger one) of the educated class, whose distinguishing characteristic was its aspiration to overcome the stagnation of the existing Russian system of government and secure a change of regime. No class distinction was made with regard to this stratum. The landowners Petrunkevich and Rodichev were considered as much members of the intelligentsia as were Mikhailovskii and Plekhanov. Not infrequently judges, civil servants, and more rarely, army officers were typical members of the intelligentsia.

There is one specific characteristic usually attributed to the Russian intelligentsia: a tendency to doctrinairism and extremism in tactics. This tendency cannot be denied; but it was by no means characteristic of the whole or even the majority of the intelligentsia. Nor was it surprising that it should be found in a country in which arbitrary rule had prevailed for generations. For explanation I would refer to what de Tocqueville wrote more than a century ago about the analogous tendency in France on the eve of the French Revolution.[4] Had the intelligentsia in Russia been given an opportunity to take part in political activities and political decisions, it would have learned to understand better the distance between the possible and the desirable, and therefore it would not have been so inclined to doctrinairism and extremism. The Russian autocracy, by its obstinate resistance to peaceful change and by its lack of sincerity when compelled to make concessions, provoked extremism. What the majority of the intelligentsia really aspired to was the rule of law; and, as we shall see, it was capable of turning to moderate methods. The left minority was undoubtedly extremist: some of them (as the Mensheviks) were doctrinaire rather than extremist, but some (as the Bolsheviks) were thoroughgoing extremists on principle.

In order to understand the stages in the development of the Russian intelligentsia in the pre-Revolutionary period we must study them against the background of political events.

At the outset of the present century, the belief that Russia urgently needed to get rid of the autocracy became nearly universal among educated society. Even the old and stubborn gradualist, Boris Chicherin, made up his mind that the establishment of a constitutional regime should not be put off any longer. The foundation in 1903 of the Union of Liberation, in which the *zemstvo* constitutionalists joined hands with representatives of the professional classes, brought about a widespread and fairly effective organization. The intelligentsia was gripped by excitement, and this infected the urban population.

It was the *zemstvo* men who set the ball rolling. In a sense, they were the only group among the intelligentsia who had gained political experience and created adequate methods of political tactics. Their conference, which took place openly in St. Petersburg in November 1904, passed resolutions demanding fundamental political reforms; as regards representative institutions, the majority demanded a legislative assembly, and the minority, a consultative one. If one wishes to fix a starting point for the revolution of 1905, we may say it was this conference.

The majority of the *zemstvo* conference consisted of members of the Union of Liberation. Members of the left wing of that union, mostly belonging to the professional intelligentsia, followed the lead of the *zemstvo* men and organized large gatherings in the cities at which the speeches and resolutions went much further than those of the *zemstvo* conference in demanding universal suffrage and the convening of a constituent assembly. The shooting down on 9 January 1905 of an unarmed workers' procession carrying a petition to the Tsar added bitterness to the general excitement.

If the monarchy then had begun to carry out an honest policy of fundamental reforms, the wind might have been taken out of the sails of the liberation movement. But the monarchy hated the very thought of a constitutional regime. Nicholas II at times promised some reforms, including the creation of a consultative assembly, but at other times declared the autocracy inviolable. The general public felt no confidence in the monarchy.

Meanwhile, the liberation movement was spreading. The professional intelligentsia started organizing itself in professional unions—unions of doctors, university professors, schoolmasters, lawyers, etc.—which, united in the Union of Unions, later played the most active part in the general assault on the monarchy in October 1905. Six months earlier, the second conference of *zemstvo* representatives took place in April 1905 and added new touches to the resolutions of November 1904; in keeping with the general radical tendency in the country, it declared for universal, direct, and equal suffrage with the secret ballot and for the preliminary assembly of elected representatives of the *zemstvos* to draw up a constitution. Thus the *zemstvo* men marched in step with the whole of the intelligentsia.

Strikes spread from city to city and reached the railways, postal communications, the bar, and all sorts of offices. The strike became a general one. All activities in the country stopped. This frightened the Tsar and forced him to give in. By the Manifesto of 17 October 1905 he proclaimed the introduction of political freedom and a legislative parliament.

Up to this moment the liberation movement, if not wholly nationwide—the mass of the peasantry were unconscious of its purely political aims—nevertheless embraced a very large part of the population and probably the whole of the intelligentsia, on whom it was dependent for its success. Even F. Dan, the leader of the Mensheviks and an unbending orthodox Marxist, admitted that

The liberal and democratic intelligentsia played a very important part in the October movement. . . . The rapid and decisive success was to a considerable extent caused by the participation of that part of the intelligentsia which performs organizing functions in a capitalist economy and in state activities and, owing to its social position, can act as a link between the movement of the masses and that of the propertied upper classes.[5]

The Socialist parties at the time were much too small to have more than a slight influence on the working class. But for the part performed by the liberal intelligentsia, the victory of 17 October would not have been possible.

The October manifesto signified the defeat of the autocracy, which for the first time in Russia's history was forced to proclaim a change-over to political freedom, and the establishment of a representative body with legislative power. However, it was only a defeat, not a surrender. Evidence exists to prove that Nicholas II realized that what he had promised was in fact a constitution;[6] but not once in the course of the next eleven years did he or any of his ministers pronounce publicly the word "constitution." This naturally fed suspicion, which was soon justified.

Pogroms of the intelligentsia and of the Jews, following the October manifesto and patently abetted by the local administration,[7] and merciless killings by military expeditions made the situation ever plainer.

Distrust and suspicion of the intentions of the monarchy were also caused by the way in which Witte, the prime minister appointed on 17 October, spoke to the liberal politicians, to whom he offered three nonpolitical ministerial posts in his cabinet. These talks made it clear that while Witte wanted to make use of their names and popularity, he was not prepared, or rather not authorized, to provide them with real power to influence the course of events and to bring about a change in the regime. The offers of ministerial posts were therefore declined, not only by the more radical Kadets, but also by such moderate politicians as Shipov and Guchkov. We know now why Witte was unable to inspire the liberal politicians with confidence. When Miliukov, from whom Witte sought counsel, advised him to bring about a democratic constitution on the Belgian or Bulgarian model and, to begin with, to make things clear by referring publicly to the popular word "constitution," Witte said in reply he could not do that, "because the Tsar does not wish it."[8] At that time the Tsar wrote his mother that he had told Witte he did not like the latter's talks with "persons of radical views" and hoped he would discontinue them.[9]

Nothing came of Witte's talks with the liberal politicians. It

would be unfair to charge Witte alone with the failure. The demand
for a constituent assembly made by the delegates from the central
office of the *zemstvo* conferences, who visited Witte for the purpose
of mutual information, was undoubtedly an error of judgment. Yet
when a fortnight later the third *zemstvo* conference, under the moderating influence of Miliukov, omitted all mention of a constituent
assembly from its resolutions and suggested that the first Duma,
which was to be elected by universal suffrage, should be given the
task of drawing up a fundamental law *to be sanctioned by the Tsar*,
Witte paid no attention to these resolutions and, no doubt under
the above-mentioned instructions of the Tsar, refused to receive
the delegates of the *zemstvo* conference. Thirty years later Maklakov,
the eminent orator of the Duma, criticizing his own Kadet party in
the light of subsequent history, blamed that error for the failure to
reach a compromise between the monarchy and the liberals. In this
Maklakov was certainly wrong. Two are needed for a compromise,
and Nicholas II was never ready to compromise with opponents of
the autocratic regime. The intelligentsia rightly felt that if the liberal
politicians had joined Witte's cabinet they would soon be either
forced to resign or simply dismissed. Witte himself had to resign
after having been the head of the government for only six months,
that is to say, until the storm of the revolution had subsided.

Hopes of a real change were fading. Still, hoping against hope,
the liberal democratic intelligentsia, the largest part of which had
joined the Kadet party, awaited the results of the elections to the
first Duma, which, it was thought, would by its moral and legal
authority force the monarchy to make concessions. The nonparty
intelligentsia (the former left wing of the Union of Liberation) based
their political activity and propaganda on their connections with
the Socialist parties. Meanwhile, the split within the Socialist
intelligentsia was widening. The Bolsheviks and the Mensheviks
were unable to reach an agreement on what their role in the "bourgeois" revolution should be. Lenin was inveighing against the liberals, who, according to his conception of Marx's teachings, were
bound to "betray" the interests of the proletariat; instead, he
preached the alliance of the proletariat with the peasant masses, and
this was to lead by way of an armed uprising to a dictatorship. He
was obsessed by the idea of such a rising, and elaborated its technical and military aspects. Besides, he gradually arrived at the idea
of the transformation of the "bourgeois" revolution into a Socialist
one. The Mensheviks, too, were in favor of an armed uprising.

With them, however, it was rather a question of doctrine and they concentrated their propaganda on the necessity for the proletariat to exert "pressure" on the "bourgeoisie"—which again remained pure theory. The hostility, or at least the suspicion the Socialists felt for the liberals created a dislocation in the front of 17 October, and contributed largely to the failure of the liberation movement.

The potential strength of the Socialist parties at that time was at any rate no greater than was that of the Kadets. They never gained ground after the initial success, common to the "bourgeois" democrats, of the October general strike. The second general strike, called by the St. Petersburg soviet in protest against the handing over of the mutinous Cronstadt sailors for trial and against martial law in Poland, proved a failure. Then the government arrested the St. Petersburg soviet. This produced another call for a general strike which, Lenin kept insisting, was to be turned into an armed uprising—and this call again met with unwillingness on the part of the working class. Efforts were then concentrated on Moscow, where the local soviet obliged. The government seemed to favor the plan of a Socialist uprising, which would offer an opportunity to crush the revolutionaries. After the suppression of the Moscow uprising, Admiral Dubassov, the governor general of Moscow, confirmed in an interview with a French journalist that the authorities shut their eyes to the preparations for an armed uprising. The Tsar wrote his mother on 15 December that, "although the events in Moscow are very distressing and cause me much pain, it seems to me that they are for the best." [10]

The ruthless suppression of the Moscow uprising determined the fate of the revolutionary movement for years to come. This was not generally realized for some time. In retrospect, the Menshevik leader Dan stated that the defeat of the Moscow uprising (in which the Mensheviks had taken part) amounted to "the liquidation of a whole period of revolutionary development"; and in this connection, Dan rightly pointed to the secession of the intelligentsia from the revolutionary movement and the failure of the revolutionaries to gain support from the lower classes of the urban population and the peasantry. It is characteristic of Menshevik mentality that in writing of the defeat of the revolutionary movement, Dan complained of "the hostile attitude of a considerable proportion of the capitalist bourgeoisie," and even "the disappearance of *zemstvo* liberalism." [11]

Nor did the liberal majority of the intelligentsia immediately understand that the defeat of the revolutionary movement was the turning point, which by its very nature would determine what followed. It was only with difficulty that the leaders of the Kadet party succeeded in withstanding the pressure of its left wing, which was seething with anger and indignation against the government. At that time S. Frank, the future coauthor of *Vekhi*, was demanding that the Kadets should "openly take their stand on the ground of a nation-wide revolution."[12]

For its part, the monarchy made immediate use of its victory in Moscow. It ceased to heed public opinion, it purged the government of ministers suspected of sympathy with public opinion (as Manukhin and Kutler) and, most important, it broke the main promise of the October manifesto, that no law would be enacted without the consent of the Duma. On 20 February 1906 it enacted the new law concerning the legislative bodies, the Duma and the State Council; on 23 April, four days before the Duma was to assemble for the first time, it enacted the Fundamental Law. Both measures limited the rights of the Duma as a legislative and supervisory body —undoubtedly, a violation of the October manifesto. Liberal public opinion, including the conservative liberal Shipov,[13] considered the enactment of the new fundamental law as illegal and incompatible with the idea of a truly constitutional regime. It was later learned that a number of high dignitaries who had taken part in the deliberative conference on the draft of the fundamental law under the chairmanship of the Tsar also expressed the opinion that the enactment of the fundamental law other than through the Duma would be a violation of the October manifesto.[14] However, public attention was focused on the Duma, which was to begin functioning in a few days' time.

The history of the period of the Dumas is well known. The first Duma was truly representative of the Russian nation, and in spite of verbal extremism on the part of its left, capable of leading the way to a peaceful change; for both these propositions there is the testimony of so penetrating an observer as Kliuchevskii.[15] The Tsar's government charged it with incapability of working—which meant that the Duma was incapable of cooperating in the anticonstitutional activities of the government led by the arch-reactionary Goremykin. From the memoirs of Kryzhanovskii, the notorious juggler with electoral laws, we know that after only about a week of the first Duma's existence Goremykin, who a few days before had been appointed prime minister, instructed Kryzhanovskii to draft alterations to the electoral law which would yield "more satisfactory results."[16]

At the time of the first Duma the landowning nobility began to exert intense pressure against the democratic plans for agrarian reform on which the Duma was working. As in the period before the reform of 1861, most of the nobility set themselves against giving land to the peasants. In 1861 Alexander II was prevailed upon not to give way to the wishes of the landowners. This time, Nicholas II was in full agreement with their views. The first Duma was dissolved after a life of seventy-two days.

Thereafter for eight whole months the government, now headed by Stolypin, ruled without the Duma. Stolypin, who was mainly responsible for instigating and carrying out the dissolution of the first Duma, had some confused plans for getting moderate liberal politicians to participate in the government; but again there were good reasons for a lack of confidence in his intentions. Instead of pacifying the country by political reforms, Stolypin governed by military executions without trial and legislated by decree. Thus, among other measures, he enacted an agrarian law aimed at performing the function of a counter-measure to a liberal agrarian reform which would assuage the land hunger of the peasantry. However this law, by which the peasants were free to abandon the land community, may be regarded (some members of the intelligentsia approved of it as a matter of principle), it was not intended to contribute to solving the problem of the peasants' hunger for land—the problem which had long constituted the greatest danger to the peaceful development of Russia.

Elections to the first Duma were boycotted by the Bolsheviks and the Social Revolutionaries; nevertheless, there were a number of Socialists in the first Duma. The boycott was given up at the time of the elections to the second Duma. Whether for that reason or as a response to the dissolution of the first Duma and the reactionary policy of Stolypin's government, the left was much more numerous in the second Duma than in the first. However, the prevailing attitude, not only of the Kadets, with whom it was party tactics, but also (at least for a while) of the majority of the left, was that care must be taken to preserve the existence of the Duma and to avoid giving the government a pretext for dissolving it a second time. In the light of what we know now, it seems that Stolypin hesitated as to the course to be taken; but the powers above him compelled him to strike,[17] because of both the political and the agrarian problems. In default of a legal pretext, a Social-Democratic plot was concocted by the political police, and the second Duma was dissolved on 3 June 1907. Simultaneously, the electoral

39

law was drastically altered by decree, in violation of the fundamental law. Under the new electoral law a majority was henceforth assured to the landowning gentry.

The dissolution of the second Duma drew a sharp line and removed all possibility of doubt. By means of the new electoral law and administrative pressure on a large scale, Stolypin got a Duma the majority of which approved his action and, indeed, granted him everything he wanted. The opposition was barely tolerated.

The intelligentsia realized that Russia was, and would be for years to come, in the power of reactionary forces. On the left, the movement away from the Socialist parties seemed to have thinned their ranks drastically. F. Dan later observed that the Social-Democratic party at that time "in reality broke up and suddenly shrank into a few tiny illegal groups which met with but slight response from among the working masses."[18] In the Social Revolutionary party a similar crisis, aggravated by the unmasking of Azev, led to its virtual disintegration.[19] There was no crisis whatsoever in the Kadet party; the Kadets admitted their defeat, but they were morally supported by the belief that right was on their side. Apart from insignificant outbursts by a few individuals (as in *Vekhi*), there were no signs of a crisis among the liberal and democratic intelligentsia.

In the third Duma the Socialist parties, ignoring the proper function of the Duma, used the debates purely for propaganda. The Kadets, on the other hand, believing firmly in the power for development inherent in representative institutions, worked hard in the committees, and after being at first ignored and even insulted, gradually forced the Duma to listen to them. In the fourth Duma, they would be called on to lead.

Among the politically minded intelligentsia there was a good deal of searching examination of the past. Although this received little public utterance, it did not pass unnoticed. The Mensheviks attributed the collapse of the revolutionary movement to the Moscow uprising of December 1905. At the London conference of the Social Revolutionaries in 1908, their leader Chernov said that "the first great victory of the liberation movement over the Tsar's autocracy was gained on credit; it was not at all the result of the adequate revolutionary elements in the community, but only of unpreparedness for the new situation on the part of the government."[20] Miliukov quotes in his memoirs the statement of the Kadet Obninskii that what took place in 1905 was not a revolution but rather a pretended revolution on the part of the intelligentsia; and he seems to approve this view, since he says that the revolutionary movement "was far from having penetrated the masses."[21] Repeatedly and insistently Miliukov warned the extreme left against the Moscow uprising, and after it had been crushed he recognized its defeat as the point from which the curve of the liberation movement must inevitably go downward.[22] The formation of open political parties was in Miliukov's view the most important achievement; but the success of the Kadets in the election for the first Duma and their great influence in it was a "doubtful victory."[23]

Our previous successes [he wrote in his memoirs, referring to the third Duma] were merely apparent and only for a short time disguised the real state of things. The wave broke, and the Duma was revealed in the same crippled state as that to which it had been reduced at the outset by the fundamental law which on all sides had cut down its rights as a representative assembly and by the existence of the State Council, which we called the "stopper" and the "graveyard" of the Duma legislation.[24]

This rather pessimistic outlook does not seem to tally with Miliukov's unyielding tactics in the negotiations for the formation of a coalition government. His justification lay in that he saw clearly what was to be expected from the monarchy by way of a compromise. Miliukov receded from his attitude at the time the Progressive Bloc was formed in the fourth Duma. But by then World War I had started.

It may seem that the slightly pessimistic tendency common to liberal and democratic public opinion in the period after the dissolution of the second Duma was not fully warranted by the facts. True, Stolypin's government moved uninterruptedly toward liquidating the gains of 1905, and it worked systematically and energetically to this end. Nevertheless, it did not complete the task. The Duma was not abolished, and its members were not deprived of their freedom of speech; in the reports of the sittings of the Duma the population read the speeches of the members of the opposition, which could not fail to broaden the political horizon of the masses. Apart from that, the abolition of the preventive censorship and of licenses for the publication of newspapers and periodicals (this took place on the eve of the first Duma) led to a great increase in the number and the circulation of newspapers, and however much the administration confiscated and fined them, the influence of the liberal and democratic newspapers continued to grow.

The intelligentsia did its political work, each of its components in its appropriate sphere. The Social Democrats split in fact, if not formally, into two parties. The Mensheviks concentrated their activities on the growing trade-union movement. The Bolsheviks organized guerrilla bands, and according to the Mensheviks committed armed raids and robberies of government funds.[25] The Social Revolutionaries failed to recover from the feeling of prostration caused by the exposure of Azev. The nonparty left wing, the former members of the Union of Liberation who did not join the Kadet party, were working in the cooperative movement, which was very successful. The Kadets continued to set their hopes on the law of development inherent in the functioning of representative institutions.

At that period, new literary and philosophical currents appeared in Russia, with a certain emphasis on pure aesthetics and religious thinking, and interest in art was growing. In 1909 a certain sensation was caused by the publication of a volume, *Vekhi*, in which seven men of letters, highly respected but rather unstable in their views, subjected the intelligentsia to a severe if uncoordinated criticism; the book was republished and was widely read, but it caused hardly any reaction, and S. Frank, one of its authors, admitted in retrospect that the effect of *Vekhi* was "essentially a *succès de scandale*."[26]

In the political field, a certain moderating wind had begun to exert its influence on the Russian left—except, of course, the Bolsheviks. We have mentioned above the concentration by the Mensheviks on the trade-union movement; under the growing leadership of Potresov their party organizations were emancipating the workers from Bolshevik influences. The numerous class of *zemstvo* employees, the so-called "third element" (doctors, teachers, and agronomists), which had been the stronghold of the Socialist parties, were also becoming more moderate; as the historian of the *zemstvo* put it, practical elements were gaining ascendancy over these classes.[27]

In the meantime, after a period of violently reactionary rule by Stolypin, signs of discontent began to show. As a result, the pendulum began to swing slowly to the left. The Octobrists, Stolypin's main support, began to feel uneasy—isolated in the country, as their leader Guchkov put it. They pointed out that constitutional reforms could not be put off any longer. But Stolypin was no longer able to cope with the reactionary forces he had helped to power, and the Tsar would not allow him to start on constitutional reforms. To save his personal position for the time being, Stolypin turned for support to the right. By this maneuver he lost his standing both with the Tsar, who could himself manage the right, and with the moderate conservatives, who realized the significance of the new wave of opposition. Stolypin became an obvious candidate for dismissal. He was spared this only by his assassination in 1911 by a Social Revolutionary in the service of the political police.

In the fourth Duma, elected in 1912, the relative numerical strength of the parties was not much different from what it had been in the third Duma; the electoral law made any change impossible. But the mood was different. The Octobrists, representing the upper propertied classes, brought with them a reflection of the growing opposition in the country. A group of so-called Left Octobrists gradually joined the opposition in the Duma.

The monarchy moved in its due direction. Kokovtsov, Stolypin's successor, in his memoirs cautiously remarked that the growth of the tendency toward absolutism in the Tsar's surroundings demonstrated that the misgivings of the intelligentsia on that score were well founded.[28]

At that time the facts that became known after 1917 from published documents and memoirs were still unknown. Nevertheless, the intelligentsia were getting wind of the Tsar's way of thinking. We now know that in 1913 he approved the suggestion by Nicholas Maklakov, the arch-reactionary Minister of the Interior, that the fourth Duma be dissolved. Moreover, he wrote to him:

> I believe it necessary and well-intentioned that the Council of Ministers should consider immediately the idea I have long entertained that an amendment should be made to that section of the Law of the Duma under which, if the Duma does not agree with the amendments proposed by the State Council and does not approve the bill, the bill lapses. As we have no constitution, that is complete nonsense. To revert to the rule by which the opinions of both the majority and the minority were submitted to the Sovereign for enactment by him would be a beneficial return to the previous orderly course of legislation and, moreover, would be in the Russian spirit.[29]

It is obvious that the Tsar's mind was working in the direction of a restoration of the autocracy by means of a *coup d'état*. The war, which started soon afterwards, put an end to the realization of Nicholas II's intentions.

The outbreak of the war evoked universal patriotism. The attitude of the overwhelming majority of the intelligentsia was identical with that of the Kadets, who declared that in the face of the common danger to the country they would lay aside their opposition to the government and unconditionally support the war effort. Defeatists were exceptional even in the ranks of the extreme left and amounted to a few isolated individuals; the great majority of the Socialists called themselves "Defensists."

The monarchy again frustrated this attitude. The government once more proved not to have prepared the defense of the country, and the task of making up for the deficiencies in supplies was beyond its capacity. The difficulties were overcome only by immense efforts on the part of unofficial bodies—the Union of Zemstvos, the Union of City Corporations, and the Military Industrial Committee, in all of which the main work was done by the intelligentsia.

The minds of the intelligentsia began to work, as in other Allied countries, in terms of a "war against war," and gradually moved to the ideas of the later "'Wilsonism." However, on the extreme left an attitude of defeatism began to be felt; among the socialist *émigrés* abroad it became a noticeable current that penetrated Russia and infected the Bolshevik and near-Bolshevik groups.

Meanwhile, unrestrained arbitrariness on the part of the monarchy was taking forms that became as unaccountable as they were intolerable. The Tsar fell under the influence of irresponsible and obscure individuals, while the appointment of ministers, who were replaced more and more frequently, became dependent on Rasputin and other rogues. Faced with the prospect of defeat in the war, Russia could not endure this situation. A majority coalition called the Progressive Bloc formed itself in the Duma, and then in the State Council, on a platform of minimal liberal reforms, and it demanded the formation of a government commanding the confidence of the country. The Tsar would not, however, give way. The military revolt decided the issue. The centuries-old Russian monarchy, completely isolated and abandoned by everyone, fell to pieces like a house of cards. Its legacy was that of all despotic regimes.

As long as the organization of the state remained intact, the majority of the Russian intelligentsia was able and prepared to manage it, thus saving its mechanism from disintegration. But after the fall of the monarchy, a new majority gained ground and began working from different premises, reducing the state organization to a vacuum. The result was chaos, in which the state power was seized by the *primus occupans*.

It is still too soon to say whether groups reminiscent of the old intelligentsia will in time emerge from among the contemporary Russian classes. If this happens, the new intelligentsia, enriched by enormous experience, is likely to be more realistic than its predecessor.

REFERENCES

1 Stuart Ramsay Tompkins, *The Russian Intelligentsia* (Norman: University of Oklahoma Press, 1957), p. 271 and *passim*.

2 George Fischer rightly says in his recent book, *Russian Liberalism* (Cambridge, Harvard University Press, 1958, p. 116), that about 1905 the revolutionaries in Russia formed "a tiny minority, whose sweeping later triumphs have too often obscured an opposite trend within the Russian intelligentsia which was at the time considerably more important." Victor Chernov, the leader of the Social Revolutionary party, said at the congress of that party in 1908 that "before the revolution [of 1905] we were an insignificant group" (V. M. Chernov, *Pered Burei: Vospominaniia* [New York, Izd. im. Chekhova, 1953, p. 283).

3 Miliukov's essay is in *Intelligentsiia v Rossii* (St. Petersburg, Knigoizd. "Zemlia," 1910).

4 Alexis de Tocqueville, *L'Ancien régime et la Révolution* (Paris, Gallimard, 1952), livre III, chapitre 1.

5 L. Martov, P. Maslov, A. Potresov (editors), *Obshchestvennoe dvizhenie v Rossii v nachale XXgo veka* (Public Opinion in Russia at the Beginning of the XXth Century; St. Petersburg, 1914), vol. IV, part 1, p. 356.

6 The Tsar admitted this in a letter to his mother written two days after 17 October (*Lettres de Nicolas II et de sa Mère, l'Impératrice douairière de Russie,* Paris, S. Kra, 1928, p. 79).

7 A short but colorful description dealing with the *zemstvo* intelligentsia is in I. I. Petrunkevich, *Iz zapisok obshchestvennago deiatelia* (From the Notes of a Public Figure), *Arkhiv Russkoi Revoliutsii*, vol. XXI, p. 404 ff.

8 P. N. Miliukov, *Vospominaniia, 1859-1917* (New York, Izd. im. Chekhova, 1955), vol. I, p. 328.

9 *Lettres de Nicolas II . . .* , letter of 27 October 1905, p. 86.

10 *Ibid.,* p. 121.

11 F. I. Dan, *Proiskhozhdenie Bolshevizma* (New York, Izd. "Novaia Demokratiia," 1946), p. 365.

12 In the weekly journal, *Poliarnaia Zvezda,* December 1905.

13 D. N. Shipov, *Vospominaniia i dumy o perezhitom* (Moscow, 1918), p. 423 ff.

14 For the records of this conference, see the review, *Byloe,* October 1917.

15 See V. O. Kliuchevskii's letter to A. F. Koni in the latter's *Na zhiznennom puti,* vol. II (St. Petersburg, 1913), p. 190.

16 See S. E. Kryzhanovskii, *Vospominaniia* (Berlin, Petropolis, 1908), p. 90.

17 Kryzhanovskii, then deputy to Stolypin as Minister of the Interior, reported in his memoirs that the Tsar in a letter to Stolypin had urged him on with the words, "It is time to strike." (Kryzhanovskii, *Vospominaniia,* p. 111.)

18 Dan, *op. cit.,* p. 434.

19 Chernov, *op. cit.,* pp. 285 ff.

20 *Ibid.,* p. 282.

21 Miliukov, *Vospominaniia,* vol. I, p. 263.

22 *Ibid.,* pp. 346 ff.

23 *Ibid.*, pp. 352 ff.

24 *Ibid.*, vol. II, p. 15.

25 The London party congress, in which the Bolsheviks had the majority, decided to disband the guerrilla bands and prohibited these robberies. According to Nikolaevsky, however, Bolshevik armed robberies continued after the
London congress (among them was the famous raid on Treasury funds in
transport in Tiflis). See B. Nikolaevsky's article on I. G. Tseretelli in *Sot-
sialisticheskii Vestnik*, November 1959, p. 221; and Dan, *Proiskhozhdenie
Bolshevizma*, p. 431.

26 See S. L. Frank's posthumous book, *Biografiia P. B. Struve* (New York, Izd.
im. Chekhova, 1956), pp. 83-84.

27 See B. B. Veselovskii, *Istoriia zemstva za sorok let* (St. Petersburg, 1909-
1911), vol. IV, pp. 63 ff.

28 Count V. N. Kokovtsov, *Iz moego proshlago* (Paris, Iz. "Zhurnala Illus-
trirovannaia Rossiia," 1933), vol. II, pp. 155 ff. (English translation, *Out of
My Past*, Stanford, Stanford University Press; London, Oxford University
Press, 1935.)

29 The Tsar's letter of 18 October 1913. See V. P. Semennikov, *Monarkhiia pered
krusheniem, 1914-1917* (Moscow, Gos. Izdat., 1927), p. 92.

RICHARD PIPES

The Historical Evolution of the Russian Intelligentsia

"Immer denk ich: mein Wunsch ist erreicht,
Und gleich geht's wieder anders her!"
Zerstückle das Leben, du machst dir's leicht;
Vereinige es, und du machst dir's schwer.
—GOETHE

IN RUSSIA the intelligentsia, both as an historical phenomenon and a social concept, has been intrinsically connected with the process of Westernization. It has come into being as a by-product of that process; its character has changed in response to changes that process has undergone, and its future still seems in large measure dependent on it.

Historically, the term Westernization has broadly speaking two connotations. One may use it to refer to the adoption of certain modes of life developed by and associated with modern European secular society, that is, to a cultural phenomenon; but one may also intend a narrower range of phenomena connected with specific ideological currents emanating from the West, in particular, with eighteenth- and nineteenth-century movements that may be loosely described as "rationalist." This narrower kind of Westernization is philosophical in character. The two types of Westernization are by no means separate and distinct, but neither are they coterminous. "Cultural" Westernization affects diverse groups of the population, and entails no political preference: it is just as compatible with conservative as with liberal and radical attitudes. "Philosophic" Westernization, on the other hand, does call for a definite commitment which, being "rationalist" in spirit, is predisposed to agree with left-of-center political and social views.

Corresponding to these two aspects of Westernization, we may distinguish in Russia two Westernized groups. Cultural Westernization, which began early in the history of the Moscow state, had already produced a small minority of liberally educated and secular-minded people by the end of the seventeenth century. In the course of the eighteenth century, this minority rapidly grew in consequence of the monarchy's introduction of compulsory education for the gentry, and particularly after 1762, when the abolition of obligatory state service led to the emergence of a leisure class. In the nineteenth and early twentieth centuries the modernization of the country helped expand this class into a large and articulate body of public opinion. Russia's gradual cultural Westernization thus produced a social group distinguished from the mass of the population by its education, its way of life, and a general sense of affinity with the Western cultural community. This was the "intelligentsia," in the broad, objective sense which gained currency in Russia sometime in the middle of the nineteenth century and first appeared in print in the novels of Boborykin and Turgenev around 1870. From the sociological point of view, the group to which this term applied was amorphous. It included the small-town, provincial elite, such as the local doctor, teacher, or journalist—what the French call *les notables*. It also included the whole professional class, as well as the enlightened gentry and bourgeoisie. And finally, it included the large and growing body of citizens of all social strata whose way of life was modeled on the European, and whose outlook was secular and broadly liberal. If the term, despite its vagueness, enjoyed wide currency, it was because there was need then for some word to denote that public body which by virtue of its education was separated from the "people," and, by virtue of its enlightened, Europe-oriented outlook, from the monarchy and its bureaucratic apparatus.

Within this cultured, objective intelligentsia there developed in the middle of the nineteenth century an intelligentsia in the narrower, more subjective sense. This was a group which accepted fully and in the more extreme form contemporary French and German positivist thought, and deliberately detached itself from the rest of the population to form something resembling a dedicated sect. To belong to this intelligentsia one had to assimilate certain philosophic notions, which included a monistic view of nature, socialism (in some one of its several forms), and the idea of revolution. The roots of this intelligentsia may be traced back to the end of the eighteenth century, when French materialist thought first made itself felt in Russia; but its real flowering occurred only in the 1860's and 1870's, in connection with the emergence among the young generation of the concept of the "critically thinking personality" as the agent of progress in a backward society. The concept of "intelligentsia" in this sense represented a Russian adaptation of the concept of the "intellectual" as it gained currency first in France, and then in Central Europe.[1]

Before the Bolshevik coup of 1917 the word intelligentsia was used in Russia simultaneously in both these senses, cultural and ideological, a fact which creates much difficulty for the historian. In 1909, for example, a group of thinkers, some of whom had evolved from Marxism to a relatively conservative position, published in a collection of essays called *Vekhi* (Signposts) a strong indictment of the Russian "intelligentsia," accusing it, among other things, of a lack of patriotism, religious spirit, and a sense of civic responsibility in general. *Vekhi* provoked a number of replies written largely (but not exclusively) by socialists, who defended the "intelligentsia" from these charges. Yet even in their attack the authors of *Vekhi* did not cease to regard themselves as members of the intelligentsia. Perhaps the disagreement between the *Vekhi* group and their opponents stemmed from their differing concepts of the Westernization of Russia. The authors of *Vekhi* thought that a profound cultural transformation of Russia was a prerequisite for far-reaching political and social reforms, while most of their opponents connected Westernization with the introduction of a specific social and economic order advocated by one school of Western thought.

However, in the twentieth century the Westernization of Russia did not proceed along the exact lines projected by either the "cultured" intelligentsia as a whole or by its critical component. Russia did not continue to Westernize in the broad cultural sense, nor has she achieved a "rational" society.[2] As a consequence, the intelligentsia in both the cultural and the critical sense has experienced a deep crisis that for most of it ended either in exile or physical annihilation. Yet the term "intelligentsia" has lost neither its significance nor its currency but has merely evolved in response to a dramatic change in Russia's Westernization, a change which first made itself felt around 1890.

It would be presumptuous, of course, to speak of the Soviet intelligentsia with any degree of certainty. Because of the absence of an articulate public opinion in Russia, and the general atomization of society, one can refer to all intellectual and social phenomena in the Soviet Union only in the broadest and most conditional manner. Even Soviet citizens themselves are probably not very clear as to what they mean by the word "intelligentsia." The outside observer is at a particular disadvantage in trying to deal with a term inherently vague and evolving, whose practical connotation, moreover, cannot be directly studied. But he can reasonably hope that by comparing developments in Russia with those in other countries which are at a similar stage of development, by tracing trends that originated before

49

the Bolshevik seizure of power, and then by confronting the hypotheses thus secured with the shreds of evidence obtainable from within the Soviet Union, he will arrive at some sort of valid general pattern.

The principal premises on which the analysis in this paper rests may be stated thus: the outstanding social fact of Russia's history since 1890 has been her industrialization; the outstanding political fact of that period has been her sudden and complete loss of freedom. Neither of these two occurrences evolved organically from Russia's development in the nineteenth century, from the era of the classical Russian intelligentsia. Industrialization as well as totalitarianism were Western imports; they were the principal forms of Russia's "Westernization" in the twentieth century. Each of these processes had direct bearing on the Russian intelligentsia, with industrialization affecting the whole broad, cultured intelligentsia, and totalitarianism in particular its critical element.

The splendid cultured class in pre-Revolutionary Russia was the product of unique circumstances. It emerged from a leisure class with extensive privileges and virtually no duties, which even after the emancipation of the serfs enjoyed very considerable social freedom, because in a country as enormous and yet as short of educated personnel as Russia, education in general, without narrow specialization, offered many opportunities for a decent livelihood. Nineteenth-century Russia provided an excellent environment for cultural and intellectual dilettantism in the best sense of the word. Furthermore, because the country was predominantly agricultural, and also suffered from a large surplus rural population, the educated class was assured of cheap food and lodging, and servants. While the lot of the average Russian *intelligent* in the nineteenth century was by no means idyllic, he could devote most of his energy to the pursuit of knowledge. In addition, there were social groups such as the gentry and some of the bourgeoisie, as well as voluntary associations, which encouraged and financially supported cultural activities. The pre-Revolutionary intelligentsia thus enjoyed a considerable degree of independence, in a large measure resulting from the backwardness of the bulk of the population and the existence of favorable (from its point of view) economic circumstances. [3]

Beginning with 1890, and especially since 1930, these conditions have radically changed, depriving the intelligentsia of its cultural and social independence and its status. For industrialization on the one hand reduces through mass education the contrast between the educated and uneducated, and on the other tends to transform the entire population, and the educated group in particular, into a body of salaried, professional civil servants. A similar process has taken place in the West, but in Russia it was more dramatic and brutal.

Mass education was initiated in Russia by the *zemstvos* (institutions of local self-government) in the second half of the nineteenth century. Greatly expanded by the Soviet government, it has produced in twentieth century Russia a large class of citizens with middle and higher education. In particular, in Soviet Russia there has arisen a sizable body of technically trained personnel, that is, people who receive a superficial education qualifying them for a variety of simple technical jobs. From the point of view of their educational attainments, the mass product of the *tekhnikumy* and most *Vuzy* is not comparable to that of the great Soviet university centers (not to speak of those of the pre-Revolutionary period), but neither is it identical with the peasant and working-class population from which it emerged. The vast majority of the graduates of Soviet schools, as of schools in other industrial, "demotic" societies, consists of a semi-educated industrial labor force whose members have a mere nodding acquaintance with the liberal arts, once considered the essence of a higher education. In other words, they constitute a semi-intelligentsia, a group indispensable to an industrial society, which, much as it may differ from the old cultured class in breadth of knowledge, spirit, and purpose, is nevertheless *formally* comparable to it. The Soviet official usage of the term "intelligentsia" takes cognizance of this fact by extending it to all those groups in Soviet society which we would call "white collar."

Mass education, implicit in industrialization, has thus considerably blurred the sharp distinction which in pre-1890 Russia had separated the educated minority from the rest of the population, and given it its sense of cultural cohesion. Side by side, there has now emerged a considerable body of technical and administrative semi-intelligentsia dispersed through many levels of Soviet society. If Soviet industrialization should continue to develop at its recent pace, it is entirely conceivable that eventually this group may come to constitute an absolute majority of the population.

This cultural blurring is accompanied by the loss of social and economic independence. Industrialization everywhere subjects the free-lance, dilettante, cultured intelligentsia to a tremendous pressure, first to become professional, and then to enter into service. This pressure had made itself felt in Russia as early as the closing decades of the nineteenth century, when a large part of the intelligentsia acquired a specialized training and then either joined the rural and urban organs of self-rule or went into the free professions. It did so not unwillingly, because it was eager to act, and because the conditions of service were not onerous, allowing much opportunity for nonprofessional, cultural pursuits. The establishment of the Soviet regime in 1917 and particularly the abolition of private property in the 1930's deprived the educated class of all the remaining vestiges of social and economic independence. Since the Soviet Union has no private enterprises and allows no focus of economic self-sufficiency, for all practical purposes the entire adult population of the country, the white collar class in particular, has been transformed into a body of salaried employees.

The traditional Russian cultured intelligentsia therefore has declined not merely owing to the persecutions to which it has been subjected by the Communists for its hostility to the Soviet regime, but also because intense and ruthless industrialization has knocked out the very social foundations from under it. Its place has been taken by a technical and administrative semi-intelligentsia. In perspective it seems that the old cultured intelligentsia has fulfilled its historic role.

Yet when this is said, the problem of the present situation and the prospects of the cultured intelligentsia is by no means fully resolved. Perhaps Marxism has conditioned us too much to think of historic changes in terms of tableaux, each of which disappears from sight when the next one takes its place on the stage. But if metaphors are needed, the process of historical change, cultural change in particular, resembles rather geological upheavals that produce convolutions and frequently leave elements of an earlier age exposed intact. Even if the old cultured class has been all but destroyed, and its survivors find conditions of modern life unfavorable, its influence is not necessarily spent nor its physical continuity entirely disrupted.

An analogy to the problem facing the cultured intelligentsia in the twentieth century may perhaps be found in the history of the ancient Russian titled nobility, the appanage princes and the members of their retinue, the so-called *boyars*. Once powerful and practically independent, these groups found themselves persecuted by the Moscow rulers, who disliked their self-sufficiency and preferred to build up a large petty servitor gentry as a counterweight. The conflict between the monarchy and the nobility lasted for nearly two centuries, and was finally resolved in favor of the monarchy and the gentry under Peter the Great, who abolished the distinction between hereditary and conditional land tenure, and made all noble status dependent on the performance of state service. This had the effect of submerging the old aristocracy in a vast body of gentry parvenus, and apparently ended its social and historic role. Yet even after the death of Peter, Russian history is replete with signs of vigor on the part of that class: the abortive attempts of the old aristocrats to limit the monarchy in 1730; the efforts of their successors in the second half of the eighteenth century to win for the gentry the status of a genuine aristocracy; the plans of the Northern Society of the Decembrists. As late as 1918-1919 the Dolgorukis and Trubetskois play a leading role in the liberal struggle, this time against Bolshevism. The continuity of this class was due to two factors: the monarchy's dependence on it for the execution of certain state obligations (e.g., administrative and diplomatic), and the process of cultural accretion by means of which a small and diminishing class constantly rejuvenated itself through voluntary self-identification with it on the part of outside groups. Its influence thus long outlasted its primary social function.

Without pushing the analogy too far, one may deduce from it certain facts about the fate of the cultured intelligentsia in modern Russia. It too had flourished freely until the state monopolized its functions; it too finds itself persecuted by the state and challenged by a state-sponsored servitor class with which it has been compelled to merge; and yet it too is needed by the state to carry out certain state functions, and provides a cultural model for the other classes.

The old cultured intelligentsia and its direct descendants have something to offer the Soviet state which the latter cannot obtain from the mass-produced white collar class, and that is a broad cultural background, linguistic competence, intellectual breadth and sophistication. Those are not qualities required by the Soviet administration, but they are very important in certain other areas of great concern to the regime. One such area is that of the natural sciences, which in modern society constitute the backbone of economic and military might; another is sophisticated propaganda, such as literature and art. In these fields of endeavor, young men and women reared in old-intelligentsia homes have a natural advantage over children of working-class families. Therefore they constitute a sizable proportion of the scholars and students in the universities, the academies of science and their numerous institutes, and of all those professions where sheer knowledge and intellectual sophistication rather than political adaptability or ability to get things done are the criteria for selection and advancement. Conversely, they seem to play an unimportant part in the political and administrative apparatus of the country. Under modern conditions, knowledge and a broad educational background are as important to the state as administrative experience was to the *ancien régime* during its conflict with the aristocracy. Since this is what the old intelligentsia can offer, it is able to secure a certain foothold in an otherwise very unfavorable social environment. From this point of view its position has unexpectedly improved since the end of World War II because the scientific developments connected with atomic energy, rocketry, etc., have helped to tip the scales a bit in favor of the scientist as contrasted with the engineer and administrator, who had the field pretty much to themselves in the 1930's.

The most profound impact of the old intelligentsia on modern Soviet Russia, however, is cultural. The Communist regime, despite the hopes of the *Proletkul't* (proletarian culture) protagonists of the 1920's, has dismally failed to create its own literature and art, and after a brief period of experimentation (in itself an offshoot of pre-Revolutionary tendencies), openly adopted the principal heritage of Russian national culture. Yet by so doing it has placed itself in a paradoxical situation, for this national culture, apart from the religious element which the Communists reject anyway, is *par excellence* the creation of the old Russian intelligentsia: it is permeated with its values and ideals. The writings of Pushkin, Herzen, Turgenev, Tolstoy, Dostoyevsky, or Chekhov (distributed in the Soviet Union in astronomical quantities) from the point of view of the Soviet government are the most subversive literature conceivable. In spirit and in letter they reject practically everything that government does and stands for—a fact that does not escape the more sensitive Russian of the present generation. And yet these writers have become assimilated into the main body of Russian secular culture to such an extent that no Russian government can reject them unless it wishes to create a cultural vacuum. The acceptance of the heritage of the old intelligentsia has gone so far that in recent years the Soviet regime has "adopted" the works of such staunch anti-Communist émigrés as Ivan Bunin and Serge Rachmaninoff.

This cultural heritage, especially as embodied in its greatest single glory, Russian classical literature, is perhaps the most effective form of impact of the old cultured class on posterity. It is a legacy far more potent than that left in its time by the old aristocracy, which, though it may have worked out a way of life, never created its own formalized culture capable of being passed on. The hold this culture exercises on Russians is so strong that through it a class which is historically dead acquires, posthumously, ever new heirs and successors.

In particular, a fraction of the technical and administrative semi-intelligentsia of the second and third generation, as it grows more secure and sophisticated, may be expected to model itself on it.[4] It is the greatest humanizing force in Soviet Russia.

The fate of the old critical intelligentsia has been if anything even more tragic, and its transformation even more fundamental. The activity of this group, as we pointed out earlier, was intrinsically connected with a current of European philosophy defined as "rationalist." In Russia a social and political doctrine that was essentially anarchistic derived from that current. The motive that inspired this intelligentsia was a striving for freedom in the widest sense, a striving that was to be realized through the application of "reason," i.e., "science," to all human affairs.

These premises have been seriously challenged by the whole development of Western thought and history from the late nineteenth century onward. As a result, the critical intelligentsia found itself in all the social and economic difficulties of the cultured class of which it was a part, and in addition it experienced a serious inner crisis.

This intellectual crisis began in the last years of the nineteenth century. It manifested itself in several ways. There was the general public reaction against the utilitarian conception of aesthetics that had held sway in Russia since the middle of the century, and accompanying this reaction, a great outburst of artistic activity; poetry, in particular, came into its own after several decades of neglect. Religious movements inspired by Tolstoy and Soloviev acquired a following among intellectuals. But perhaps the most important expression of this countermovement was philosophic "idealism," and particularly the ideas emanating from the various Western neo-Kantian schools. Neo-Kantian thinkers challenged the monistic world view, and postulated the existence of autonomous "ideas," absolute values, and a natural limit to human knowledge. They sought to create—parallel to but independent of the "material" world—a realm of ideas and values which required no justification from the point of view of their social utility, and which developed in accordance with their own inner needs and laws. Neo-Kantianism, which in one way or another has dominated European thought since its emergence, penetrated Russia in the 1890's, and in the next decade won over some of the ablest, most perceptive minds in the country. It is probably no exaggeration to say that the decade immediately preceding the outbreak of World War I in Russia was intellectually a period of neo-Kantian ("idealist") hegemony, much as that of the 1840's was dominated by Hegelianism, and that of the 1860's by Feuerbachian doctrines. The "materialism" of the immediately preceding period seemed now to have lost its fascination for the intellectual elite, though it still attracted the middlebrows. Even the Marxists, who at the time claimed the most intelligent radical youths, found it necessary to adjust their philosophy to neo-Kantianism by adapting some of its elements (empiriocriticism).

The whole shift in the content and spirit of European philosophy around the turn of the century had a demoralizing effect on the Russian critical intelligentsia. Much of that élan which drove it into a suicidal struggle against autocracy had derived from a faith that it was in the vanguard of history by virtue of its rational, scientific attitude. The triumphs of "idealism" abroad and the conversions it made within Russia, and, worst of all, the apparent affinity of twentieth-century science for "idealist" philosophy, seriously menaced this faith. The drift was obvious: whereas until the end of the century the ablest, most vigorous Russian youths were connected in one way or another with philosophic "rationalism," after 1900 they turned their backs on it and in increasing numbers became converted to idealism, aestheticism, even religious mysticism. Even had there been no Bolshevik coup, the critical intelligentsia would have found the going difficult in the twentieth century, because its ideas (a legacy of the mid-nineteenth century, by and large) were out of step with the main movements of modern thought.

A similar statement may be made about the social program of this intelligentsia. Originally it was anarchist and socialist, because anarchism and socialism were against capitalism, and capitalism was held responsible for those obstacles which prevented man from attaining a rounded, free existence: the alienation from the tools of economic production, the separation of town from village and industry from agriculture, the accumulation of surplus value, and a degree of specialization which reduced men to mere "toes" of an economic organism. This kind of reasoning was perhaps valid in the nineteenth century because at that time industrialization was only known as a by-product of capitalism, and could not have been clearly distinguished from it.

Today, however, it is fairly evident that the socialist and anarchist sentiments of the Russian critical intelligentsia (as of its counterpart in Western Europe) derived from a misunderstanding of the nature of modern economic development. The qualities which the intelligentsia ascribed to capitalism proved actually to be inherent in all industrial life. The subsequent development of industrialization in "capitalist," "socialist," and "Communist" countries alike has shown striking similarities, moving toward ever greater alienation, capital accumulation, and specialization, with the result that freedom and the rounded, harmonious development of the human personality have everywhere suffered serious setbacks. This holds particularly true of modern Russia, where all the ills of the industrial system have been intensified by a single-minded concentration on industrial growth at all costs.

In considering the possible modern successor to the traditional critical intelligentsia, one must first of all keep in mind that its "rationalism" was an historical coincidence. It is not the "rationalism" which constitutes the essence of this group, but the critical spirit of which "rationalism" is merely one expression. Indeed, the critical function can be just as readily exercised from a conservative, anti-rationalist position (for instance, when a society is condemned for its departure from established religion or from national tradition). The Russian critical force in the nineteenth century expressed itself in a rationalistic form because at the time "rationalism" (in the loose sense in which it is defined in a footnote to this essay) was in the air, and seemed to offer the best opportunity for a complete emancipation of man. In particular, a rational reorganization of the economic and social order was believed essential to this end. This hope has not been fulfilled. The violent destruction of traditional society in Russia has indeed led to rationalization, but it is a rationalization of a quite different order from what the old intelligentsia had in mind; instead of emancipating man, it has enslaved him.

Yet obviously the disillusionment with "rationalism" has not obviated the need for a critical element in society: it has only changed its character. What this change is may be gleaned from modern Western history.

It is often observed that in the West there has occurred over the past century and a half a progressive "alienation" of the intellectual from society: the enlightened, public-minded, *engagé* thinker of the seventeenth and eighteenth centuries has gradually given way to the *dégagé* intellectual who shuns society and public obligation and withdraws into a private world of personal problems, personal images and symbols, even a personal language. The reason is that, as the political and economic system "rationalizes," it acquires a life of its own which has less and less relevance to the problems that face the individual, especially the intellectually independent individual. Detaching itself from the human foundations from which it originally sprang and which it is meant to serve, this system reaches a level at which it transforms itself from a "base" into something resembling a "superstructure." Somewhere along the way, the intellectual, who at first assists and encourages this process, begins to withdraw. Romanticism may perhaps be viewed as the first manifestation of this withdrawal, and socialism, as a force which temporarily halted it. The enormous success of socialism among European intellectuals may be ascribed to the fact that it seemed to resolve the conflict between the intellectual's striving for freedom and his awareness that the industrial revolution contains powerful antilibertarian elements. But socialism failed, dissolving into a program of social welfare on the one hand, and one of forced economic growth on the other, neither of which has much to do with the problem which faced and still faces intellectuals. The disillusionment of European intellectuals with socialism may well have broken the main bond still connecting many of them with society, thus bringing about the rapid "alienation" of the intellectual that is characteristic of the present century.

In so far as the Soviet Union embodies in an extreme form the forces which have impelled the European intellectuals in this direction, it is not unreasonable to assume that, *mutatis mutandis*, a similar change has occurred within the Russian critical intelligentsia. The resistance to the regime in Russia today probably cannot be carried on in the classical nineteenth-century fashion, that is, by challenging some of its features or by endeavoring to abolish the regime altogether. The regime is too strong to yield to such an assault; nor is the Russian intelligentsia, after the disillusioning experience of the Revolution and the subsequent failure of reform movements, likely to have much enthusiasm for political action. The complete political disorientation brought about by several decades of the systematic suppression of some facts and the falsification of others, and by a thoroughgoing befuddling of the entire vocabulary of politics would be likely to confound seriously even those intellectuals who might be politically oriented.[5]

Among a large number of Soviet *intelligenty* all these factors induce a mood of cynicism and pessimism which usually leads to some degree of adjustment to Soviet life and to a loss of all interest in public affairs. But there is evidence of a body of intelligentsia which does retain a sense of civic awareness, however inarticulate and unsophisticated, and therefore cannot quite escape the conflict inherent in the relationship between the individual and society. This intelligentsia appears to resemble its contemporary European counterpart more than its own national predecessor. That is to say, unlike the old Russian intelligentsia, it tends to seek a resolution of the conflict between the individual and society, not in a transformation of society in accord with some preconceived image, but rather, like the modern "alienated" intellectual of the West, in the establishment of the firmest and most generous line possible separating the realms of public and private life. In other words, the modern critical intelligentsia, instead of striving to reform the regime, seeks to escape it. The previous effort to subordinate everything to a single, all-embracing principle seems to have given way to an effort to atomize, to break up the state, society, institutions, and the many functions connected with public life into the greatest number of maximally autonomous units. This "autonomization" may well represent the principal form the critical movement assumes in the Soviet Union today, and, because its purpose is ultimately the same, it may be regarded as the direct successor of the rationalization of the nineteenth-century intelligentsia—despite the fact that the methods implicit in the two expressions of the critical spirit are diametrically opposite.

To illustrate what this involves in practice, let us call attention to two areas of Soviet life in which such efforts to "autonomize" seem to have been particularly intense. One of these areas embraces institutions and functions which may be considered not essential to the security and might of the Communist regime—or, to put it more precisely, which have a relatively low priority rating, for in a totalitarian society everything is "essential," since everything has some relevance to the system as a whole. In that category one may include, for instance, the sphere of domestic life. The degree of Soviet control over the family has been alternately intensified and relaxed over the past forty years, but the tendency in recent years has been toward a general recognition of the autonomy of that basic social institution. Private property, though limited to an infinitesimal fraction of the national wealth, has also tended in recent years to be defined in more precise legal terms and to gain institutional recognition. More important is the whole range of cultural activities, especially in literature. Leading representatives of the professional organizations representing cultural activities have been waging a constant and sometimes successful struggle for the past several years to secure for themselves and their colleagues a certain amount of aesthetic freedom. Their plea is for freedom as a prerequisite of creativity; the motive behind the limited concessions granted them is the realization on the part of the rulers that these occupations are not so critical as to justify the trouble and expense of constant and close supervision. During the past three or four years the lines of cultural autonomy have by no means been firmly fixed; Dudintsev's *Not by Bread Alone* represents an important test case in this dispute. But the need for such a line seems to be recognized in certain governmental circles, and therefore there are grounds for believing that a certain amount of "critical" spirit may find legitimate outlets.[6]

The other important area in which a certain degree of autonomy may be won from the government embraces some of the public activities which are most essential, but which the government may subject to strict controls and ideological strait jackets only at grave risk to its external power and security. Here the plea is for professional competence. First and foremost in this category are the natural sciences and several applied sciences, including economics. All these fields of activity have this in common, that they are of vital concern to the regime, but in order to flourish they demand intellectual freedom. It is not possible to develop atomic energy if scientists are compelled to turn their backs on modern "idealist" physics and accept seriously, as an operative doctrine, the primitive cosmology of official Communism. Nor is it possible to derive the maximum benefit from the industrial and agricultural plant if one ignores modern techniques of economic analysis, such as "linear programing," even if they are difficult to reconcile with what has come to be accepted as orthodox Marxist economic doctrine.[7] The more the rulers of the Soviet Union commit themselves to a struggle for world supremacy, the more they are compelled to grant the scientists and other specialists full access to foreign sources of information, and a very extensive freedom within the area of their professional competence. Here too the lines have not been firmly drawn. Whereas scholars in disciplines of such obvious bearing on national security as physics and mathematics have won virtually full professional freedom, others, whose practical contribution is less indisputable, have had to fight a tug-of-war, the outcome of which is not yet certain (this applies to the biologists, especially the geneticists).[8] In any event, it is certain that in so far as complete ideological control is incompatible with scientific and economic leadership in the world, the regime must make more and more concessions to the professions.

There is no certainty at all that these processes need weaken the totalitarian features of the Soviet regime. It is perfectly conceivable that the regime may voluntarily withdraw from certain fields of activity—whether because these are not essential enough to warrant constant interference, or because they are so essential that such interference represents a serious danger to the state—without surrendering any of its principal dictatorial prerogatives. But it is not unreasonable to assume that these autonomous areas, however limited, do foster a critical spirit, and hence make it possible for a critical intelligentsia to survive. In that respect the system contains serious contradictions. The authorities seem to be aware of this, and since 1956 many of the vacillations on the ideological and cultural battle-fronts may be ascribed to the difficulty of reconciling the demands of external security, which call for the maximum of freedom, with the demands of internal security, which require that freedom be reduced to a minimum.

The autonomous tendencies inherent in the arts and sciences are particularly significant, because, as we have pointed out earlier, they are pursuits that tend anyway to attract descendants of the old cultured intelligentsia. In these fields, professional tendencies are bolstered by the social and cultural background of their practitioners. But the tendencies toward "autonomization" are by no means restricted to the arts and sciences: in some measure they affect every aspect of Soviet life. In a sense, like the old critical intelligentsia it destroyed, the Communist regime finds its "total," "rational" outlook and practice challenged by modern developments.

REFERENCES

1 Polish dictionaries as early as the 1840's and 1850's defined "intellectual" (*intelektualista*) as one acting in accord with reason. See M. Olgebrandt, *Slownik jezyka polskiego* (Wilno, 1861), p. 422.

Roughly speaking, the distinction drawn here between the "cultured," "objective" and the "philosophic," "subjective" intelligentsia corresponds to that which Theodor Geiger makes between the "academicians" and the "educated" on the one hand, and the "intelligentsia" proper, on the other. See his *Aufgaben und Stellung der Intelligenz in der Gesellschaft* (Stuttgart, 1949), pp. 4-19. For the sake of convenience, I shall refer to the one group as the "cultured" intelligentsia, and to the other as the "critical" intelligentsia.

2 I use the term "rational" here in the sense in which it is applicable to the Russian intelligentsia, that is, in its original eighteenth-century sense, "in accord with reason," and contrary to "arbitrary," "fanatical," or "despotic." In the twentieth century this term has undergone a subtle evolution. As a result of the emergence of the idea and the term "rationalization" (in the sense of economic streamlining), "rational" has tended to acquire the meaning of "efficient." In some ways this connotation is antithetical to the older one, since "rational" in its original sense implied "free," whereas in the modern one it is perfectly compatible with "despotic" and "fanatical." It is the older sense I have in mind when I say that the Soviet Union is not "rational."

3 That is not to imply that the intelligentsia condoned these circumstances. On the contrary, the majority of educated Russians wished to change them. But

in historical retrospect it appears that the existence of the cultured elite in Russia in large measure depended on their preservation.

4 Cultural syncretism of this kind is observable in contemporary Poland, where intellectuals of peasant and working-class origin tend to model themselves on the pre-1939 Polish intellectual, who was of gentry or middle-class origin.

5 The extremely naïve political program of young Seriozha in A. Terts's recent story, "The Court is in Session," is probably characteristic of much of the contemporary Soviet youth.

6 I would regard the Soviet students' striving for a clearly defined sphere of private life as brought out in Mr. Burg's paper in this volume, and the Soviet writers' struggle against extreme party control described by Mr. Hayward, as among the manifestations of this tendency.

In so far as "ideological" disciplines such as history and political theory are considered critical for the system, they have been emphatically exempt from this kind of "autonomization." The attempt of Burdzhalov in 1956 to win for history the same relative autonomy that had been granted literature and the visual arts, as is known, ended in disaster.

7 See, for example, a recent book by L. B. Kantorovich, *Ekonomicheskii raschet nailuchshego ispol'zovaniia resursov* (Moscow, 1959) which adopts some of the modern methods of mathematical economic analysis. The author is criticised from a more orthodox Soviet viewpoint in a foreword written by V. S. Nemchinov.

8 Professor Wetter's remarks in this issue on the conflict between science and official ideology, as well as the document cited below (pp. 192-207), provide materials illustrating this point.

LEOPOLD LABEDZ

The Structure of the Soviet Intelligentsia

DURING THE FIRST WORLD WAR an American writer published a series
of articles on Russia in *Collier's*, in *Everybody's Magazine*, and in the
Century Magazine. These reports by Richard Washburn Child later
appeared in his *Potential Russia* (1916), including this passage:

Among Russian women as among Russian men there is a third class
characterized not by its exclusion from the other two classes which are
classes of high birth or lack of it, or wealth, or lack of it, or position in
governmental service, or lack of it, but by intellectual characteristics.
Among women as among men this class is called the Intelligentsia, and an
individual of it is called an intelligent.

"Define an intelligent," suggested a war correspondent from the United
States who had a distaste for generalities.

The Englishman who writes articles upon Russian manners and customs
slid down into his chair, the French diplomatic attaché scowled, an
American who has done business in Kiev, Moscow, and Warsaw for seven
years coughed, and the two Russians, one a journalist and the other a
member of the Lower House of the Empire, the Duma, smiled sourly.

"What is meant is something which has escaped before it is captured,"
said the Petrograd editor, running his long forefinger about his collar as if
seeking relief from asphyxiation. "An intelligent is an educated person—
from a University—perhaps engaged in a profession—and perhaps with
ideas of reform of Russia."

"And yet there is Leonid H. — !" said the Frenchman dreamily, looking
across the tables at which well-gowned and smiling ladies, so different
from the women of London and Paris, sat just as if war were not going on.
"He never saw a University. His hobby was individual study. He is in no
learned profession. He has no idea of reforming Russia. And he is a
bureaucrat."

"But he, too, is an intelligent," the Englishman said, and the others
nodded.

"Ah, there it is as always—an intelligent is an intelligent," the journalist
cried out in despair.

63

The member of the Duma said, "Let us say that an intelligent is one who thinks."

"Who thinks—" repeated the Englishman, waiting for more.

"Who thinks and talks and writes of change," finished the Russian. "An intelligent is an intelligent."

"It will do," they all said.

Forty-five years later the intelligentsia is still referred to as a third category. It is officially described as "a social stratum consisting of people who are occupied professionally with mental labor," which, unlike the workers and peasants, does not form a separate class since it does not occupy an independent position in the system of social production. Yet the difficulties with defining the intelligentsia are as great in Soviet Russia as in Tsarist Russia, but for other reasons.

One difficulty is that the Marxist determinant of class—the relation to the means of production—is clearly insufficient for distinguishing between "the new Soviet intelligentsia" and the working class. Neither owns the means of production, privately or cooperatively. Obviously, other criteria must be used to differentiate between them if one is to describe the composition of the Soviet intelligentsia and its position in the Soviet social structure.

The difficulties in using other criteria in the official Soviet pronouncements on the subject stem from doctrinal embarrassments.[1] One of the distinguishing marks of Communist society, according to Marxist theory, is the disappearance of differences between mental and manual labor, and consequently, of the intelligentsia as a separate social category. Yet there are few signs in Soviet Russia of the withering-away of occupations professionally concerned with mental labor, despite the claim that the building of socialism has been accomplished and that the country has already entered the phase of the construction of Communism. Specialization, professionalization, and a wide range of skills based on scientific education are inherent in the modern industrial division of labor, not in a particular system of property relationships under which industrialism is promoted.

The second difficulty concerns the scope of the definition, i.e., the question of where to draw the line between mental and manual occupations in the general occupational structure. Here, too, the doctrinal precepts do not meet the actual social situation. Even under the dictatorship of the proletariat the population finds it more desirable to belong to the intelligentsia than to the working class, since intellectual occupations enjoy greater prestige than do manual ones, in Soviet society as in the West. This results in conceptual confusion and statistical ambiguities. The intelligentsia include not only occupations that do not fit the historical Russian usage of the term, but also some that transcend the formal Soviet definition.

It is clear why the traditional concept of the intelligentsia does not fit "the new Soviet intelligentsia." The old intelligentsia was not an occupational group, and its membership was not determined by educational criteria: it was the attitude toward the existing order that was the decisive factor. With the new Soviet intelligentsia, education and occupation play a far more important role, although they do not suffice to account for the current Soviet statistical definition, which includes some nonintellectual pursuits. The group designated as intelligentsia in Soviet statistics differs not only from that historically included in the Russian meaning of the concept, or from its Western derivatives, but also from that described by the official Soviet definition. This discrepancy is probably a result of the gap between the doctrinal formulation of the problem (dating from 1934 when Stalin gave his stamp to it) and the more general usage of the term, which in effect facilitated "the entry" into the intelligentsia of some working-class categories. This discrepancy between the doctrinal and statistical definitions of the term is not to be confused with the Western distinction between the subjective and objective criteria of status—unascertainable without relevant surveys inside the USSR.

The current application of the concept of the intelligentsia evolved from a pre-Revolutionary usage, which, because the intelligentsia was changing its character, was becoming obsolete even before 1917. The penitent nobles and *raznochintsy* no longer dominated it, its political and social preoccupations were being diluted by more individualistic pursuits and aesthetic interests, and the free professions were becoming more numerous. It was at this transitional stage that the Russian intelligentsia faced the Revolution, still as a carrier of the Russian revolutionary tradition, but no longer a dedicated order as in the beginning, when as a self-conscious group it was totally alienated. When Zaichnevski's cali to the axe finally materialized, the Russian intelligentsia had already changed in composition, and the tough-minded, radical descendants of Tkachev and Nechaev formed only one stream among many. The intelligentsia as a whole enthusiastically welcomed the February revolution, but its attitude toward the October coup was far more ambivalent, as exemplified by Sukhanov, "the Hamlet of the revolution," or by Dr. Zhivago. Its attitude soon crystallized into muted hostility toward the "Soviet power," though it had no sympathy for the Whites either.

The ruling Communist Party, however, needed the services of the bourgeois *spets* (specialist) for the management of the state and the economy, and it was then that the phrase "the toiling intelligentsia" (*trudyashchaya intelligentsia*) first came into general use. It was a hybrid term, in which the adjective "toiling" had an expiatory overtone, for the word *intelligent* had by then acquired a pejorative meaning, signifying for the Party not revolutionary ardor (as it did for the Tsarist officials) but "petty-bourgeois vacillations." For the members of the intelligentsia itself, it was a saving clause, that legitimized its existence, and distinguished it from other social categories condemned to extinction, like the bourgeoisie and the landowners. The term *trudyashchaya intelligentsia* persisted until the early 'thirties, when Stalin announced a new policy regarding it: discrimination on the basis of "social origin" was to be alleviated. The decision to proceed with enforced industrialization in a country short of technological cadres put the old specialists at a premium, but they were never really accepted, as the trial of the Industrial Party and the subsequent show-trials, *inter alia*, indicated. They were to be replaced by a new generation of specialists, educated and formed under the Soviet regime, who were expected to display entirely new characteristics, not only in respect to their political loyalty, but also in the wider social sense. The break with the old Russian intelligentsia was to be complete. And indeed, with Stalin's proclamation in 1934 of the achievement of socialism, and with his formulation then of the new theory of the Soviet social structure, the Soviet leaders never ceased to repeat that "the new Soviet intelligentsia" is a wholly new phenomenon, a stratum with characteristics never before seen in history.

In fact, even before the Revolution the Russian intelligentsia had been undergoing an evolution comparable to that which took place in other countries that had entered on the path of industrialization. There were differences, of course, because of the Russian historical background and the peculiarities of the Russian social structure. Such differences notwithstanding, there were certain basic similarities which made the effects of industrialization comparable to those in other countries. Enforced industrialization in the Soviet era has naturally increased these trends, in respect to the composition of the intelligentsia and its position in the general social structure.

The Occupational Dynamics of the Soviet Intelligentsia

Until recently only a very incomplete picture of the occupational structure of the Soviet intelligentsia could have been drawn on the basis of the information available. However, the newly published Soviet statistical yearbook contains the following table[2] (p. 672):

The Composition of the Soviet Intelligentsia

		1926	1956
All intelligentsia	(in thousands)	2,725	15,460
Heads of enterprises, constructions, sovkhozes, kolkhozes, machine tractor stations, establishments and organizations, including heads of all structural subdivisions of enterprises, establishments and organizations*		365	2,240
Technical personnel ("engineers" including chief and senior engineers, architects, technicians, foremen, dispatchers, norm-controllers, station-masters, etc.)		225	2,570
Agronomical, veterinary, and agricultural personnel (agronomists, zootechnicians, veterinary workers, surveyors, geodesists, meliorators, etc.)		45	376
Scientific workers (professors, lecturers in higher educational establishments, research workers), excluding heads of scientific institutions and of higher educational establishments		14	231
Teachers, lecturers, and educators (including heads of schools and preschool establishments)		381	2,080
Cultural-educational workers (including those in charge of clubs, libraries, publishing enterprises) and art workers		90	572
Physicians (excluding dentists), heads of medical and curative institutions†		57	329
Intermediate medical personnel (dentists, *feldshers* [medical aides], midwives, nurses, laboratory workers, pharmacists, etc.)		128	1,047
Planning and accountancy personnel		650	2,161
Judiciary staff		27	67
Students of higher educational establishments (excluding evening and correspondence courses)		168	1,178
Other groups of intelligentsia		575	2,609

* Excluding the heads of schools, preschool establishments, medical and curative institutions, juridical institutions, clubs, libraries, and publishing enterprises.

† Including physicians occupied in research or teaching in scientific institutes and higher educational establishments.

The table is accompanied by a note explaining that "these data about the intelligentsia do not include a great number of workers *(rabochiye)* and other categories of workmen *(rabotniki)* with a secondary education who are studying without leaving their work in secondary special and higher educational establishments."

In previous Soviet references to the intelligentsia, it was not made clear that such categories as foremen (*proraby, mastera, desyatniki*), dispatchers, norm-controllers *(normirovshchiki)*, etc., were included.

The *Bol'shaya sovetskaya entsiklopediya* listed scientists, civil engineers, teachers, writers, artists, physicians, agronomists, etc., as examples of occupations which form the "new Soviet intelligentsia," but not these other occupations, hardly describable as intellectual.

However, it seems that although the actual criteria for the Soviet statistical definition of the intelligentsia were never made explicit, the scope of the net has probably been fairly consistent, at least since the 'thirties. During the 18th Congress of the Party in 1939 Molotov disclosed the figures on the intelligentsia, with a breakdown slightly different from the one presented in the current Statistical Yearbook. He gave this analysis of the Soviet intelligentsia as of January 1937:

(all figures in thousands)	
1. Directors and other executives of enterprises, institutions, factory departments, sovkhozes, kolkhozes, etc.	1,751
2. Engineers, architects, etc.	250
3. Intermediate technical personnel	810
4. Agronomists	80
5. Miscellaneous scientific personnel for agriculture	96
6. Scientific workers (professors, etc.)	80
7. Teachers	969
8. Cultural workers (journalists, librarians, etc.)	297
9. Art workers	159
10. Physicians	132
11. Intermediate medical personnel (nurses, etc.)	382
12. Economists and statisticians	822
13. Bookkeepers and accountants	1,617
14. Judiciary staff	46
15. University and college students	550
16. Other groups of intelligentsia (including those in the armed forces)	1,550
Total:	9,591

Source: *The Land of Socialism Today and Tomorrow* (Moscow, 1939), p. 149.

It seems probable that the current breakdown has been arrived at by amalgamating some categories from the above table, namely, 2 and 3, 4 and 5, 8 and 9, and 12 and 13. Assuming that this is so, and that comparable types of occupations were consistently included (some of them did not exist in 1926) in the over-all categories, one can construct the following table of the occupational dynamics of the Soviet intelligentsia on the basis of the official breakdown:

(all figures in thousands)					
1926 = 100	1926	1937	% increase	1956	% increase
All intelligentsia	2,725	9,591	350	15,460	570
Executives	365	1,751	480	2,240	610
Technical-industrial personnel	225	1,060	470	2,570	1,140
Technical-agricultural personnel	45	176	390	376	830
Scientific workers	14	80	570	231	1,650
Teachers	381	969	250	2,080	540
Cultural workers	90	453	500	572	520
Physicians	57	132	230	329	580
Intermediate medical personnel	128	382	300	1,047	820
Planning and accountancy personnel	650	2,439	370	2,161	330
Judiciary staff	27	46	170	67	250
University and college students	168	550	330	1,178	700
Other groups of intelligentsia	575	1,550	270	2,609	450

Leaving aside problems of definition, one can get a general idea of the development of the professional composition of the Soviet intelligentsia from this (not very satisfactory) breakdown.

The greatest increase in the size of the intelligentsia occurred before the war; in the decade 1926-1936 it rose by almost 7 millions, while in the subsequent two decades by only 6 millions. Not surprisingly, the greatest over-all percentage increase occurred among the technical industrial and scientific personnel, and the postwar growth was no less spectacular than that of the prewar period. The technical industrial personnel increased more quickly than the technical agricultural personnel, but the latter also rose very substantially. This is another reminder that, contrary to the general view, Soviet investments in agriculture, both capital and educational, were quite substantial (their effect on productivity in agriculture relative to the effect of such investment in industry is another matter). The number of teachers and educators has also shown a uniform tendency for rapid growth throughout the period, and so has the medical personnel. The Soviet Union not only claims that it is now graduating almost three times more civil engineers yearly than is the United States (94,000 and 35,000, respectively, in 1958), but also that it has the highest number of physicians relative to population (16.4 and 12.0 per 10,000, respectively, in 1956). The expansion of the Soviet educational system is visible in the growth of the number of students maintained throughout the postwar period.

In contrast, three other categories have not shown a comparable tendency to increase. The most striking is the slow growth of the legal profession; the number of jurists has increased only two and one-half times during this period, less than half the average for the whole intelligentsia. There is, of course, no reason to suppose that this is owing to the insignificance of the Soviet penal system or to the low incidence of crime (criminal statistics are not published), rather it is a reflection of the weak development of the *Rechtstaat* in the Soviet system.

As for "cultural workers" and "art workers," categories which include journalists and librarians, writers and painters, as well as the more humble *kulturniki* (lowbrow *Kulturtraegers* at a grass-roots level, dealing with posters and anniversaries, "red corners" and manifestations), and similar occupations, in the first decade there was a spectacular increase in their number (perhaps reflecting the growth not only of "culture" but also of the propaganda apparatus), but there was hardly any increase in the subsequent two decades.

Planning and accountancy personnel have also shown a tendency to become stationary since the period of quick growth; their numbers have actually fallen during the last twenty years, owing perhaps to a slight decrease in the army of Soviet accountants and bookkeepers. It may indicate that the days of that most popular Soviet counting machine, the abacus, are limited.

The two remaining categories are executives and the "other groups of intelligentsia." Throughout Soviet history they consistently formed about 30 percent of the total. Their interest for us lies in the fact that they comprise most of what is designated in the Soviet Union as *rukovodiashchie kadry* (the leading cadres) or what in popular parlance is referred to as *nachalstvo* (the bosses). The first group includes managers, directors, and state administrators, the second, the officer staff of the armed forces, and perhaps the cadres of other apparatuses of power as well (Party *apparatchiki* might well be included). One may gain an idea of what the first group is like. Its total for 1937 consisted of the following subgroups:

(all figures in thousands)	
Heads of administration, health services and cultural institutions	450
Directors and other executives of industrial enterprises, shops and departments	350
Chairmen and deputy-chairmen of kolkhozes, and superintendents of their dairy and livestock departments	582
Heads of machine-tractor stations, of sovkhozes, and superintendents of their dairy and livestock departments	19
Heads of producers' cooperatives	40
Store managers and heads of departments	250
Managers of restaurants and other public eating places	60
Total:	1,751

Source: *The Land of Socialism Today and Tomorrow* (Moscow, 1939), p. 148.

No corresponding figures for the present composition of this group, however, are provided in the current Statistical Yearbook. No doubt there were great changes in it; with the amalgamation of kolkhozes (reduced from 243,000 in 1937 to 69,000 in 1958) the number of their chairmen and deputy chairmen must have correspondingly diminished; the reform of the industrial administration and the establishment of *sovnarkhozy* must have affected other subgroups. Not long ago the head of the Central Statistical Administration, Professor V. N. Starovskii, promised in *Pravda* (5 February 1960) that when the full results of the recent census (January 1959) become available, they will provide detailed information "about the distribution of the population according to social groups, branches of production and occupations." One can only hope that this new data will not be tabulated, as Naum Jasny said in his *The Soviet 1956 Statistical Handbook: A Commentary* (East Lansing:

Michigan State University Press, 1957, p. 159), "according to the best
rules of riddlemaking."

The Intelligentsia in the General Economic Structure

In 1926 the Soviet urban population accounted for 18 percent of
the total, and in 1959, 48 percent. In 1928, at the beginning of the
planning era, "the workers and employees" *(rabochiye i sluzha-
shchiye)* amounted to 10.8 millions, and in 1959, to 56.3 millions.[2]
The changes in the distribution of labor roughly followed Colin
Clark's familiar scheme:[3]

	1928	1937	1958
Total labor force (without the students and the military)	100%	100%	100%
of this total:			
1 Agriculture and forestry	80%	56%	42%
2 Industry	8%	24%	31%
3 Services	12%	20%	27%

The planned growth of employment for the period 1958-1965 is
15.5 percent, but the tertiary sector is expected to grow by 22.7 percent.[4]

Thus in broad outline the Soviet occupational structure follows
developments in other countries undergoing industrialization. The
trends are similar enough, although the rates of development in
different sectors are specific and reflect both the tempo and method
of Soviet industrialization. In 1958 the number of wage and salary
workers in the USSR reached the American figure, but it has increased more rapidly since 1928.[5] On the other hand, American
agriculture employs less than 10 percent of the total labor force as
compared with 42 percent in the USSR. (Strictly speaking, the above
figures are not analytically comparable, because some of the respec-
tive occupations in America belong to the category of the self-em-
ployed, while the American labor force here includes the military,
but these minor adjustments do not change the over-all picture.)
One could say that the Soviet occupational structure reflects the
coexistence of the kolkhoz, the abacus, and the sputnik. No doubt
automation will cause further shifts in the Soviet occupational structure, and BESM (the Soviet counterpart of UNIVAC) may displace
some clerical staff; but it is wildly improbable that by the time the
Soviet Union plans to overtake the economy of the USA (i.e., in

1975) Soviet agricultural employment will comprise only 5 percent of the total labor force, a figure estimated by the American Assistant Secretary of Labor as the proportion to be employed in United States agriculture fifteen years hence. What is likely is that the percentage of industrial workers will become stabilized (with an internal shift from the unskilled to the skilled), while the number of employees will grow and the percentage of labor employed in agriculture will gradually diminish, although not to the British or American proportion.

According to the 1959 census, people with higher and secondary specialist education numbered 13.4 million, those with general secondary education numbered 9.9 million, and those with incomplete secondary education, 35.4 million.[6] Of these about 20 million are now said to be occupied with intellectual work,[7] but this may not quite coincide with the present number of intelligentsia, as neither this general criterion nor the above quoted educational levels entirely determine this figure.

The position of the intelligentsia in the general social structure is affected by the ascending scale of prestige and income on the educational and occupational ladder of the intelligentsia. The upper half consists of specialists with a higher or secondary education in their specialties; their numbers increased between 1928 and 1959 from 521,000 to 7,476,000.[8] Those with a higher education increased by 13 times, and those with a secondary specialized education, 15.4 times (from 233,000 to 3,027,000, and from 288,000 to 4,449,000, respectively). But not all specialists are listed among the intelligentsia according to their ostensible specialization. The number of jurists in 1956 is given as 79,500 (56,500 with a higher, and 23,000 with a secondary education.)[9] But the table showing the composition of the Soviet intelligentsia reproduced above gives the figure of only 67,000 as the number of the judicial personnel in that year. Perhaps some of these jurists (specialists with at least a secondary education, who seem not to appear among the intelligentsia) belong nevertheless to some category pertaining to the judicial system, such as MVD (Ministry of the Interior) or KGB (Committee of State Security). Since by 1957 the number of jurists with a secondary education actually fell to 20,400, this may have reflected reductions in the security police. Some of its personnel is probably listed among "other categories," and some among "juridical staff" in the table on the intelligentsia, but they may all be considered "jurists" in the table on specialists.

The changes in professional distribution among the branches of the economy are unfortunately given only since 1941. They are as follows: [10]

	1941			1958		
	Total	With higher education	With secondary education	Total	With higher education	With secondary education
All specialists	100%	100%	100%	100%	100%	100%
Agriculture	2%	1%	2%	5%	4%	7%
Industry and construction	15%	18%	12%	19%	15%	21%
Services	83%	81%	86%	76%	81%	72%

As elsewhere, the majority of the professionals are occupied in the services, and the specialists among the rural intelligentsia (kolkhoznaya intelligentsia) constitute only a small part of the total, although the percentage of the agriculturalists has increased, as has that of the specialists in industry. The upper educational layer of the intelligentsia rises faster in towns than in the countryside. According to the last census the number of people with a higher education increased by 3.3 times in urban centers, and by only 2.8 times in rural localities. [11] This does not necessarily contradict the figures in the above table, as some of the specialists listed under "services" are engaged in occupations which, although not urban, are not agricultural, either.

The number of women among the intelligentsia is not given, but some idea of its magnitude can be derived from the figures on the occupational and professional distribution of female labor. According to the 1959 census, women make up 55 percent of the total population (52 percent in 1926 and 1939) and the disproportion between men and women, reflecting wartime losses, is particularly striking in the groups above the age of 32, where for every 100 men there are 166 women. [12] Between 1929 and 1958 the proportion of women among the "workers and employees" increased from 27 percent to 46 percent, but they formed a much greater percentage in some branches such as teaching and health services, where they now constitute 69 percent and 85 percent of the total, respectively. [13] They also form almost half of all those with a higher education (1,845,000 out of 3,778,000) and their numbers have increased much faster than those for men; since 1939 the total has risen by 4.9 times, while the number of men with a higher education has risen by only 2.4 times.[14] Among the specialists with a higher education, women constituted 34 percent in 1941 and 52 percent in 1958 (75 percent of all physicians).[15]

Intelligentsia in the General Social Structure

The difficulties in defining the intelligentsia are also at the root of the difficulties in relating this group to the general social structure. Writers, artists, technical specialists, managers, *apparatchiki,* army officers, state bureaucrats, doctors, teachers—all these and the army of clerks and foremen do not seem to form a very cohesive social group. Is it conscious of itself as a group and of its opposition to other groups? No clear-cut answer can be given to such a question. The operation of the Soviet system prevents classes from acquiring too much class-consciousness, let alone a "stratum" with a range of occupations stretching into the working class. Inkeles subdivided the Soviet intelligentsia into four strata,[16] others have made different subdivisions,[17] but whatever the scheme, the heterogeneity of the intelligentsia is obvious. As respects the usual determinants of social position (prestige, income, and power) it includes very divergent categories. Yet, despite all the changes in the composition of the intelligentsia, the increased role of the technical specialists and the inclusion of "non-*intelligent*" occupations, the break with the old intelligentsia is not complete. A residual element of continuity is visible in that part of the "new Soviet intelligentsia" which is referred to as *tvorcheskaya intelligentsia* (the creative intelligentsia) rather than in the *tekhnicheskaya intelligentsia* (the technical intelligentsia). The title of *intelligent,* however, must still carry some general prestige if the head of the Soviet Writers Union denied it so hotly to Pasternak. Nevertheless there is little doubt that during the Soviet era it is the technical intelligentsia which has been on the upgrade, and through its performance it has gained a genuine social prestige, while the opposite holds true of the "creative intelligentsia,"[18] whose intellectual activity was crippled through Party controls.

If there is some argument about the quasi-class character of the intelligentsia, there cannot be any about its being a new "ruling class." As early as 1918 Waclaw Machajski wrote that "as long as the working class is condemned to ignorance, the intelligentsia will rule through the workers' deputies."[19] According to his theory, the intelligentsia, having eliminated private capitalism with the help of the proletariat, becomes the new ruling class on the basis of its possession of the "capital" of knowledge and education. Ever since Bakunin's *State and Anarchy*[20] there has been no dearth of theories about the ruling class in the "new society." Burnham's "managers" and Djilas' "new class" are the two best-known examples. All these theories have a correct perception (or presentiment) of the inevitable inequality of power and privilege in post-Revolutionary society; but in their effort to present the new elite as a post-capitalist counterpart of the bourgeoisie in the era of capitalism, or of the landed aristocracy in feudalism, they all miss a point. That is, they oversimplify by applying concepts that might have been relevant in the past, but which are no longer applicable to the present era of mass-organization; for today the more pertinent questions to be asked are not about the relations between classes, but about the relation of the classes (or other social categories) to the system of organized political power. To present the Party as a representative of a class does not make sense, whether it is done in apologetics, by identifying it with the working class, or in criticism, by equating it with the interests of some other class or social group, technocratic or otherwise. In either case we face a piece of sociological fiction.

The "new Soviet intelligentsia" is emphatically not a "ruling class," whether in Marx's or Mosca's sense of the term. Even if, despite its heterogeneity, it has a degree of group consciousness, it still has no power to compel the Party to act in its interests, it cannot even act as a pressure or veto group. The increased membership in the Party of the scions of the intelligentsia no doubt affects its profile socially, but they do not act as representatives of a class, and even though they may indirectly influence some decisions on policy, they most certainly do not determine the Party policy as such. The changes in Soviet wage and salary structure, the raising of the minimum wage and a reduction of some of the higher salaries do not look like acts of the "executive committee" of the intelligentsia. What the long-term effects of the *embourgeoisement* of the intelligentsia might be, and how they may affect the Party, is anybody's guess. So far, it is not the intelligentsia that controls the Party, but the Party that controls the intelligentsia through *nomenklatura* (the system of control of appointments) and the network of political controls. This Party grip is incomparably more pronounced in the humanities than in the natural sciences, and therefore it affects the "creative intelligentsia" even more than the technical intelligentsia; but both are dependent on Party patronage.

However, now that the Soviet economy is becoming more mature,

Party control may be exercised in a different way. In the future, economic inequality may be less directly transformed into social inequality, as the more indispensable goods (food, clothing, housing), which so directly determine the style of life, become more widely available. This does not mean, of course, that social differences will disappear in the USSR: economic inequalities will persist (incentives are a matter of differentials) as well as differences in power and education; as elsewhere they will be expressed through the symbols of status. But both the Party and the intelligentsia will have to operate in a new social context.

Marx and Engels failed to establish a clear definition of class, and they did not see that the problems of political power and social mobility, of economic privilege and social distance, continue to exist, whether society is stratified or "classless." They did notice the growth of a professional intelligentsia, but they did not visualize how this would affect the society that was to emerge from the "dictatorship of the proletariat." Soviet ideologists, therefore, have to explain away some of the facts which do not fit into the doctrinal scheme. On the one hand, they present the universal effects of industrial development on the occupational structure as a unique socialist achievement: "The Soviet intelligentsia is a social stratum of a new socialist type, unknown in all the history of a humanity,"[21] as if doctors and teachers, managers and scientists, clerks and technicians, existed only in the USSR. On the other hand, the ideologists assert that "with the victory of Communism there will be no intelligentsia as a separate social stratum."[22] Since full Communism is now officially a not-too-distant prospect, "the new Soviet intelligentsia" should by then be proclaimed out of existence. But as doctors and teachers will presumably continue to exist, and the advantages of specialization are not going to be abandoned, only a purely semantic solution of the doctrinal problem is feasible. Such a terminological operation on the "separate social stratum" may or may not be impending, but in any case the real problems of a society entering the second stage of its industrial revolution will remain.

Social mobility is one of these problems. As in other industrial societies, social mobility will remain high in the Soviet Union, but despite the expanding economy, there will be some downward social mobility.[23] In the United States, one-third of the sons of professionals, semiprofessionals, proprietors, managers, and public officials are in manual occupations. As S. L. Lipset indicates (in his *Political Man: The Social Bases of Politics*) these categories on the whole are profoundly conservative in the States. Will the scions of the Soviet intelligentsia also remain so if faced with the prospect of being déclassé in a classless society? Or will they display the more radical attitudes historically associated with bourgeois youth without the prospects of a career?

The problem may arise, and if so, it may contribute to the re-emergence of that "ability to generalize facts" which was a characteristic of the old intelligentsia. Historical continuity may yet reassert itself, but if it does it will be in a very diluted form. This time the Sons are not likely to be too rebellious against the Fathers.[24] With the rise of the professional and technical cadres, the structure of the intelligentsia is now different, and so is its profile. It is not alienated from the general social order, and only students and some elements connected with the "creative intelligentsia" display dangerous thoughts. In a bureaucratic structure, as Max Weber has observed, an ascending social mobility requires conformity, rather than searching intelligence.

REFERENCES

1 A short account of the doctrinal treatment of the problem is given in the present writer's article, "The New Soviet Intelligentsia, Origins and Recruitment," *Soviet Survey*, July-September 1959, pp. 103-111.

2 *Narodnoe khoziaystvo SSSR v 1958 godu* (The National Economy of the USSR in 1958; Moscow, 1959), pp. 656, 672.

3 *Ibid.*, p. 654. The distribution of occupational categories is not entirely comparable to Colin Clark's.

4 *Voprosy Ekonomiki,* No. 1, 1960, p. 105.

5 Warren W. Eason, *Comparisons of the United States and Soviet Economies: The Labor Force* (papers submitted by panelists appearing before the Subcommittee on Economic Statistics, Joint Economic Committee of the U. S. Congress).

6 *Pravda*, 4 February 1960.

7 Starovskii in *Pravda,* 5 February 1960.

8 *The National Economy . . . 1958*, p. 102.

9 *Ibid.*, p. 674.

10 *Ibid.*, p. 615. As in the previous table, the three branches are not entirely comparable to Colin Clark's.

11 *Pravda*, 4 February 1960.

12 *Ibid.*

13 *The National Economy . . . 1958*, p. 664.

14 *Pravda*, 4 February 1960.

15 *The National Economy . . . 1958*, pp. 690-691.

16 A. Inkeles, "Social Stratification and Mobility in the Soviet Union, 1940-50," *American Sociological Review,* 1950, *15:* 465-479.

17 A summary of such schemes is given in a paper delivered by S. V. Utechin at the First International Congress of Sociology in Liège, "Social Stratification and Social Mobility in the USSR," (ISA/SSM/Cong. 2/27).

18 It is interesting to note that a recent survey conducted in Poland has shown that "the highest prestige among children is enjoyed by the so-called 'professions' and creative intelligentsia" (*Zycie Gospodarcze,* 24 January 1960). But then in Poland one can still read matrimonial advertisements seeking a wife from "the true intelligentsia" (*Kulisy,* No. 3, 1960).

19 Quoted in Max Nomad, *Rebels and Renegades,* New York, The Macmillan Company, 1932.

20 See a neglected text by Marx on Bakunin recently published by Henry Mayer in *Etudes de Marxologie,* No. 91, October 1959, Paris; Bakunin asserted that the "would-be people's state will be nothing else but a despotic rule over the toiling masses by a new, numerically small aristocracy of genuine or sham scientists." Elsewhere, he referred to the "rule of the great mass of the people by a small minority who, once they become rulers or representatives of the people, cease to be workers . . . from that time on they represent not the people but themselves and their own claims to govern the people. Those who doubt this know precious little about human nature." Marx evidently doubted it, because he commented on the margin: "No more than a manufacturer today ceases to be a capitalist when he becomes a member of the municipal council." Obviously, Bakunin had a better grasp of the problem of power, but retrospectively, it is clear that neither of them could see the new aspects of the problem, which only emerged in the twentieth century.

21 F. Konstantinov, "Sovetskaya Intelligentsia," *Kommunist,* No. 15, October 1959, p. 49.

22 *Ibid.*

23 Zinaïda Shakhovskoy reports the following conversation in *Ma Russie habilée en URSS* (Paris, Grasset, 1958; also published as: Zinaïda Schakovskoy, *The Privilege Was Mine,* New York, G. P. Putnam's Sons, 1959): "Au cours d'une réception la réflexion d'un diplomate occidental jeta dans la confusion un haut personnage du Kremlin. Celui-ci faisait remarquer au diplomate que tous ses collègues étaient fils d'ouvriers. Ce qui d'ailleurs n'est pas vrai.—C'est très bien, dit le diplomate, mais j'aimerais savoir si, parmi les fils de vos hommes d'Etat, il y en a qui soient des ouvriers" (page 71).

24 On different currents in the old Russian intelligentsia, see George Fischer, *Russian Liberalism* (Cambridge, Harvard University Press, 1958). Fischer argues that under the impact of industrialization, the erstwhile "superfluous" and radical Sons of Turgenev, who "reacted to Russia's halting modernization by forming a new isolated group," were partly transformed into responsible, professionally trained "grandsons" at the end of the nineteenth and the beginning of the twentieth centuries.

DAVID BURG

Observations on Soviet University Students

THIS ARTICLE is based on observations of Moscow students, one of whom I was for five years (1951-1956). The observations are limited to three faculties of the University—one of science and two of arts—and four or five "institutes," e.g., specialized colleges. Whenever possible, I have tried not to rely entirely on my impressions, but to quote Soviet printed sources as well. All generalizations relate specifically to Moscow students, who, I believe, are typical as far as students in big cities are concerned. Whenever no sources are quoted I am fully responsible for the information.

Although the million and a half university and institute students in the USSR comprise no more than three-quarters of one percent of the total population, their significance seems to be inversely proportional to their numbers. According to Khrushchev, only one-third of these advanced students are the children of workers and peasants; that is to say, a distinct majority are by birth members of the intelligentsia.[1] (Khrushchev was speaking of Soviet students as a whole.) A closer analysis reveals that the Soviet intelligentsia, which plays a leading role in the society and provides its ruling elite, has in fact become largely hereditary.

Soviet institutions of higher education may be divided into two groups, the "prestige" and "nonprestige" institutions. A student at Moscow University and a student at, say, the Poltava Pedagogical Institute are not equal in terms of learning, social prestige, or postgraduate opportunity. Only a handful of students attending the prestige institutions come from families outside the intelligentsia; it is the children of the intelligentsia who virtually monopolize the better known universities and such distinguished institutions as the Aviation

Translated from the Russian by Judith Davison.

Institute and the Institute of Foreign Relations in Moscow. The greater the prestige of a university or institute, the more "elite" are those who attend it. It is true that the majority of the students' parents (and increasingly their parents' parents) were once, long ago, promoted from "the people," but this fact in no way affects the lives of their offspring. If during the last few years preference in admissions has been given to applicants coming from "the factory," this does not indicate that university lecture rooms are being filled with manual laborers. In the first place, now, as always, a large percentage of places in the "prestige" institutions are set aside for graduates of the secondary schools. In the second place, even if the Soviet press is to be believed, the majority of those coming directly from the factory are not real workers either, but children of intelligentsia families who have spent two years working in a factory in order to qualify for further study.

These remarks may serve to define the basic social position of those with whom this article is concerned. It is a new generation of a hereditary Soviet elite, some of whom will in the future attain the highest rung of the social ladder. This is especially true of the students in Moscow University and in certain Moscow institutes, among whom I have lived. Rather than survey all the varied problems that face the young Soviet elite, I shall concentrate on the problem that seems to me to be central. This is, in brief, the attitude of the elite to Russia's present-day social and political structure.

Even to suggest that such a problem exists may appear to some nonsensical; one may ask how can an elite be anything but vitally interested in the preservation of existing conditions? How can it hold any but a conformist attitude toward the system that guarantees its dominant place in society? The uneasy tone in which the Soviet press has discussed student attitudes since 1956, however, indicates that such a simplistic reaction is unwarranted. According to these reports, there are people in Soviet institutions "whose individual shortcomings prevent them from perceiving the blessings of Soviet life."[2] Student circles of "ultra-revolutionaries," "nihilists creating a transvaluation of values," "apolitical, ideologically foreign persons," "disturbers of the social order," have been discovered in Leningrad institutes.[3] The *Tribune,* the wall newspaper of Moscow University, has permitted the appearance of "slanderous attacks on Soviet power, borrowed from the bourgeois press."[4] "Gossips and demagogues have come forth with speeches" in the Moscow Institute of Energetics.[5] In the Ural University and Polytechnical Institute "demagogic appearances of individual students" have been reported.[6] And in Voronezh, "petty bourgeois individualists" have been uncovered.[7] On 28 February 1957 the Central Committee of the Young Communist League (the Komsomol) issued a resolution admitting serious deficiencies in its own ideological-educational work. On 26 March 1957 the *Komsomolskaia Pravda*, abandoning the accepted practice of Soviet journalists of emphasizing the atypicality of any negative event, wrote: "We must consider not only how to eliminate individual shortcomings, but also how to improve decisively all ideological work [among students]." Earlier, on 8 November 1956 Khrushchev himself had spoken of an "unhealthy frame of mind among students"; he later returned again and again, directly and indirectly, to the same theme.

Thus a host of official Soviet comments indicate that there are persons in student circles of prestige and nonprestige institutions whose attitudes suit neither the Soviet press nor the Soviet rulers. The attitude of these students is paradoxical; those at the very height of the social order "do not perceive the blessings" of their position. The historical parallel of the nineteenth-century gentry—seeking expiation, repentant of a position they felt sinned against the people —comes immediately to mind. It is tempting to say that the present dissatisfaction of youth is simply a repetition of the Russian revolutionary movement, an expression of that uncompromising aspiration toward justice with which every Russian is eternally imbued. It is tempting to say that the Russian intelligentsia, failing to find justice in Communist reality, has turned away from it, to seek out truth "despite good sense, despite the elements," in Griboyedov's words. This would only partly explain it, however. Fathers live on in their children, and children emulate their fathers; nonetheless, it is impossible not to notice the difference between the old Russian *intelligent*, marching off to revolution in the same frame of mind in which some men join a particularly strict monastic order, and today's Soviet *intelligent*.

The old *intelligent* was basically déclassé, lacking both a firm position and an occupation. Educated, sensitive, bright, he first found in the Revolution an employment for his otherwise wasted talents. The old revolutionary was essentially such a "superfluous man" (*lishniy chelovek*) who had found his place in life. The professional class, as distinct from the unattached nineteenth- and early twentieth-century intelligentsia, though bearing many of the latter's psychological birthmarks—had only begun to come into being in pre-Revolutionary Russia, at a time when Russia was entering the industrial stage of her development. In contrast, today's Soviet in-

telligentsia is in no sense déclassé. It is first of all composed of professional people, of men of affairs: scholars, industrial experts, engineers, doctors, teachers, agronomists, all of whom have clearly
defined functions in society. The difference between the old revolutionaries and the new intelligentsia is the difference between déclassé
truth-seekers, free from all social bonds, and men who are practical,
active members of a society to which they are bound by a thousand
ties. It is deeply symbolic that the revolutionary (Kibalchich) whose
bomb killed Alexander II was a talented engineer and one of the
first Russians to work on space travel. Yet for all his calculations, he
won a place only in the police archives.

Since the new intelligentsia, as distinguished from the old, par-
ticipates actively in society, it may seem puzzling that precisely
within this group "antisocial" attitudes reminiscent of the old revolutionary spirit should have appeared. Khrushchev offered the official explanation of the phenomenon at the XXIst Party Congress,
when he said that the young people of today lack experience of life
and have not personally endured the hell of capitalism, and that they
are therefore open to the influence of bourgeois ideology imported
into the USSR from abroad and disseminated by certain members
of the older generation.[8] "Unhealthy attitudes" are thus represented
as foreign superficialities. The possibility that they might originate
within Soviet society is not even considered. Even so, the official
explanation tacitly acknowledges two important facts: that something in Soviet ideology does not satisfy some people (for otherwise,
why turn to bourgeois ideology?); and that "bourgeois ideology" is
attractive in itself to persons ignorant of the realities of capitalism.

The lure of "bourgeois ideology" evidently contradicts the widely
held Western belief that the farther the pre-Revolutionary era re-
cedes into the past, the stronger will be the younger generations'
resistance to all foreign influence. One cannot help asking why a
person raised in the spirit of socialism succumbs to bourgeois ideological influence merely because he has not lived under capitalism. To
carry the point further: why "bourgeois ideology"—by the admission
of the Soviet press—exercises its strongest influence on the students
who belong to the privileged few. To answer the question, one must
examine more carefully the social position of the Soviet elite.

The cardinal factor here, I think, lies in the fact that today's elite
is not monolithic but differentiated. In the first place there are the
professional people already discussed. They appeared in large numbers during the process of industrialization, and are tied to an indus-

trial society that values technology and civilization; apart from these conditions such an elite cannot exist. This element, however, is not necessarily tied to the Soviet totalitarian system, for an executive or a doctor will be needed wherever factories and hospitals exist. There is another group within the Soviet elite, however, which can maintain its position only under the conditions peculiar to this regime. This is above all the party machine, and to a smaller degree the "ideological" intelligentsia allied with it. The party bureaucrat, or *apparatchik*, is distinguished from the ordinary party member by his professional attachment to the party, for as a rule he devotes himself exclusively to party activity. It is in his hands that real power today lies. The unpretentious "intraparty democracy" of the post-Stalinist period is the democracy of the *apparatchiki*, the democracy within an oligarchy.

The other members of the Soviet elite have neither political nor personal rights: they do not participate in decisions affecting their country's fate and, further, they do not even have command over their own lives. An incident in a recent Soviet novel reflects the powerlessness of even a prominent representative of the professional class when confronted by the authority of an *apparatchik*.[9] It recounts how a member of the Central Committee bureaucracy informs an important engineer of his transfer to the provinces. The engineer is reluctant to leave Moscow, where he is conducting his research and has his apartment, his position, and his family, but he is warned that his refusal to go will cause his expulsion from the party, and thus put a final and irrevocable end to his career, not only in the ministry that employs him but anywhere in Russia. Reconciling himself to abandoning his research, living among strangers, and leaving his children, who would remain in Moscow, he goes to his new job. The incident sums up clearly the frustrating paradox of his situation. On the one hand he, and many like him, are engaged in responsible, professional work; materially speaking, they live far more comfortable lives than the rest of the population. On the other hand, they have no rights, either political or personal. This very contradiction engenders the dissatisfaction of the professional intelligentsia, particularly among the young generation who have not yet been worn down by life, who have not yet learned the art of compromise, and who have not carried the burden of family responsibilities.

The division of the Soviet elite into "party workers" and "professional intelligentsia" begins in the universities and goes on through the Komsomol, to which more than ninety percent of all Soviet students belong. The overwhelming majority of students conceive of their future careers as divided between research and the practice of their professions, but there is a minority of some ten to fifteen percent who prefer to concentrate instead on what is called "social work." This "social work" is, in fact, nothing more than work in Komsomol positions, to which students are formally elected but actually appointed by the Party Bureau. Their activity in the Komsomol does not leave them enough time for the remarkably intensive academic schedule common to all Soviet educational institutions. While they do not receive the necessary professional training, however, they do acquire the experience of "organizational work with the masses"— party work, in other words—and it is from them that as a rule the professional party bureaucrats emerge.

Some of them frankly declare that they do not expect to pursue their chosen professions after graduation, but instead count on holding office in the Komsomol and later in the party. I shall later return to the question of how this sort of person becomes a professional party worker; now let me turn to the work they actually perform. Briefly, it is this: paying close attention to the behavior and attitude of each student, they seek by means ranging from persuasion to outright compulsion to ensure political and social conformity. The fundamental assignment of every Komsomol worker is to repress "nonconformity" in everyday life.

The basic demand of Soviet conformity is clearly and unequivocally expressed in the slogan, "Personal sacrifice for the sake of social welfare." "Social" is interpreted to mean whatever demands the regime may make of students at any given moment. The "hero of labor," ready to work selflessly wherever he is sent, never thinking of reward, treating natural human emotions as nothing more than an unavoidable irritant, symbolizes the official ethical ideal. The insistence upon sacrifice and submission in everything, whether or not it is important, is fundamental to this ideal. Laws do not restrict the choice of profession, but a "conscious Soviet man" must choose whatever the government needs. In the 1930's the government needed technicians, and the Komsomoltsy, regardless of their own inclinations, were put into technology. Now, in contrast, the government needs labor—and pressure from the Komsomol organizations turns graduates of high schools into milkmaids and locksmiths. The perfect "young builder of communism" must leave his family, fiancée, friends, and all the comforts of life to set out, for instance, for the virgin lands in Siberia. To set out uncomplainingly is not enough; he must go enthusiastically. At the present time it is law, and no longer a sense of duty that compels students to spend three years after graduation on an assigned job. Anyone refusing an assignment may be denied his diploma and is usually expelled from the Komsomol, by which means he is effectively denied forever the opportunity of holding an important or well-paying job.

"Personal sacrifices for the sake of social welfare" entail, furthermore, an unconditional surrender of leisure time. The perfect Young Communist must always be ready to undertake "social work" at the end of his own working day. For many long years much of the "social work" of Moscow University students consisted in explaining to the inhabitants of workers' barracks at the construction site of the new university how fortunate they were to be citizens of the world's first proletarian state. During the last several years it has become traditional for students to spend at least a part of their vacations and some Sundays working for little or no pay on construction gangs or, during the harvest season, on the farms. The job of organizing this "enthusiasm for labor" falls to the same professional Komsomol workers.

Finally, the Komsomol interferes even in the relations between the sexes, regulating tangled relations, demanding that transgressors confess publicly at Komsomol meetings, expelling those who refuse to account satisfactorily for themselves and those who deviate too radically from accepted "moral standards."

Such are the fundamental demands of Soviet conformity in everyday life. The attempt to organize all aspects of the life of Russian youth naturally arouses the resistance of those who are being organized, and the task of the organizers is to overcome this resistance. They are more successful, I would say, in the universities than in factories or collective farms, for to be expelled from the Komsomol or even only to be censured or given a "deficient" character rating is tantamount to being denied possibilities of advancement. In order to avoid any "unpleasantness over the Komsomol," therefore, many persons are willing to make serious sacrifices. Nonetheless, the Komsomol's meddling in private affairs arouses resentment among what appears to be the majority of students, including those who rarely concern themselves with politics and those who theoretically (especially to foreigners) defend the existing system. Frustration over the government's insistence on deciding the student's fate and determining his manner of life draws together not only the majority of students but also the majority of all young people. The first and basic cause of what the Soviet press calls "unhealthy attitudes" is, in my opinion, the interference by the party and the Komsomol in private affairs; and because it affects the largest number of people, it is the most widespread cause as well.

For most young people, escape from this interference is possible only through outright evasion, which is easiest, of course, for those who have important connections. There are always stories in the Soviet press of influential parents who arrange interesting and profitable jobs for their children, and manage to have them kept in one large city or another. The most egregious case of nepotism is perhaps the one the Soviet press has never mentioned, that of Alexei Adzhubei, Khrushchev's son-in-law, who was made foreign editor of *Komsomolskaia Pravda* upon his graduation from the university and has since been appointed editor-in-chief of *Izvestiia*, although he is little more than thirty years old. In spite of all attempts at evasion, however, the majority eventually do conform, but the feeling that their own interests are at odds with the demands from above remains. Under these circumstances the "organizers of the masses" naturally inspire distrust, ill will, and hostility.

This is a frame of mind, an emotional reaction to the Soviet system, rather than an opinion about it. Mentally, therefore, such malcontents find themselves living in two different worlds. They do not presume to doubt the system, and are theoretically prepared to defend it. But in practice, they seek as much as possible to elude all officialdom, all "social work." They run away from the virgin lands; they feign illness to avoid being sent to a collective farm for the harvest season; they invent one pretext after another for not attending the endless series of meetings and conferences. In short, they use every honest and dishonest means at their disposal to protect their private lives from the ponderous intrusion of the Soviet system. Whether consciously or not, these "private lifers," by their very existence, stand in opposition to the totalitarian regime which demands of everyone "self-sacrificing participation in the building of communism."

Only for a few persons has the exclusive concentration on "private life" become a matter of conscious attention; for most it remains simply the natural reaction of average, normal people to the abnormal demands of their environment. It is the reaction of those who, as one contemporary writer said, "understand little about politics, but feel in their lives that they are not happy." Although the average man may not articulate his attitude in just these terms, he nonetheless resents the totalitarian system most for its continuous attempts to meddle in his private life and to deflect it from its normal course. This reaction has engendered a passive opposition that the regime must for the moment take even more seriously than it would deliberate political rebellion. In his article commemorating the fortieth anniversary of the founding of the Komsomol, the well-known publicist David Zaslavskii had good reason for calling "indifference" the greatest threat to Komsomol goals.[10]

Perhaps the most interesting of all the "private lifers" are to be found among those whom one would suspect least: the "activists," the young *apparatchiki*. Today's Young Communist leader bears little resemblance to the enthusiast of the 1920's and the First Five-Year Plan, who was sure of his righteousness, and could be as ruthless to himself as to others. True, the modern activist is still ruthless to others but he is no longer ruthless with himself. On the whole, he is likely to be a person who quietly and deliberately begins his career as a party worker at the institute or university. The type is personified by A. E., an acquaintance of mine. In his first year at the philological faculty of Moscow University, A. was a square peg in a round hole. He was crude, spoke with a strong northern accent, and read very little. The son of a regional party official in the Urals, he had managed somehow to enter a university which annually turns down from nineteen to twenty-four applicants for every candidate accepted. He was by no means stupid. He learned his way around quickly and realized that he would never qualify as a scholar or a teacher. Accordingly, he took up Komsomol work: he was forever organizing, rallying, "working people over," discussing. At the same time his pleasant appearance, his simple manners, his apparent devotion to principles, his readiness to help other students find dormitory space or procure loans from the mutual benefit fund gave him a certain authority, which he began to exercise freely. During the official anti-Semitic campaign in 1953, he "exposed" as a daughter of one of the "doctor-assassins" a girl then studying at the university. In the winter of 1955-1956, when a question concerning the bribing of the administration in order that students be admitted to the university was raised at a meeting, he skillfully suppressed it. This service did not go unrewarded by the administration. Although he failed his examinations twice, he was not expelled from the university. When he came to the end of his five-year course but did not seem ready to present his thesis, he was allowed an altogether unprecedented sixth year. In his fourth year he was accepted as a candidate for party membership. He admitted openly that his ambition was to become a party worker.

This man symbolizes the Komsomol worker although, of course, not all of them are as simple as he. But what matters is the paradox-

ical fact that these warriors of conformity are themselves only superficially conformist. They preach the rule of "personal sacrifice for the
sake of social welfare," but do not practice it; clearly, careerism is
not compatible with self-effacement. The idealist *Komsomolets*, prepared to offer himself up to the cause of Communist triumph, belongs
to the past. He is dead, undone by the visible gap between word and
deed, between ideology and reality.

There are other cases of death by ideological strangulation. The
poet-activist E. Iodkovskii was among the first to go to the virgin
lands. There he wrote the song, "And we shall go, my friends, to
distant lands," which has become the semiofficial hymn of all workers
in the virgin lands. Iodkovskii, however, returned to Moscow within
four months on the pretext of attending a writers' conference; he was
never again seen in the wilderness. His superficially heroic gesture
concealed a perfectly justified calculation. He, and others like him,
are dependent on the regime, but the regime for them is only a kind
of feeding trough.

Despite their exhorting others to idealism and sacrifice, these men
remain essentially unprincipled. Nothing reveals this more strikingly
than their private interests and hobbies. The professional *Komsomoltsy* find all political and ideological arguments disconcerting, even
when they are carried on in the spirit of purest orthodoxy; shop-talk,
clothes, sports, apolitical but often off-color jokes form the common
themes of their conversation. It might be inferred that these activists are simply cynics; but while some cynics do appear, they are
the exception rather than the rule. As a rule they are men doing
their job, living from one task to the next, who do not concern themselves with the obvious gap between their daily activity and the
ideology this activity supposedly serves. Ideology is one thing and
everyday Komsomol work another. Such a situation may seem incredible, and indeed is not possible where freedom of expression and
discussion exist. But Komsomol workers do not bother with the discrepancy between ideology and reality, for even to suspect its existence is to violate one of the most sacred precepts of totalitarianism,
to pass the point at which "slander on Soviet reality" and "anti-Soviet
propaganda" begin. At this point, too, prosecution begins: because
it is from the realization of the discrepancy between ideology and
reality that conscious opposition arises.

Thus far I have confined my discussion to the conformity in
everyday life and the resentment of official interference in private
affairs. Both affect the majority of Soviet students and young people

in general, and both tend to encourage conscious opposition. But resentment and conscious opposition are not identical: not everyone has related his anger at the government's meddling to his attitude toward the system as a whole. In the final years of Stalinist terror people were so secretive that one could draw the most contradictory conclusions about their frame of mind. Everyone could have seemed ready for revolution; or everyone, with the exception of oneself and a few friends, could have appeared absolutely content with everything. It is difficult to give exact figures, but my estimate of the proportion of Soviet students whose political[11] discontent was revealed during the thaw of 1956 would be from one-fourth to one-third of the total. With the exception of the professional activists, the remaining played the familiar role of "the masses": their attitude toward the political avant-garde was sometimes sympathetic, sometimes uncomprehending, but rarely hostile.

In 1956-1957, after the XXth Party Congress, opposition elements within the institutes and universities began to wage an open battle against Komsomol leadership. They sought, first of all, to gain freedom of criticism and expression, and second to introduce a degree of intra-Komsomol democracy that would make the Komsomol a truly representative organization with an honestly elected leadership. Freedom of expression was in fact gradually achieved at that period by a kind of procedure of protestation, and extraordinarily sharp critical comments were heard more and more commonly at meetings.[12] At the same time, illegal and semilegal student journals with such characteristic titles as *Heresy* and *Fresh Voices* began to appear; they discussed art and ideology, ridiculed socialist realism, and attacked the local Komsomol leaders.[13] Wall newspapers began to print "undesirable" articles. In official literary conferences literary enthusiasts began to raise subjects formerly discussed only among intimate friends—for example, the question as to whether Soviet literature was basically truthful. The articles and pamphlets that made their appearance during this period were not wholly political, but also contained verse and prose which, in Soviet terminology, was condemned as decadent. Their themes were the confusion, depression, and impotence of man, as these typical lines reveal:

> And I do not know where to go,
> Which path to choose and to where,
> My voice is intimate and low—
> Have you a hand for a blind girl?

Finally, during the Hungarian uprising an account of the events, as gathered from a British Broadcasting Company broadcast, was posted on a bulletin board in the University of Moscow.[14]

As for intra-Komsomol democracy, many institutes and universities did attempt to use such externally democratic forms as general meetings and election of officers by secret ballot in their Komsomol organizations. In many places the rank and file of Komsomol leadership refused to accept secretaries and bureau members recommended from above and instead elected their own candidates. As a rule the regional committees then refused to confirm the "people's choice" and elections were held repeatedly as long as the Komsomol hierarchy and "the masses" failed to find mutually acceptable candidates. In certain institutes, however, it proved necessary to take the extreme step of breaking up the Komsomol organization altogether.

In some places, semilegal means of carrying out the struggle were supplemented by the creation of illegal political groups that had far-reaching political aspirations. In the history faculty at the University of Moscow, for example, a group of some ten to fifteen graduate students and young research workers printed and distributed leaflets directed against Khrushchev personally and the party dictatorship generally, and calling for the establishment of Soviet democracy and a return to the "Leninist line"; a French student in the University has since told me that the members of this group were arrested during the summer of 1957 and given the relatively mild sentence of from three to eight years in prison. In his article "Strength and Faith" in the 6 September 1959 issue of *Izvestiia*, the well-known jurist and writer Sheinin describes a typical student conspiracy of this sort:

In that perplexing time three years ago, when Stalin's cult of personality was being subjected to serious criticism, the agencies of state security discovered that a few students, estranged from reality and corrupted by an easy and comfortable life, had succumbed to enemy influence. (Radio stations like Radio Free Europe worked day and night, and various other transmitters of foreign intelligence were operating as well.) These young people met together and often carried on openly anti-Soviet conversations. They praised each other, superciliously condemned everything else, and went so far as to state their political views in essay form . . . . Later they admitted that certain of them had even proposed to write and distribute harmful leaflets.

Sheinin does not specify where the conspiracy took place or what the political views of the conspirators were, but his sketch is accurate enough.

91

Today, of course, the real strength of the student groups hardly corresponds to the magnitude of their political goals. But it must be remembered that the revolutionary movement that brought down the autocracy also began in student circles, and that the young intelligentsia's authority and influence in society is not determined exclusively by its numerical strength. Furthermore, in the period of relatively open opposition in 1956, members of the various student groups discovered that there is a broader body of sympathizers beyond their own, limited numbers. It may well be that the real significance of the "thaw" lies in the fact that it marked the beginning of a spiritual, though not politically organized, union between the radical opposition and "the masses"; that it ended the complete isolation of one tiny group from the next, and laid the foundation that may make it possible in the future to overcome the atomization and dispersion that now characterize the opponents of the regime. And though it is true that there have been almost no open pronouncements by the opposition, there is no ground for thinking that all illegal activity has also come to an end.

The party machine, recovering in mid-1957 from the shock of Poland and Hungary, turned its attention in earnest to the internal opposition: to the artistic intelligentsia and to the students about whom I am writing. The Soviet press began to speak of the appearance in educational institutions of "demagogues" and "critics" who carried on "hostile conversations" and stepped forth "with noisy speeches at meetings."[15] The journalistic lynching of demagogues and critics began; and although it was not as ferocious as it would have been in Stalin's time, it was severe enough. The victims were expelled from the institutes, some of them arrested and others simply exiled, while the newspapers waged an active campaign against them.[16] Evidently afraid that their readers' sympathies might be on the wrong side of the conflict, the popular newspapers at first neglected to define "demagogy" and "criticism" and restricted themselves instead to abuse. Some time later, they pasted the label of "revisionism" on the opposition. This, too, was left distinctly undefined: the popular press, adhering to the Orwellian prescription, simply repeated that revisionism is an evil. Even so, revisionist demands inevitably found expression in some articles. The most systematic of these, "Raise higher the banner of Marxist-Leninist ideology," appeared in the first issue for 1957 of the intraparty journal *Kommunist.*[17] First of all, the revisionists, it explained, rejected "the guiding role of the party in the life of the country"—which meant, put bluntly, the party dictatorship. In the second place, they opposed party leadership in art and in spiritual affairs generally: in other words, the party ought not to have the last word on what is, or is not, the truth. Speaking of the opposition's positive political program, *Kommunist* noted, in the third place, that "some persons subsist by talking about pure democracy."

What *Kommunist* says of the revisionist opposition in general is wholly applicable to the politically active students with whom I am concerned. But the pattern of hostile attitudes concealed by a common label of "revisionism" is in fact a good deal more interesting and complex than the *Kommunist* depicts it. It is true that the opposition is united in denying the party's monopoly of power, and its claims to the possession of absolute truth on all matters, and in rejecting dictatorship. With respect to a desirable alternative to the present regime, however, opinion is by no means unanimous. Among Soviet students and the younger intelligentsia one observes three principal opposition tendencies.

The first of these is a widespread attitude that might tentatively be called "neo-Bolshevism" or "neo-Leninism." It springs from the striking incongruity between Bolshevik goals before and during the Revolution on the one hand, and the entire Soviet social system on the other. The discovery of this very incongruity, the cry, "What are we fighting for?", has led many persons onto the path to an ideological revolution. The neo-Bolsheviks attack the regime for its failure to fulfill its pledges of 1917, and especially for its failure to create the egalitarian society that Lenin prescribed in *State and Revolution* and *The Basic Tasks of Soviet Power*. "The elimination of exploitation, democracy without officials, police or a regular army, each citizen fulfilling his obligation to administer the state." Lenin's program of 1917 is well known, and no extraordinary perspicacity is neccessary to see that Soviet reality does not conform to his definition of socialism. At the same time, in the reasoning of the neo-Bolsheviks, neither is contemporary Russia a capitalist state. The old exploiting classes, bourgeois and kulak alike, have been liquidated. Agriculture is essentially socialist because it is co-operative. Industry is nationalized. Thus the neo-Bolshevik opposition is confronted with the dilemma of reconciling the accomplishment of socialist goals in economic life with the fact that as far as social organization is concerned, the original program was more nearly achieved in the early years of the Revolution than it is today.

According to the neo-Leninists, the explanation of this paradox lies in the distortion and even the total inversion of all the goals of socialism by a party bureaucracy that eliminated the original leaders of the socialist revolution. Perhaps, they concede, dictatorship by the bureaucracy was indispensable for the liquidation of the exploiting classes: but it has now outlived its usefulness. The party *apparat* has been transformed into a new ruling class, using all the power at its disposal not to build the socialism outlined by Lenin, but to preserve its own privileged position. Consequently the neo-Bolsheviks believe that if Lenin's legacy is to be realized, bureaucratic domination must be done away with, the "Leninist norms of party life"— intraparty democracy—must be re-established, and the Communist party converted from a society devoted to the protection of its secretaries' interests into a real political party with a Leninist platform. This must be done not hypocritically, as Khrushchev's men are doing it, but in all sincerity.

The neo-Bolsheviks think that power should not fall to the party automatically; it ought rather to belong, as the famous Leninist slogan proposed, to democratically elected and genuinely representative soviets. To preserve its power the party would then be compelled to fight constantly for popular support. The collective farms would have to become real co-operatives in which the members regulated their own affairs. All industrial enterprises would have to be placed under the control of the workers. In so far as the exploiting classes have vanished, internal police repression ought to vanish, too, for repression now can only be directed against the workers. Social self-sufficiency ought to replace governmental organization. Persecution of dissenters ought not to be permitted under any circumstances; anyone retaining the marks of bourgeois ideology ought to be educated and convinced, but not persecuted. There ought also to be free discussion of all interpretations of Marxist and Leninist socialism, as there should be free discussion in scientific research and in art. On the other hand, the neo-Bolsheviks are opposed to a multiparty system; they support instead a single, internally democratic party with a Leninist program. At the same time they favor the retention of a centrally planned industry and oppose the development of a free-market economy, which they believe would lead to inequality.

The principal quality of the neo-Bolshevik program is the vision of a free society of equal men, the vision of a realized Marxist utopia, in the feasibility of which they have complete faith. That society might not follow the path laid out for it after the introduction of a broad democracy does not concern them. They are certain that free men properly educated could accept no other but a genuine classless society, "an association of free producers," and would naturally prefer it to the injustice and cruelty of a society based on privilege. Such a conviction of course leads them to condemn the West. The neo-Bolsheviks usually argue that while the West is politically freer than the USSR, the Soviet economic structure is more progressive because it is no longer under capitalist control. All that remains to be accomplished, therefore, is the modification of the political structure to prevent the consolidation of power in the hands of a new exploiting class. In contrast, the West is still faced with the problem of wresting economic power from a strongly entrenched bourgeoisie.

Such, in brief, is the neo-Bolshevik point of view. Its inconsistencies are obvious. Equally clear is its social naïveté, in view of the conditions of modern industrial society: the increasing division of labor and the concomitant development of managerial functions. The theory itself is a remnant from an earlier, arcadian age of egalitarian ideals. It is nevertheless widely held, and there are many reasons for its popularity. Especially to the young, the principle of equality and the eternal temptation to equate equality with justice are attractive, and their strength must not be underestimated. It is also clear that to point out the discrepancies between the familiar "legacies of Lenin" and the facts of social life is a rather obvious line of criticism, which strikes at the Achilles' heel of a political opponent. But it seems to me that the fundamental rationale behind the slogan "Back to Lenin!" lies elsewhere. Many persons find it psychologically impossible to admit that such enormous sacrifices have been made in the name of ideals that were at best only noble dreams. It is much more comforting to believe that the ideals of the Revolution were good and just, that calamity resulted from their perversion by dishonorable men, and that recovery lies in returning to them.[18] How to effect the return is another problem. The neo-Bolsheviks feel that the "dishonorable men" are intent upon preserving current conditions. They recall their teacher's admonition that no privileged class ever willingly surrenders its position. Furthermore, because they consider themselves heirs to the Russian revolutionary tradition, the neo-Leninists seek revolutionary forms of struggle; this is not only because they imitate, but because there are no opportunities for a legal opposition. In any event, the leaflets issued by clandestine groups generally expound the neo-Bolshevik line, as did the history students at the University of Moscow to whom I have referred above.

While the neo-Bolsheviks ask, "What are we fighting for?" a second opposition group replies with the proverbial, "You find what you are looking for." This is the attitude of the liberal socialists, who might also be considered exponents of social democracy—although in rather changed historic circumstances. Like the neo-Bolsheviks, the liberal socialists argue that the early revolutionary ideals have been perverted; unlike them, they do not think the ideals could possibly have survived intact. The question as to whether or not the October Revolution was inevitable, they reason, is a purely academic one. But the lifelessness of the ideals of this revolution was revealed beyond doubt as society moved away from, and not toward, their realization. In rejecting the idea of a return to October, however, they do not advocate a return to pre-October society: not only would this be impossible, but there was nothing in the political, social, or economic structure of the old regime to recommend it. Retreat is impossible because Russia has created an entirely new society that must be emancipated rather than uprooted and replaced with another brave new world. More particularly, Russia's new society must be emancipated from the domination of a single small group— the party bureaucracy—which is intent on forcibly subordinating everything to its own interests. For the *apparat* has gone beyond the corruption of socialism. It has created a state-capitalist system in which the wielders of political power are also the "collective capitalists." The liberal socialists thus conclude that a pluralist socialist society must be established, in which industry would be placed under the direct control of labor and agriculture under the direction of free co-operatives, and political power would be transferred to democratically elected soviets or other representative institutions. The dispersion of power would guarantee the free play of social forces, which in turn would assure personal freedom.

Although they present their arguments differently, the liberal socialists differ little from the neo-Bolsheviks on overtly political questions. The basic disagreement between them is economic: the neo-Bolsheviks would permit independent enterprise only on the periphery of a central plan directed toward the ultimate goal of an egalitarian society (the same goal, incidentally, that the neo-Bolshe-viks would have political freedom serve); the "liberals" on the other hand believe that if industries are to belong to separate organizations of producers, each must enter and submit to a free market, and social forces must be left free to act even if it requires the creation of a multiparty system. Obviously, therefore, the liberals do not look upon socialism as a prelude to an egalitarian communist society. They deny that such a society can even exist; and while they accept the basic Marxist critique of capitalism, they reject the Leninist and even the Marxist prescriptions for getting rid of it. They do not worry about problems of total social justice and harmony, they consider all promises of earthly paradise to be either unintentional or deliberate deceit. Instead, they concern themselves with improving life for the individual; it is a matter of little consequence to them whether progress is achieved by socialism in Russia or by a synthesis of socialism and capitalism in the West. The moral they draw from the Russian revolutionary experiment is simply that violent upheavals intensify rather than relieve human suffering. Consequently, whenever and wherever possible, they are reformers, and only wherever and whenever they have no alternative do they favor revolution. Here again they differ from the neo-Bolsheviks, who, perennially striving after "final purposes," remain revolutionaries in spite of everything.

In formulating any general difference between the neo-Bolsheviks and the liberal socialists, it is important to remember that the two groups are united in their desire to free and to reform Russian society without destroying it as a whole. At the same time, they have different conceptions of the purpose of reform. The neo-Bolsheviks, favoring an egalitarian society, advocate political democracy as the best means of achieving it, and insist upon a centralized economic structure to ensure equality. The liberal socialists, on the other hand, look upon political democracy as an end in itself; economically, they seek a peculiar socialist *laissez-faire* system in which ownership would fall within the province of producers' collectives, and not to the state.

The third and final student opposition, a tendency observed principally in the technological institutes, may be called "anti-socialist." Although many people in such places follow the neo-Bolshevik or the liberal socialist line, many more have no taste for the involved ideological arguments of both groups. They have undergone a different kind of intellectual training, and they tend to despise all such arguments, for they feel not at home with them. Many "technologists" tend to think politically in more familiar terms of "pluses" and "minuses." The anti-socialists argue that although socialism has been established in Russia, it has not made life easier for anyone. Life in the West is freer and more comfortable; and, as the West is capitalist, capitalism must be superior to socialism. The anti-socialists usually have only a very general notion of today's capitalism, acquired not without the help of the Voice of America. They conceive it simply as private ownership of industries. Capitalism even assumes certain utopian features: to the anti-socialists it stands as the very antithesis of their own poor, unfree existence, and they endow it with all the qualities lacking in their own lives. (Trotsky was thus partially right when he prophesied that, were Stalin to come to power, the word "socialism" would be discredited forever.) As far as I know, the extreme forms of anti-socialism—the tendency to transfigure the West into a utopia—exist mostly on the fringes of student circles. Many "men in the street" are enthralled by the luster of a Western life they have barely glimpsed, in much the same way as a "small man" in the West may be enchanted by the mysteriously alluring life of a movie star or millionaire.[19]

One occasionally meets the same kind of exaggerated notions of Western justice and material welfare among the students as well, but on the whole even the "pro-capitalists'" attitudes are relatively sober. For one thing, Soviet students have had greater access to information in the last few years, especially as Western literature has become available; such information does not readily support utopian visions. Furthermore, "anti-socialist" and unreservedly "pro-Western" attitudes are characteristic of those social groups that have nothing to lose and seek fundamentally to destroy Soviet society. Students do not fall into this category. If they are not part of the "new class" Djilas describes, at least they belong to the new Soviet elite. Student opposition does not wish to relegate the elite to the lowest rung on the social ladder, but rather to set it and all of Soviet society free from the total domination of the party bureaucrats, who constitute numerically a relatively insignificant and unproductive group within the elite.

It would be pointless to assert that admiration for the West and for capitalism is tied to an unconditional acceptance of Western political democracy. And, if misunderstanding is to be avoided, it must be remembered that "anti-socialism" does not imply restoration: anti-socialists are concerned not with returning to a Russia dead and gone, but with creating a new society founded on political freedom and private property. This program is, of course, little more than a slogan. It is not clear to anyone how the monstrous state economic machinery is to be set rolling on the path of private property. The demand for "private property" is simply a demand for radical change in the course of the country's development. Perhaps the most important of all the aspects of anti-socialism is its insistence upon political democracy and spiritual freedom as the necessary preconditions of any normal society. This sentiment it shares with other oppositional tendencies.

From the exemplary conformity of the professional activists, to the resentment of individuals at totalitarian meddling in private affairs, to political opposition—this, in bare outline, is the spectrum of the political attitudes of Soviet students. Though I have neglected to mention a number of fundamental problems—attitudes toward culture and history, for example, or the dilemmas of patriotism—I have focused on what seems to me crucial for future Russian development. If one takes the long historical view of present conditions, one can, I think, be optimistic. Orwell's nightmare has not come to pass in Russia. The younger Soviet intelligentsia looks upon totalitarianism with irritation or outright hostility. Historical optimism, however, does not necessarily involve political optimism. The events of 1956 revealed where real police strength lay: behind the *apparatchik*, and not with the opposition. It proved relatively easy for the bureaucrats to drive an emergent opposition underground, although not to the depths of the Stalinist period. Nonetheless, the very fact that anti-totalitarian currents exist within the young intelligentsia is important, for at the historically opportune moment they will make their presence felt. When that moment will come cannot be foretold; indeed, we cannot even say whether it will come at all, or whether a new terror will not annihilate the younger generation as the Stalinist terror did the old. Over the last fifty years Russia has tumbled from one pit to another, ever deeper, and each successive generation has held the same high hopes of embarking on a new and better life.

REFERENCES

1 According to Soviet statistics, there are 2 million students in the USSR. This figure, however, includes those enrolled in correspondence courses. By taking the total number of students accepted as freshmen in 1957 (280,000) and multiplying it by five (the average number of years in the programs of Soviet institutes and universities), one arrives at the more accurate estimate of 1½ million. Khrushchev's statement can be found in *Pravda*, 21 September 1958.

2 *Komsomolskaia Pravda*, 26 February 1957.

3 *Ibid.*, 14 December 1956; *Leningradskaia Pravda*, 13 December 1956, and 14 December 1956; *Trud*, 8 January 1957.

4 *Trud*, 8 January 1957.

5 *Sovietskaia Rossiia*, 19 December 1956.

6 *Loc. cit.*

7 *Meditsinskii Rabotnik*, 15 January 1957.

8 See N. S. Khrushchev, Report at the XXIst Congress of the Communist Party of the Soviet Union.

9 Lev Ovalov, "Partiinoe Poruchenie," *Moskva*, No. 7, 1959.

10 See D. Zaslavskii, "Dan Molodosti," *Krokodil*, No. 25, 1958.

11 In so far as a totalitarian regime conceives politics as including everything from terrorism to aesthetic theory, in dealing with Soviet theory one has no alternative but to accept this interpretation.

12 An instance of public criticism is vividly described by the Stalinist writer Kochetov in his novel, *The Ershov Brothers*. "If we want to root out the consequences of the cult of personality," asks a student, "oughtn't we destroy the old *apparat*?" Someone asks him in return, "Which *apparat*?" He replies, "All of it, but first of all the bureaucratic one." (In *Neva*, 1958, No. 7, p. 73.) Here the question of changing the leadership of the country is being raised directly.

13 *Komsomolskaia Pravda*, 26 December 1956.

14 The London *Daily Telegraph*, 26 November 1956 and 8 January 1957.

15 *Komsomolskaia Pravda*, 15 December 1956; and *Trud*, 8 January 1957.

16 A foreign inmate of many Soviet concentration camps who spent 1957-1958 at one of the corrective work colonies in Pot'ma told me that during those years the population of the colony was significantly reinforced by young intellectuals from the large cities.

17 "Vyshe znamia marksistko-leninskoi ideologii," *Kommunist*, No. 1, 1957.

18 The young poet Evtushenko is in many ways typical of the neo-Bolsheviks. He has written of the October ideals:

> The great cannot be a deception,
> But it can be deceived by men.

And he draws this conclusion:

> Comrades!
> Give back to the word
> Its original meaning!

Evtushenko was one of the leaders in the 1956 upsurge, and has been repeatedly the object of critical attacks by the party. He has never recanted, however, and in fact has been distinguished by his extreme aggressiveness. Speaking of his critics, he declared in March, 1957, "We'll rap their knuckles!" His enormous talent and his popularity have saved him from the fate that has overtaken writers less notable than he.

19 After visiting the United States exhibition in Moscow, an unsympathetic Soviet journalist thus described a man he had observed there: "With darting, rabbity glances he took in the kitchen, the women's nylon blouses, and the tiny, pointed slippers, exclaiming again and again, 'Ah, America! They have really shown us something! This is what I call polish!'" (*Sovetskaia Rossiia*, 4 October 1959.)

LEOPOLD H. HAIMSON

The Solitary Hero and the Philistines
A Note on the Heritage of the Stalin Era

AMONG THE HESITANT and discordant notes that have been sounded in Soviet life during the seven years of the post-Stalin "thaw," one major theme has been struck: with Stalin's death an era in the history of Soviet culture came to an end, and another, however uncharted, began. This theme has been sounded, both in the published literature and in conversations, in statements of often quite different attitudes and purpose: in the efforts of official spokesmen to justify the cost and stress the value of Stalin's "historic works," just as in the appeals of a handful of bold literary critics for the reassertion of humane and aesthetic values in the wastes of Socialist Realist literature; in the torrential harangues about the advances of Russian science and technology, as in the occasional voicing of individual hopes for the recognition by state and society of wider areas of personal autonomy and privacy. Thus it has become a convenient and by now an established article of faith that between Stalin and Khrushchev a millennium was passed; in celebration of the passage of this historic corner a new scheme of periodization has come into usage: *do rozhdeniia Khrushcheva* (before the "birth" of K.) and *posle rozhdeniia Khrushcheva* (after the "birth" of K.).

Just because this belief in the birth of a new age has been sounded by so many voices and has lent itself to so many uses, it affords few definite clues to the future of Soviet culture. But it has already provided an irresistible, if often unwanted, impulse for a wider registering of its recent past. Indeed, it would be more accurate to say that for a majority of the contemporary intelligentsia the past few years have presented the first real occasion to reflect on the experience in which they were caught during the quarter-century of Stalin's rule. The occasion has come about in part because the new gov-

101

ernment's indications, however qualified, that the Stalin era was no longer beyond the pale of criticism opened a channel for the articulation of long suppressed feelings and thoughts. But even these official signals have been but the reflection of a diffuse sense, shared by state and society alike, that the experience of this era was no longer an eternal present. This conviction has impelled many, even among the more cautious members of the intelligentsia and the more turgid of its writers, to look back for the first time at this now detached past, with however veiled or timid eyes.

What major impressions has this initial confrontation of the Stalin era brought forth? Most striking, of course, are the references that have appeared to the traumatic aspects of this era: the bewildered accounts of the arbitrary arrests and disappearances during the purges of innocent "little people" and dedicated supporters of the regime; the embittered or shamed recollections of the unwillingness of frightened colleagues and friends to lift a finger in defense of the victims, even to assist their abandoned wives and children. But these flashing impressions of terror and chaos have been far outweighed by a quite different image: that of the growth of a vast bureaucratic establishment, populated by a service caste, whose existence, while occasionally punctuated by uncertainty, had gradually hardened into a stable if complex ritual almost completely detached from the particular areas of activity this caste was supposed to rule. Even if we recognize its pragmatic value to a regime now bent on "organizational" reforms, this grotesque Gogolian picture of a vast official establishment, seemingly suspended in mid-air, unquestionably constitutes a genuine facet of the contemporary view of Stalin's Russia and its heritage.[1]

One major age group in the Soviet intelligentsia is almost irretrievably identified with this image of the exorcised past—that generation of men and women roughly between the ages of forty and sixty, whose adult roles and personalities were shaped almost entirely under the shadow of Stalin's rule. Now, as under Stalin, members of this generation still occupy most of the responsible administrative posts in the ruling organs of Soviet cultural life and in the various technical and industrial establishments. It is they who usually warm the chairs of the editorial boards of Soviet professional and literary journals and who ponderously voice the canons of Socialist Realism in the *Literary Gazette* and at the meetings of the Union of Soviet Writers. Yet the image now drawn of these men—indeed the image many of them hold of themselves—has been hopelessly soiled. Almost invariably, it is they who are now elected to personify the ills of the discovered past; it is they who are chosen as the targets of denunciation in private conversations and in the climactic scenes of many contemporary novels and plays. "I, Sergei Kirpichev, declare war on you, Peter Kirpichev," a son cries out at his bloated careerist father who has already been renounced by *his* father, one of the sacred elderly "Knights" of October, in one such melodrama of the contemporary Soviet stage. "And wherever I encounter you—in whatever office, sitting in whatever chair, whatever your visage or your name—I will recognize you at once and fight you to the death. You hear! I will fight you to the death."[2]

In these confrontations by both its fathers and its sons, the generation of the Stalin era stands accused of many formidable sins: an overriding concern for enhancing their own personal power or safety, a callous disregard for the dignity of other human beings, a wholesale contempt for all genuinely creative activity, indeed, a general blunting of all feeling and sensibility. Some of the items in this bill of indictment are of course suggestive of the hackneyed image of the heartless bureaucrat who provided the target for so many earlier agitational campaigns. But what is novel, and also characteristic of the current climate, is that criticism is now leveled, not at individuals who have strayed from the righteous path of the Positive Hero, but at a whole stratum, a whole self-contained community in the upper reaches of Soviet society, and that it ranges ruthlessly over its members' private as well as public life.

Indeed, the composite image that emerges of this official establishment reminds one of another image of official society drawn by the Russian intelligentsia in a much earlier age—to be exact, in those middle decades of the nineteenth century when its tradition of social criticism was founded. The sweeping philosophical and political conclusions are absent, to be sure, but we find comparable images of social morass and conformism, of noisy, meaningless public activity and stunted private lives, of rigid, narrow social mores, of intolerance for any seemingly aberrant behavior, of the complete absence of autonomous, let alone critical, values and perceptions. And, as an epithet for this morass, even the old battle slogan of the nineteenth-century intelligentsia, together with its old denotations, is finding its way back into the language. Like the official society of Nicholas I, the official establishment of the Stalin era and the generation of the intelligentsia that it absorbed now stand accused of *meshchanstvo*.

To appreciate the significance of this indictment, it is necessary to recall that the self-image of the Russian intelligentsia was originally shaped as a counterpoint to the *meshchanstvo*, to the servile yet complacent philistinism to be discerned in existing privileged society. This self-image underwent many variations and transformations in the course of the history of the intelligentsia, but most of its guardians never really wavered from the view that they were distinct from the stagnant and undifferentiated world at large, in a position of intellectual and moral autonomy which made them the chosen carriers for the creation and implementation of new ideas, new values, new truths.

In the light of this traditional view, the indictment now being returned against the intelligentsia of the Stalin era constitutes, far more irretrievably than any accusation of ideological failing or perfidity, a judgment of symbolic death.

As a counterpoint to the image of the tentacular official establishment, a new image of the Positive Hero has appeared in the literature about the Stalin era and its heritage. This hero often appears in familiar dress: he may be a rugged engineer who has thrown himself into the backbreaking work of organizing a continuous production stream in a creaking industrial establishment,[3] or a veteran returned from the wars who, despite his lost years, enrolls in a technological institute to prepare himself for a properly useful role in the rebuilding of his devastated land;[4] or, in his most famous contemporary variant, the fanatically dedicated inventor of a new tube-making machine.[5] But before long we are introduced to a new and dominant quality in his life—its complete loneliness.

Neither at his work nor in his personal life does the hero find, within the framework of the collective life of the establishment, any channel for expressing the values, the feelings, the desires, that animate him. At the factory or the institute he encounters a collection of officials who, in their absorption with the rituals of bureaucratic existence, seem to him not to comprehend, let alone support, his desire to produce, to innovate, to create something that would be a direct, tangible expression of himself—even when his creative urge is focused on a design for a better tractor or a tube-making machine. And after his backbreaking work is done, when he returns to his lonely bachelor's quarters, or to an officious spouse who is ministering with equal attention to the physical needs of the children and to her array of stuffed furniture, he is confronted by the pattern of an equally empty personal life.

It is in this oppressive environment, in which people's concerns with the cares of public life—with the possible opinion or responses of others—appear to him to have extinguished any genuine inner drives, that the hero desperately searches for suitable objects for his feelings and his creative impulses. He is unable to find them in a pattern of collective existence in which all human relationships have become manipulative, circular, static. And so he is impelled to immerse himself in the creation of inanimate but personal expressions of his individuality through the design of lifeless (but by the same token incorruptible) machines; or he is drawn to the figure of a pure young woman with whom he might establish a relationship free from convention—and find in her a suitably detached, unsoiled recipient for the "pent-up poetry" in his soul.

If we go back in the history of Soviet culture beyond the arid years of the late 1930's and 1940's—beyond the wooden archetype of the Positive Hero, happily leading the collective in Socialist construction, a figure which became dominant after Stalin decreed that life had become happy in the society over which he ruled—we encounter an earlier Soviet version of the solitary hero, the figure of the ascetic, leather-jacketed Party man who led the heroic battles of the Civil War and the First Five Year Plan. But the isolation of this earlier version of the solitary hero stemmed from quite different sources. Self-imposed, born out of the necessity to lead unswervingly the anarchic, "spontaneous" elements under his command in accordance with the directives of the Party and the demands of his own "conscious" rationality and will, that isolation involved the deliberate denial of the hero's own personal feelings and needs as much as the suppression of the human frailties of those under his command. [6]

The hero's perception of the inescapable conflict between his "spontaneous" impulses and the stern demands of his consciousness, and his attendant sacrifice of the needs of his private life to public duty reflected, however distortedly, an image of self and of life that had long animated certain radical circles of the pre-Revolutionary intelligentsia. To be sure, the self-consciously proletarian hero of the 1920's and early 1930's usually looked down with contempt at the "soft," untrustworthy descendants of the old intelligentsia whom he encountered in the course of his herculean labors. But even his contempt, ruthlessly expressed in real life by the men whom the Party recruited from below to direct the shaping of the new Soviet culture, had been prefigured in the nineteenth century in the attitudes of other "New Men" of the intelligentsia toward their forebears.

Even in the distorted mirror of Soviet literature, it is not difficult to discern how this early, classical Soviet prototype of the solitary hero underwent his first transformation. Impelled by his image of public duty, and by his distrust for all uncontrolled individual expression, to manipulate all the relationships in which he was involved, he gradually lost the sense of humanity in his followers; he came to view them merely as "detached hands in the building of vast edifices," as cogs in the intricate machine it was his task to direct.

Davidov, the dry ascetic chap who leads the drive for collectivization in Sholokhov's novel of the early 'thirties, *Virgin Soil Upturned*, is already undergoing such an atrophy: [7]

All the inhabitants of Gremyachi passed before Davidov's mental vision. And there was much in them that was incomprehensible to him, that was hidden behind an impalpable curtain. The village was like a new type of complicated motor, and Davidov studied it intently and tensely, trying to understand its mechanism, to see clearly every detail, to note any interruption in the daily incessant throbbing of this involved machine.

Even among the descendants of the old intelligentsia there were many who succumbed to such inhuman visions. To be sure, they succumbed partly because of the pressures to which they were subjected as totalitarian controls were imposed on cultural life—pressures which compelled them to deny their humanity until they lost sight of it. Yet we should also recognize the degree to which these men themselves had prepared the way for their own downfall by their initial readiness to sacrifice individual moral issues to "broader" social ends, current humane values and needs to the building of the future utopia in which man's nature would be at last fulfilled. Indeed, we must recall that in their dogmatic zeal many of them had invited the Party to arbitrate their intellectual differences and thus to control their destiny even before the Party was prepared to do so.

But it was the members of the "new intelligentsia" whom the Party hastily trained during the late 'twenties and early 'thirties who most readily underwent this wholesale blunting of sensibility. Lacking any independent cultural tradition, thrust into responsibilities utterly divorced from their earlier experience, these New Men found in the Party's ideological and organizational prescriptions their only explanation for the vast process of social transformation over which they were to preside, their only key to their own role in the building of a disciplined socialist culture and a modern industrial order. They brought to their new roles, particularly to their contacts with any traces of the old humane culture, an added element of impersonality and brusqueness which reflected their own sense of social discomfort and antagonism when confronted by the human beings they were now to lead.

It took but a little over a decade for these hardened and impersonal men to undergo one more transformation—to turn, at least in the eyes of the young, into the bloated bureaucrats now discernible among the inheritors of the Stalin era. One motif is usually emphasized in contemporary Soviet critiques to explain this rapid degeneration: the morally debilitating effect on all layers of Soviet society of the exercise of arbitrary power. I have already implied that this generation's original vision of collective endeavor—resting as it did on the assumption that all human strivings, all human relationships, could be and should be controlled—was the original source of this concern for the exercise of power, and that this concern was merely intensified as the instruments of totalitarianism became consolidated in Soviet life. Yet there is a haunting note in some of the current literary descriptions of the effects of the Cult of Personality. As Stalin consolidated his personal rule over Soviet society, as he made himself the fountainhead of every major creative activity in Soviet life, there were apparently many, particularly among the new intelligentsia of this generation, who developed around the omnipotent image of the master a cult of the attributes of power. The art of dissimulation that began to mar their every human contact, the awe and fear that they sought to produce among their subordinates, were seemingly inspired not merely by the harsh lessons of bureaucratic infighting but also by an exalted and mysterious example of personal power which they sought to emulate but never completely understood. [8]

Yet however valid, such diagnoses of the effects of the Cult of Personality should not be allowed to obscure a quite different and perhaps more enduring aspect of the transformation that many now underwent. Once the abstract and impersonal vision of leadership and organization that had originally animated this generation was translated into realized and relatively stabilized institutions, a pattern of collective life, a web of human relationships and loyalties usually reasserted itself—an involvement in family, colleagues, and friends, which was all the more tenacious because of the pressures to which the members of the establishment, however highly placed, continued to be subjected from above.

Like the official spokesmen of the regime, most of the idealistic young critics who have now come to the fore are unable to recognize that the absorption of these men of the Stalin era into the life of the establishment constituted a partial reassertion of their humanity. And they usually discern in the "family relations" in which they became involved, in public as well as in private life, merely a complete subordination of public duties to selfish, calculated, private ends.

107

Actually, in the tight-knit collective existence of the members of the establishment, such dichotomies ceased to seem relevant. After all, did not the achievement of any public ends—whether increases in industrial production or the development of a vigorous Socialist Realist literature—require a properly co-ordinated collective effort, and did not the achievement of such co-operation demand, even at the occasional cost of individual achievements, the mutual adjustment and accommodation of the members of the collective, or at least of the men entrusted with its leadership? Ultimately, it is probably true that this pattern of collective life and the mutual concessions and obligations on which it rested became more sacred in the eyes of many bureaucrats than did any of the tangible achievements that they were supposed to promote in the building of a new Socialist society.

It is against this background that the conflict between the new solitary hero and the establishment has now been drawn. No more than the members of the establishment is this new hero subject to the inner conflicts, to the clash between consciousness and affective impulses, public duty and private needs, that preyed on earlier heroes in the tradition of the intelligentsia. At first sight, indeed, he is a curious prototype of the rebel, for he is usually represented as a man who has fully internalized the purposiveness, the self-discipline, the urge and the ability to produce the artifacts of an industrial culture which the regime strove so hard to implant in the new generation of Soviet man. But, of course, it is precisely because he has become so firmly implanted in his new role, precisely because he has absorbed its values and its skills so much more surely than have the bureaucrats who direct him, that he can now subject it to personal interpretation. His new role now affords him standards he can oppose to the collective judgment of society, and it is through the expression of these standards—whether in the application of mathematical logic to the building of calculating machines, or in the design of machine parts for a continuous production stream—that he seeks and partially finds an anchor for his individuality, a channel for his rebellious creative impulses.

Thus it is as a real (if largely unforeseen) expression of the very vision of man and of life they once sought to create that the hero now challenges the members of the establishment. And the ruthlessness of the conflict in which they engage merely reflects their mutual recognition that each constitutes a denial of the legitimate existence, indeed of the very humanity, of the other. At every step on his solitary path, the hero is confirmed in the view that the, to him, impersonal, collec-

tive figure of the establishment is intent on quashing any living expression of his individuality. And equally persuaded that, in his
reckless self-affirmation, this ascetic and incorruptible figure is bent
on tearing down the whole world of collective effort and collective life
in which their humanity has been so painfully realized, the members
of the establishment feel it not only imperative but justified to destroy
him and his works.

"You do not understand that we can do without your invention,
even if it is a genuine, a great discovery," Drozdov, the spokesman for
the establishment, exclaims at Lopatkin, the solitary inventor, who
from the start has threatened to take away his wife and ruin his
official position, at the climax of Dudintsev's *Not By Bread Alone*: [9]

> We can do without it and, just imagine, without suffering any loss,
> because of our accurate calculations and planning which insure us a
> steady advance. Let us even assume that your invention is a work of
> genius! When on the basis of statesmanlike calculations, it becomes
> necessary to put on the agenda the task which you are elementally
> [*stikhiino*] trying to fulfill . . . our designers' and technicians' collectives
> will find a solution. And this solution will be better than yours, because
> collective research always leads to the quickest and best solution of any
> problem. The collective has more genius than any individual genius. . . .
> And the result, Comrade Lopatkin, is something you cannot under-
> stand. Yes, we building ants. . . . When he said these words a cold
> monster of hatred stirred at the back of his ordinarily jolly eyes—Yes, we
> building ants are necessary.

Those of us in the Western world who have seen in the growth of
modern industrialized societies and the emergence of technically
oriented intelligentsias the threatened extinction of any human individuality and autonomy are left with an altogether ironic picture.
Whereas the men who oppress him are continuously involved in
human contacts, in a web of personal relations, the new hero who has
emerged in the wake of the Stalin era finds his individuality largely in
relation to the machine. Yet, however incongruous, it is not difficult
to discern why this hero and the code of life that he espouses should
have become an ideal image for so many in the new generation of
the intelligentsia who are now coming to the fore. While continuing
to feel loyal to the foundations of their social order—to socialism and
its values as they variously choose to define them—many of the members of this new generation appear driven by a compelling urge to
discover and to defend an area of personal autonomy, to find a channel, however narrow, for uncontrolled, unmanipulated individual
expression. As I have noted elsewhere,[10] the intense professional-
ism that most of them assert, their almost ritualistic insistence on the

sanctity of technical standards and criteria, has provided them with the safest, but also the most impenetrable, defense against the manipulated world of ideas and human relations which they inherited from their fathers' generation. With the image of the solitary hero, these youths have now discovered in the past, and in the still uncertain present, a figure who, while holding onto the same modest values and expressing his individuality within the same narrow channels, has managed against all odds to keep himself pure and irrepressibly free.

REFERENCES

1 The most curious literary example of the new image of the Establishment that has emerged in the glare of the post-Stalin thaw is Fedor Panferov's novel *Razdum'e* (*Znamya*, Nos. 7, 8, 1958). This work is actually the continuation of an earlier unfinished novel published shortly after Stalin's death (*Volga-Matushka*, in *Znamya*, Nos. 8, 9, 1953). But although the locale and the chief protagonists of the action have remained the same in Panferov's second installment, the images that are now drawn of them have undergone an incredible transformation. In 1953, we were presented with a standard orthodox description of successful Socialist construction led by virtuous Positive Heroes. Five years later, this happy land has turned into a denuded countryside, pockmarked by deserted, overgrown, experimental stations and broken-down collective farms in which starving peasants are held under the capricious yoke of elderly and almost demented Party veterans. Indeed, the chief representative of the Party power in the region, a Party Secretary, once depicted as the usual embodiment of all public virtues, has suddenly been transformed into a ruthless and wholly corrupted intriguer who is finally exposed by the Party's Central Committee.

2 Leonid Zorin, "Gosti," *Teatr'*, No. 2, 1954, p. 54.

3 Galina Nikolaeva, "Bitva v puti," *Oktyabr'*, Nos. 3-6, 1957.

4 Viktor Nekrasov, "V rodnom gorode," *Novyi Mir*, Nos. 10, 11, 1954.

5 Vladimir Dudintsev, "Ne khlebom edinym," *Novyi Mir*, Nos. 8-10, 1956. The American edition of the work, *Not By Bread Alone*, is published by E. P. Dutton & Company, 1957.

6 The classical prototypes are probably the figures of Klychkov in Dmitri Furmanov's *Chapaev*, and Levinson in Alexander Fadeev's *The Nineteen*.

7 Mikhail Sholokhov, *Virgin Soil Upturned* (London, Putnam & Company, 1948), p. 137.

8 See particularly the description of Blinkii in Galina Nikolaeva's "Bitva v puti," *Oktyabr'*, No. 6, 1957, pp. 44-45.

9 In *Novyi Mir*, No. 8, 1956, p. 109.

10 See "Three Generations of the Soviet Intelligentsia," *Foreign Affairs*, January 1959.

The Thaw and the Writers

BEFORE STALIN'S DEATH Soviet writers were discussed almost exclusively in terms of the various pressures—ideological, political and administrative—of the system within which they lived and worked. They were seen as the victims of a uniquely efficient censorship, as the captives of a muddled and contradictory literary doctrine, and as ventriloquist's dummies in the hands of a capricious Leader.

This, indeed, is how they saw themselves. Not long before Stalin's death a prominent Soviet writer, asked why there was no poetry in the Soviet Union, replied: "Because we live in a ventilator." The origin of this phrase is interesting. It derives from an audacious fable published by Lev Kassil at the end of the last war.[1] It was evidently current in writers' circles as an apt description of their plight. Though written in the form of a child's fantasy, its meaning, no doubt, was not lost on the censor—but what censor would have had the courage in those days to admit that he saw a resemblance between the state of affairs in the luckless kingdom of Sinegoria and the realities of life under Stalin?

In the story, we are told how the once happy and flourishing land of Sinegoria had come under the rule of the wicked and stupid King Fanfaron, who was able to command the services of the Winds. The Winds blew into every nook and cranny of every house and reported the most secret words and deeds of his subjects to the King. The country had once been famous for its three great craftsmen, John Greenfingers the gardener, Isobar the smith, and Amalgama the mirror maker. When Fanfaron came to power, the gardener was forbidden to grow anything but dandelions, the mirror maker was not allowed to practice his art at all, lest the King should see his own ugliness and his subjects the misery to which he had reduced them, and the smith was permitted to make only weather vanes, so that people could see "which way the wind was blowing." The supreme penalty for disobedience was to be placed in the Ventilator, where you were "blown over" by the Winds until you learned more sense.

There is not much more to be said about the situation in Russia in those days. By the time of Stalin's death a highly sensitive "weather vane" was standard equipment for all writers, the cultivation of officially approved "weeds" was the only way to achieve merit, and to hold up a mirror to life—even a mildly distorted one—meant consignment to the Ventilator of public objurgation, or worse.

As a result of the changes—sometimes dramatic, but for the most part almost imperceptible—that have taken place over the last seven years, the fable has lost much of its value. The Winds no longer have the same force and blow only fitfully, weather vanes have grown a bit rusty and sometimes are not even consulted, and the Ventilator, though still used, no longer inspires the same terror. It has now become possible to view many Soviet writers, not just as helpless victims of *force majeure*, but as rebels against their manipulators and even—with all due caution—as leaders of public opinion against some aspects of the established order. The possibility of their playing this latter role has excited much interest in recent years, and this article will try to consider their potentialities as an "organic ferment" in the light of what has happened since the death of Stalin-Fanfaron.

First, what is meant by "Soviet writers"? To talk of them collectively makes little sense except with reference to the highly concentrated literary communities of the two metropolitan centers. It is only in Moscow and Leningrad that numbers and proximity create the sort of contagious atmosphere that makes it possible for them to take a more or less common stand—at variance with the official one—on controversial issues. Moreover, it is only here that new, unofficial trends may be studied. The central press has grown increasingly incapable of disguising or minimizing the extent and strength of heterodox opinion. The hinterland for the most part remains a closed book, and accounts of writers' activities in the provincial papers suggest that writers outside the big centers can do little more than echo approved sentiment. It is only in Moscow and Leningrad, therefore, that the writers have felt strong enough to answer the official reaction to the literary ferment of 1956 with a "conspiracy of silence," that Dudintsev's novel was acclaimed at stormy meetings of young intellectuals, while it was in Moscow that a general meeting of writers called to condemn Pasternak was virtually boycotted.

While the degree of this new-found solidarity has been remarkable and on occasion has led to the virtual isolation of the small minority of eternal hacks—making them as pathetically conspicuous as the plain-clothes policemen who used to loiter among the crowd on Arbat Street—it has varied considerably according to an obvious pattern. Roughly speaking, it has been greatest in what might be called negative protest—that is, in a refusal to take part in campaigns of victimization against individual members of their ranks, in giving only token assent (or none at all) to reaffirmations of official literary policy, and generally in "dragging their feet." There has been only one case in recent years when it was possible to obtain the signatures of all the writers to a document which must have been distasteful to most of them. This was a condemnation of the Hungarian "counter-revolution." In literary affairs, however, it now seems impossible to organize the "round robins" so characteristic of Stalin's day. Solidarity is far less impressive when it comes to the active support of revolutionary or reformist demands for a basic revision of the official literary doctrine and the abolition of Party and administrative controls. Not that these demands are not widely sympathized with, but the cautious and the waverers invariably split the ranks, thus enabling the authorities to dilute and divide opposition, even at moments of extreme crisis.

There have been two such crises. The first was at the end of 1953 when the exhilarating sense of liberation from the Stalinist nightmare and the "panic and disarray" in higher circles combined to create an atmosphere in which anything seemed possible. The second one came three years later in the wake of Khrushchev's secret speech, and drew its strength from the same explosive revulsion against the horrors of the past and the hypocrisies of the present that in Poland and Hungary led to outright revolt.

As a result of these two crises, a new relationship has been worked out between the Party and the writers. It may best be described as a compromise—with tacit concessions on both sides—in the spirit of the Russian folk maxim: "Do not tease the goose."

The small group of writers who spearheaded the reconnaissance in depth of 1953 and the attempted breakthrough of 1956 soon found themselves in the position of tank crews who fail to receive infantry support. Their deed evoked admiration and sympathy, but the majority were swayed by caution and the fear of jeopardizing the limited gains that had resulted from the end of terror. In a word, the "revolutionaries" found themselves as isolated as were the hacks and time-servers.

For their part, the authorities were remarkably restrained in the measures they took to close the breach. Their counter-measures—reactionary as they appeared at the time—were vastly different from the brutal and carefully orchestrated campaigns of Stalin's time, and were noticeably half-hearted in execution. This may have been due partly to divided councils and the weakening of the secular arm, but the main reason is certainly that the Party itself was committed to (and genuinely desired) reform. It had the delicate task, therefore, of disarming the extremists without alienating the moderates.

The "maximum" program of the rebels may be inferred from the articles of the *Novyi Mir* group at the end of 1953 and from many even more outspoken articles after the XXth Congress in 1956. This program included the abandonment of socialist realism, an end to Party control of literature, and the establishment of autonomous literary organizations. The organs responsible for cultural policy evidently realized that to counter these demands merely with vilification would be not only ineffective (without the resumption of terror) but would also militate against their plans for enlisting the writers as more persuasive and subtle propagandists of post-Stalin reform. Everything, therefore, was done to create the impression that the writers themselves were setting their house in order, and not, as in former days, merely responding to a crack of the whip from the Party. This tactic served to encourage the moderates in the belief that they had much to gain by restraining the hotheads in their midst—and perhaps everything to lose by not doing so. The experience of 1956 (when Khrushchev came near to laying down the line à la Zhdanov) showed that head-on attacks were futile. The new opportunities for flouting socialist realism in practice and circumventing censorship controls—as long as one did so without being too provocative—have given the writers more freedom than they have enjoyed since the 'twenties. They no longer *have* to cultivate dandelions. They have been given much more latitude to write realistically about the past, and they are no longer obliged to falsify the present to anything like the same extent as formerly.

The signal failure of the Soviet writers to gain anything more than piecemeal concessions, and their apparent inability to parallel the exploits of writers in Poland and Hungary, have understandably strengthened the arguments of the school that takes a pessimistic view of the influence and "specific gravity" of the Soviet intelligentsia as a whole (understood as that minority which is temperamentally inclined to question the status quo). The post-mortem on 1956 has led some to proclaim the "intelligentsia" dead, and others to assert its increasing vitality. One can find ample arguments to support both views. It seems to me, however, that the controversy arises from a misunderstanding on both sides. Rather like the "big-enders" and the "little-enders," they tend to overlook the egg in their preoccupation with its extremities. While the "pro-intelligentsia" faction undoubtedly exaggerates the revolutionary potential of the critically thinking minority, the "anti-intelligentsia" faction errs more gravely by underrating its importance. They say that an intelligentsia no longer exists, or at least only as a ludicrously helpless and antique rump. I find this view singularly perverse. The existence of an intelligentsia (in the sense in which we have defined it above) is a plain fact of all modern societies. The only question is the extent of its ability to communicate with, and hence influence, the educated public, if not the "masses." In some countries the link between the intelligentsia and the public has been institutionalized (parliament, press, etc.).

In Soviet Russia, on the other hand, intellectuals for many years have not even been able to communicate with one another, let alone the public. Since they have for so long given no signs of life, it is hardly surprising that many have thought them to be either extinct or so small in numbers as to be totally ineffectual. Yet one of the most interesting things about post-Stalin Soviet literature is that its most significant products are deeply concerned with the problem of the intellectuals (this is one of the reasons why it has been so "controversial"). In the last few years literature has become a forum for the intellectuals, by means of which they communicate with the public. For the first time in decades it has given them the sense of community and the possibility of communion without which they must remain an inarticulate underground. Literature has given them opportunities that in other countries would be provided by political parties, newspapers, or clubs. Only in this forum can their ideas, their self-awareness, and their moods, in however veiled a form, be expressed. One occasionally hears it said that the so-called "literary intelligentsia" represents an isolated phenomenon of an archaic type, and that its mood is untypical of the nonliterary intelligentsia. But absorption in everyday practical activity in a rapidly expanding industrial society, and the flatteringly high premium that this society puts on him, do not make the average scientist, engineer, or doctor immune to the stresses and frustrations of Soviet life, and he will certainly not lack understanding and sympathy for such a work as *Not by Bread Alone*. The immense response to the novel and the uneasiness this response caused in official bureaucratic circles are sufficient proof that Dudintsev was not a lone voice crying in the wilderness.

What primarily distinguishes Soviet intellectuals, as they have emerged since Stalin's death, from the pre-Soviet intelligentsia is that they live today in an industrially advanced society with a vast educated and professional class. This does not, however, make them archaic or anomalous or ineffectual It was the pre-Soviet intelligentsia that was anomalous and ineffectual, because it existed in a social vacuum, and its hot-house extravagances contributed much to the final disaster.

It is wrong, therefore, to think of the Soviet intellectual as a kind of Rip Van Winkle. Much of the disappointment he arouses comes from a misleading and largely meaningless comparison with the old intelligentsia. The neo-intellectuals are, for the most part, of the younger generation and are conscious of belonging to a complex and literate society in which they should be an enzyme rather than an abnormal growth. They want to be, and indeed already are, part of the chemistry of the body politic. Their main battle—and it is more clearly reflected in literature than anywhere else—is to gain recognition for themselves in this modest role, a role taken for granted in Western societies. In their struggle they have to contend not only with bureaucratic controls but also with a definition of the word *intelligent*, which is somewhat similar to the definition of "organization man" in American sociological caricature. In Stalin's day an intellectual who ventured to stray beyond the strictly demarcated limits adjudged useful and productive in his field into the realm of speculation on fundamental political or philosophical matters was lucky not to lose his head ("With ideas you can only break your neck," says the cynical young artist in Ehrenburg's *The Thaw*). Nowadays he will be charged with revisionism and may lose his job. From this it might seem that there has been a change of degree only. The penalties have been scaled down and are applied more haphazardly, but the doctrinal trammels remain, and the concept of *partiinost*, according to which the intellectual accepts the Party's guidance and conforms to its views on all basic questions, has been vigorously reasserted. Revisionism (and what is a true intellectual but a revisionist?) has been sternly dealt with whenever it has been too explicit. In 1956, for example, the historian Strochkov exposed the whole idea of *partiinost* as a chicanery. He showed that the exploitation in Stalinist literary doctrine of Lenin's famous article, "The Party Principle in Literature," was illegitimate, since Lenin did not intend to apply this doctrine to belles-lettres, and, furthermore, he was thinking only of conditions in which the Bolsheviks were an opposition Party.[2] Strochkov was severely criticized for his views. At about the same time the whole editorial board of *Questions of History* was dismissed on account of a series of articles in which there were cautious attempts to rehabilitate the political opposition in the period of the 1917 Revolution. Since then no direct attacks on the Party's right to control intellectual activity have been tolerated.

But this is far less serious for literature than it appears. The novelist or the poet can challenge official ideas by means of subtle implication that is sometimes difficult to pin down. By his choice and handling of a theme, by means of elusive nuance and inflection, he is able to suggest with relative impunity things that cannot be stated *en toutes lettres* by intellectuals in other fields.

The main implication of Ehrenburg's *Thaw* and Dudintsev's *Not by Bread Alone* is that the lone, independent-minded intellectual is a legitimate and vital member of society. This idea, of course, is in flat contradiction to *partiinost*. Both books, which have now been reluctantly accepted, despite all the criticism at the time of their appearance, have done more to demolish and discredit the Party's claim to total "guidance" of intellectual life than the outspoken articles of Pomerantsev[3] and Strochkov. They both reflect a wide-spread feeling throughout the country that the individual is the best judge of how he can serve society and that the dictates of conscience are more important than the impositions of a specious "collective wisdom." *The Thaw* has another important implication generally overlooked at the time of its appearance. In the last few years Ehrenburg has clearly emerged as the most powerful and influential spokesman of the neo-intelligentsia.[4] With his almost infallible flair for atmospheric changes, he would not have made himself the leader of what might be called the loyal opposition if he had thought it had no prospects. Ehrenburg is the type of fellow-traveling intellectual described by Pasternak in *Dr. Zhivago*. Like Zhivago's two friends, Gordon and Dudorov, he was able to "idealise his own bondage." Like them, he was probably quite sincere. Together with many other pre-Soviet intellectuals who survived into the 'thirties, he abdicated his right to intellectual freedom, not only because of external pressure, but also because he believed that of the two mass movements dominating Europe, only Communism gave any hope for civilization. He could see no third way. The intellectuals of the West (particularly those of France, which he knew well) appeared as unlikely to influence the course of events as the Russian intelligentsia to which he belonged. Their variegated individualism seemed a dangerous luxury in a world on the threshold of Armageddon. The intellectual had a choice between two evils, and the lesser choice not unexpectedly fell on complete submission to the Party, which was at least nominally "left wing," "on the side of the people," and "internationalist."

In Ehrenburg's case the choice was not made lightly. In his novel *The Second Day* (1932) he describes the tragic dilemma of a young "hereditary" intellectual who desperately tries to submit body and soul to the Party. He endeavors to be an exemplary member of the Komsomol, but, as he writes in his diary, he is unable to "sacrifice eternal truth to a temporary truth." His father, a Social-Democrat doctor, who had often been in trouble before the Revolution for speaking up against injustice, is arrested by the Cheka after the Revolution for refusing to allow them to interrogate a sick man under his care. The son, Volodya Sofronov, eventually leaves the Komsomol in disgust because his is the only dissenting vote against a resolution to expel a member of the group who had concealed his social origin. The boy is the son of an attorney who had persecuted Volodya's father before the Revolution. As Volodya leaves the group he shouts to them: "You are not Komsomols, but cowards. Nobody can be held responsible for the sins of his parents!" Thus his attempt to become part of the new society fails because, as the author puts it, he cannot cure himself of his father's old disease—conscience. Ehrenburg's handling of Sofronov's moral dilemma is curiously contradictory. The dilemma is obviously his own as well, and his portrayal of Sofronov is full of insight and sympathy; but, to support his thesis that in that period the intellectual had only two choices, he makes Sofronov go over to the enemy camp. At the end of the novel he becomes a traitor and then commits suicide. He had already committed moral suicide by putting his conscience above the "will of the collective."

Some time in the last years of the Stalinist regime Ehrenburg must have become painfully aware how false this solution really was. To a certain extent the War had appeared to justify it, but with the annihilation of Nazi Germany the idea of the Communist dictatorship as a "lesser evil" lost its substance. With the disappearance of its Nazi rival, the Stalinist regime not only stood out as the greater evil, but it was also beginning to take on the most odious distinctive feature of its erstwhile rival. Ehrenburg, and many others like him, could no longer say, "At least there is no anti-Semitism in the Soviet Union." The ferocious anti-Americanism of his postwar novels should be judged mainly in the light of this new dilemma. The only way in which Ehrenburg could possibly justify his previous—and now irrevocable—choice was to pass off the United States as a successor to Nazi Germany. Unfortunately for him the United States was a very unsatisfactory substitute. Ehrenburg was too intelligent not to see the difference between Truman and Hitler, and in the last years of Stalin's life he seems to have taken refuge in a resigned cynicism.

This much one can judge from *The Thaw*. There are considerable elements of self-portraiture in the young artist Volodya Pukhov, who cynically paints crude socialist-realist canvases because it is "advantageous." He hates himself and the environment, which gives him no choice between this prostitution of his talent and starvation, or worse. He envies and admires another artist, Saburov, who has chosen starvation. Saburov paints for himself and has no chance to exhibit his work. In other words, he protests in the only way open to a dissident intellectual under Stalin—by silence and a stubborn refusal to collaborate.

The Thaw is thus something in the nature of a reply to *The Second Day*. Ehrenburg has completely reversed his judgment of the lone protesting intellectual. Since *The Thaw* is a seminal work in post-Stalin literature (like Gogol's *The Greatcoat* in the nineteenth century, it has introduced a new outlook and new themes into literature), the importance of this volte-face by such a hitherto staunch apologist for the regime as Ehrenburg is immense. Dudintsev and a number of other younger members of the neo-intelligentsia have been, if not inspired, at least emboldened by his example.

Apart from rehabilitating the intellectual, the literature of the "thaw" has quietly modified many other sacrosanct values of the Stalin era. The sharp division between "positive" and "negative" characters has been blurred. Various shades of grey have been added to the monotonous black-and-white color scheme of Soviet novels. The implication that Soviet society generates its own specific defects, which cannot be lightly dismissed as "the birth-marks of capitalism," has become accepted. Undertones of pity for the victims of injustice and a gentle concern for the underdog pervade much of the new writing.

Perhaps one of the most striking new features (particularly in the work of younger poets like Evtushenko) is a revulsion against moral relativism; "good," "truth," and "honesty" are spoken of in absolute terms. This may seem naïve to Western eyes, but it is revolutionary for a generation reared in the Marxist ethic. Side by side with this tendency to universalize moral categories, there is a strong undercurrent of distaste for the material allurements of the final goal of Communism.[5] Dudintsev casts doubt on the idea of "full Communism" as it has always been crassly presented to the Soviet public. What Lopatkin, the hero of the novel, says here amounts to a subtle redefinition of Communism as devoted service to a personal yet unselfish ideal unconnected with any hope of gain. [6]

> I have never believed in Philistine Communism. Those who think that under Communism they will go round in gold-braided clothes are mistaken. . . . When I realized the importance of this machine [the invention Lopatkin is vainly trying to get accepted by the authorities] and understood that I should have to tighten my belt for the sake of it, I didn't hesitate for one second and gladly plunged into this whirlpool. . . . And now I have suddenly realized that Communism is not a scheme invented by philosophers, but a force which has existed for a very long time and which is gradually preparing cadres for the society of the future. This force has already entered into me. How did I come to feel this? Because I have never in my life worked as hard as I am working now. I am working according to my abilities. . . . As for my needs, I could go right now and get a job in a factory, earn two thousand roubles and buy a mountain of food . . . or set down my name to buy a car. I could put my money in the savings bank, and the account would grow as I earned more and more! But I am just not like that! I don't want the sort of happiness you see in the movies: lots of food, an apartment, a bedroom and lace curtains. . . . I could do with Communism now, not so that I might receive, but so that I might be able to give without hindrance.

This passage is a fascinating example of a new type of Aesopian language. Under Stalin it was impossible to discuss Communism except in rigidly orthodox terms. Now "Communism" is quite often identified with a kind of timeless ascetic idealism that owes nothing to the schemes of Marx and Engels. Hence there is an implied contrast between "Communism" seen as a new embodiment of ancient virtue ("a force that has existed for a very long time") and official Party-guided Communism. Moreover, the "good Communist" is now commonly not just an incarnation of "collective" wisdom, a *deus ex machina* who solves difficulties and conflicts by virtue of his inside knowledge of an inscrutable Party line, but rather he is a rebel who swims against the current and tries to correct wrongs in the light of his personal convictions. In works dealing with the Stalin period the lone rebel often pays for his protest with persecution and arrest.

This emphasis on the responsibility of the individual is far more important than criticism of social and economic abuses. In its present phase of reforming zeal, the Party has the advantage over the writers of being able to outbid them in this respect. Addressing the Third Congress of the Soviet writers in May 1959, Khrushchev said that *Not by Bread Alone* echoed some of his own private remarks. When it came to blunt criticism, he added, it was very difficult to outdo the

Central Committee. His listeners will have understood that this mocking challenge "to do your damnedest" is also an implicit recognition that the Central Committee must heed independent criticism.

For the first time in decades, therefore, the intellectuals must feel that they have some scope for influence, however circumscribed, in the affairs of their country. There has been no formal change in their status, but they have gained a foothold.

REFERENCES

1 Lev Kassil, *Izbrannye povesti* (Moscow, 1948), pp. 345 ff.
2 Y. M. Strochkov, "K stat'e V. I. Lenina, 'Partiinaia organizatsiia i partiinaia literatura,'" *Voprosy istorii*, April, 1956.
3 "Ob iskrennosti v literature," *Novyi Mir*, December, 1953.
4 He is also the author of two articles in Aesopian language that express in a most dramatic way the intelligentsia's desire for more independence and freedom of conscience. "The Lessons of Stendhal" is in effect an apologia for Pasternak and a justification of his stand against the authorities. "Rereading Chekhov" (published in the June 1958 number of *Novyi Mir*) pointedly dwells on the right of protest that leading intellectuals enjoyed under the regime of Nicholas II.
5 Evtushenko, quoting the Russian saying, "Truth is good, but happiness is better," adds, "but without truth there is no happiness."
6 *Novyi Mir*, October, 1956.

DAVID JORAVSKY

Soviet Scientists and the Great Break

MIDWAY THROUGH THE FURY of his first Five Year Plan Stalin singled out 1929 as "the year of the great break [*perelom*]," the year of shattering transformation on all fronts of socialist construction. He had in mind the beginning of "the decisive offensive of socialism on the capitalist elements of town and country," and of course he did not mean to suggest that the offensive would be completed in 1929. The shattering and transforming, he made clear, had only begun. Academic historians, who like to speak of the period as a watershed or turning point, ought to concede that Stalin's more violent image is more appropriate for the crisis of forced industrialization and collectivization, though they are probably right in shunning his effort to dramatize the great break by marking it with the number of a single year. On "the scientific front of the cultural revolution" the great break took about two and a half years, from the end of 1929 to the middle of 1932—which is short enough, considering the magnitude of the changes accomplished, to require no further dramatization. In this brief period "the scientific change-over [*smena*]" from "bourgeois" to "red" specialists, and the accompanying search for a suitable philosophy or ideology of science, reached a crisis, a breaking point, by which past trends were selected, some for destruction, others for increasing dominance over a generation of Soviet scientists and philosophers of science. In the present essay the break in "the scientific change-over" is examined; the corresponding break in the

This essay is a version of a chapter from the author's book, *Soviet Marxism and Natural Science, 1917-1932*, to be published by Columbia University Press in the United States, and by Routledge and Kegan Paul in England in 1961. The chapter as it will appear in the book is extensively documented.

Soviet Marxist philosophy of science is left for treatment elsewhere.

From its start the Bolshevik regime had been convinced that Russia's scientific and technical personnel were inadequate for "the construction of socialism." They were far too few, and most of them were basically hostile or at least skeptical toward Bolshevism. But their work was essential for the mere existence of the Soviet state, while its improvement was dependent on them in a painfully para-doxical manner: the great army of "red" specialists that was supposed to emerge from the peasant and proletarian supporters of the regime could receive its training only from these "bourgeois" specialists. The result of this paradox, clearly perceived by the Bolsheviks, was a cautious mixture of policies in the search for the scientific change-over, and a correspondingly slow rate of progress, throughout the period of the New Economic Policy (NEP). Forceful measures were not used against the old specialists, who were assured by word and deed that as long as they worked conscientiously at their individual trades and abstained from political action, they were free to have whatever ideology they liked. Kalinin, indeed, in a speech to a convention of doctors at the end of 1925 (*Izvestiia*, No 287), implied that they could have whatever political ideology they liked, even anti-Communist, as long as they did not act on it. He and other high Soviet officials appealed to the older specialists on a level where Bolshevik ideals coincided with those of Russian scien-tists: heavy financial support for scientific research and training, the dissemination of scientific knowledge to the widest possible audi-ence, and the practical application of scientific discoveries to the modernization and strengthening of the native land. Invidious com-parisons with the record of the pre-Revolutionary regime were made on all three scores, and some older scientists were brought round to praise the Bolsheviks. For example, the biochemist A. N. Bakh, who had been a member of the People's Will when Lenin was an eight-year-old, and, more significantly, a Socialist Revolutionary at the time of Lenin's Revolution in 1917, became the president of VAR-NITSO, the Association of Scientific and Technical Workers for Sup-port to Socialist Construction; and the physicist O. D. Khvol'son, who had been past fifty in 1909, when Lenin attacked him as a fideist, lent his considerable reputation to support of the Union of Scientific Workers, which, like all Soviet trade unions, taught its members to identify the improvement of their lot with the enhancement of the Soviet regime. In order to broaden its appeal, the Union abstained almost completely from the dissemination of Marxism as a philosophy of natural science, but even so, at the end of 1927, the last year of

NEP, it could claim barely six percent of all scientific workers as its members. Moreover, the Communist Academy's societies of materialist scientists, which *had* campaigned for the acceptance of Marxism as a general philosophy, had a combined membership by the most generous estimate of only a few hundred. Obviously, peaceful persuasion was a slow method of transforming mature scientists into dedicated supporters of the regime. Yet precisely such scientists, the government was convinced, were essential to the success of the Plan.

The progress of the new "red" specialists was hardly more encouraging, as the Plan began in 1928. The law required that the sons and daughters of manual workers and peasants be favored in admissions to higher schools, and there was an impressive network of *rabfaki* or "workmen's faculties" to give them the academic prerequisites for higher education. But this system had been in effective operation only six years, not enough time for even the first contingent of predominantly proletarian students to have received graduate degrees. They were reaching the universities as undergraduates, but in 1928 the children of nonproletarian elements were still the majority of first-year graduate students. To the Bolshevik authorities this seemed the main reason that the majority of graduate students in the natural sciences either were uninterested in Bolshevik ideology or shared their "bourgeois" professors' skepticism. Beginning in 1927 all graduate students were required to pass an examination in Marxism, but when an examiner asked a future mathematician for an appraisal of dialectical materialism, his question was answered with another: "Why should I bother with such nonsense?"[1] Nor was this "contradiction between the ever-growing role of the scientific worker in socialist construction and his ideological and socio-political backwardness" the only cause of deepening Bolshevik anxiety. The elementary problem of numbers threatened to get out of hand; the rate of production of new technicians and scientists seemed to be falling hopelessly behind the staggering increase in the Plan's demand for them.

"Military measures" designed to achieve "maximum results in the shortest time" seemed the only way out, as Andrei Vyshinsky, then an important official in higher education, wrote in 1928. The Party's Central Committee ordered a detachment of one thousand Communists to be enrolled in higher schools in the fall of 1928 with scant regard for academic prerequisites. A spirited public drive was set in motion to "renew" the Academy of Sciences, that is, to swell its ranks with many new pro-Soviet members nominated by institutions outside the hitherto autonomous Academy. In the universities professors of ten or more years' standing were ordered to undergo "re-election": in public meetings their fitness both as specialists and as "social men" (*obshchestvenniki*) was to be examined by colleagues, students, and representatives of the Party. Of course, membership in the Union of Scientific Workers or in VARNITSO counted heavily in a candidate's favor, especially since the Union, early in 1929, formally established the Marxist-Leninist *Weltanschauung* as a requirement for membership. In short, efforts to push forward new "red" specialists, and pressure on mature specialists to give up "neutralism" or "the so-called simply legal relationship to the Soviet regime" were considerably intensified in 1928 and the first half of 1929.[2]

Still, as the Soviet regime approached its supreme test, the drive for the "solid" collectivization of agriculture, it showed growing dissatisfaction with the progress of the scientific change-over. Professors were reportedly sneering at the dispatch of "the thousand" as an effort "to prove the theorem that any illiterate can become a university student." And it appeared that such professors usually had little to fear from the re-elections. In most institutions there had as yet been none; in others, all candidates, regardless of their "social physiognomy," were being "re-elected" by a formal ritual of meetings and eulogies; and when there were genuine "re-elections," the Communists on the spot (students for the most part) tended toward one of two extremes, equally denounced as deviations in the central press. Either they attacked the professorial candidates as if they were *lishentsy* (a Soviet neologism for such people as priests and former gendarmes, who were deprived of civil rights), or, more often, the Communists succumbed to the mysteries of the academic guild and agreed to use professional competence as the sole basis for judging the candidates.

The renovation of the Academy of Sciences also moved forward haltingly. In January, 1929, A. M. Deborin and V. M. Friche, the chief Soviet Marxists in the fields of philosophy and art criticism, though nominated to membership by many Communist institutions, were voted down by the Academy, while the mathematician N. N. Luzin, an intuitionist in the theory of mathematics, was elected qua philosopher. To be sure, the Academy quickly reconsidered this affront to the Bolsheviks, and elected the two Marxists at an extraordinary session in February. At the public celebration that followed, the Secretary of the Academy, the 67-year-old orientalist S. F. Ol'denburg, reassured the Bolsheviks: "We feel still more our close connection with public opinion; we feel that there is no 'we' and 'you,' but only 'we.'" Apparently not all shared this feeling. A meeting of the Academy's graduate students (*praktikanty*) seems to have resolved that compulsory training in Marxism should *not* be made a part of their program. And in the fall of 1929 a special investigating commission descended on the Academy and dismissed at least one hundred and twenty-eight people, some of whom appear to have been prosecuted subsequently in secret before administrative tribunals.[3] For Soviet scientists the great break had begun in earnest.

Without access to the archives one cannot know much about secret arrests and punishments, but the public record does reveal some things. In the first place it shows pretty clearly that mass terror, which had not been used against scholars, made its appearance after the purge of the Academy of Sciences in November, 1929. From the spring of 1928, to be sure, there had been intensely publicized trials of specialists accused of wrecking, that is, of activity "bringing economic and political harm to the Soviet state with the purpose of sapping its power and preparing for an anti-Soviet intervention." Such loud admonitory shouts at the "bourgeois" specialist did not cease at the end of 1929, but they were joined by less definite warnings, by obscure, unexplained acts of terror. For example, the only published allegations of malfeasance in the Academy of Sciences concerned some historical documents found in the Academy library; they were supposedly "of political importance," and the Librarian, the historian S. F. Platonov, was "relieved of all administrative posts" for failing to turn them over to the proper agency and for allowing unauthorized people to see them. Platonov's further fate was not publicized, nor was any light shed on the misdeeds or the further punishment of those dismissed with him. A similar obscurity, an equally ominous omission of specifics, characterized most of the references in 1930 and 1931 to "methods of terrorizing the accomplices of counter-revolution," methods that were being used, if we can believe the journal of the Communist Academy (1931, No. 1, p. 83), against "that whole upper-echelon bourgeois intelligentsia, which, though not caught *flagrante delicto*, fosters wrecking activity by its sympathy or by its neutrality."

There was no longer any question whether antipathy to Communism was permissible. The great outcry was against "apoliticism" and "neutralism." VARNITSO took scientific workers out on the streets of Moscow to demonstrate against these sins, and a 38-year-old Bolshevik mathematician warned against the most refined kind of "apoliticism": verbal endorsements of Marxism-Leninism unaccompanied by deeds to prove sincerity. "Never," he exclaimed, "has the class struggle in science been carried on with such bitterness as just now. Never has the demand for *our* science, a science that really serves socialist construction, been as great as today. Whoever now is not with us, whoever is still neutral, is against us."

Nor were lesser Bolsheviks the only ones to erase the former distinction between political loyalty and ideological solidarity. Lunacharsky, the former Commissar of Education who, early in 1928, had given scientists one of the last assurances of their right to reject Marxism, in 1930 spoke to them with a new toughness, saying nothing of rights but only of obligations. Perhaps Karl Radek's exhortation, "On One Side of the Barricades or the Other," which appeared in the journal VARNITSO in August, 1930, was the most revealing. *"The broad mass of specialists,"* he wrote, underscoring the extensiveness of such feelings, "stunned by shootings and arrests, dash off in various directions, and frightened by the hostile atmosphere that events have created about them, do not know where to submit, but try in the meantime to hide their heads under their wings, in expectation of better times."

Radek warned such "Philistines" that "the mistrustful attitude of the working class cannot be assuaged by correct declarations of loyalty or by silence." Still, declarations of loyalty abounded, culminating at the end of 1930 in a birthday greeting from the Unions of Scientific and Educational Workers to the Star Chamber itself: the Unions thanked the OGPU, on the occasion of its thirteenth anniversary, for purging their ranks of those not worthy of the honorable title of Soviet scientific worker.

One also gets a vivid sense of the hostile atmosphere surrounding the mature specialist in 1930-1931 from the plays and novels of the time. Gorky's irritation with the Russian intelligentsia was given new expression in a play about a counter-Revolutionary engineer, whose villainy is inspired by arrogant pride in his special knowledge and by contempt for the working man's ignorance. "The workers have seized state power," he explains to his wife, "but they can't manage. . . . In general, the dictatorship of workers, and socialism, are fantasies, illusions, which we the intelligentsia involuntarily support by our work. . . . Machinists, housepainters, weavers, they're not capable of state power; it must be taken over by scientists [*uchenye*], by engineers."

When his troubled wife asks whether he is not two-faced, he exclaims: "Am I two-faced? Yes! Any other way is impossible! . . . The role of the defeated, the prisoner's role, is not my role!" This was one of Gorky's exceptional individuals (gone wrong, to be sure), but a similar sense of outraged pride was presumed to be hidden behind the mask of complaisance worn by the ordinary "Philistine" (*obyvatel'-skii*) specialist, the type who had no stomach for plots against the Soviet state but might, if the proletarian dictatorship relaxed the threat over him. Anyone educated before 1917 was a "bourgeois" specialist unless he proved himself otherwise. He belonged to that "long-winded, weak-kneed intelligentsia [as Gorky described the type in *Izvestiia* (12-13 December 1929)] . . . which met the October Revolution with passive sabotage or with active, armed resistance, and which in part continues to struggle 'in word and deed' against the Soviet regime even to the present day, wrecking consciously and unconsciously."

Was the suggestion in Gorky's final phrase—that a specialist might *unknowingly* commit the capital crime of wrecking—simply an extravagant flight of rhetoric? Probably not, for the central problem of a very popular play written in 1930 by Afinogenov was precisely a scientist's unwitting wrecking. The play, significantly entitled *Fear*, dealt with an eminent professor of human physiology (was Pavlov the author's original inspiration?) who was not one of the conscious enemies of the Soviet state, but played into their hands by working out a theory that fear was the essential motive in the behavior of Soviet people. His theory was "exposed" in a public meeting by an old Bolshevik woman, whose rich political experience compensated for her lack of formal education. When she concluded her indictment of the professor with a cry to the audience on stage to be vigilant and merciless toward the class enemy, the real audience in the theater responded with loud applause (*Pravda*, 7 January 1932). The response lends verisimilitude to the dramatist's picture of "public opinion" (*obshchestvennost'*) working with the OGPU to make the professor a Soviet patriot or else break him. Certainly, the *vydvizhentsy* in the audience (a Soviet coinage for proletarians "pushed up" into scientific or other responsible work) must have felt a tightness in their throats at the symbolism of the play's ending. The professor, converted, promises to give a public criticism of his wrecking theory and to hand over the keys of all the offices to the *vydvizhentsy* in his institute.

One naturally wonders whether the great break of 1929-1931 was actually the triumphal completion of the scientific change-over, as this play suggests. Were Russia's mature scientists actually forced to choose between full-throated Bolshevism and self-destruction by "wrecking"? Did the actual management of scientific institutes and university departments pass in this brief period to the "pushed up" new generation of "red" specialists? Certainly there is nonfictional evidence that suggests an affirmative answer to both questions.

"The thousand" of the academic year 1928-1929 (that is, the detachment of Communists pushed into universities and institutes with little regard for academic prerequisites) were joined by two thousand more in 1929-1930, and by still more in the next two academic years. Even without such special detachments, the staggering overall expansion of higher education between 1928 and 1932 (the student body trebled and the teaching staff doubled) suggests that the older specialists were being "dissolved in a sea of new forces," as a report of the State Planning Commission put it in 1930. "A young man who studies our science," said the Bolshevik mathematician who helped write the report, "has every chance of becoming a professor at twenty-five."

At the same time, drastic measures were taken to reduce the sense of need for highly trained professors. In November 1929 the Party's Central Committee ordered "continuous productive practice" for students in higher technical education, with the result that abstract, theoretical subjects, the stronghold of the old specialists, were pushed into the background. Some institutes even abandoned courses in theoretical physics and chemistry altogether, brushing aside as reactionary—or worse—the professors who protested that technicians rather than engineers would be the result. New methods of teaching and grading in "brigades" were designed to get round the need for individual *expertise* in students as well as teachers. Even in research it seemed that the masses might break down the *tsekhovshchina* or guild-like seclusion of the old specialists. When T. D. Lysenko, a virtually unknown 31-year-old seedman from the Caucasus, failed to impress a scientific convention in 1929 with a report of his experiments on plant physiology, he got some dirt farmers to try them out, and the Commissariat of Agriculture was so impressed that in 1931 it ordered collective farms to experiment with Lysenko's allegedly new methods "on a mass scale. . . . Only in this way," the Commissar of Agriculture declared, "will the enterprise be set up in a really scientific way, in a really revolutionary way." Such things seem to confirm the playwright's vision of the great break as a time when the old specialists surrendered the keys of their institutes to the *vydvizhentsy*, to those pushed up from bench and plow.

Moreover, one can find real analogies to the fictional indictment of a scientist for unwitting wrecking, in apparent confirmation of the notion that the older scientists were actually forced to choose be-

tween full-throated Bolshevism and self-destruction by "wrecking."
The calm, objective tone of a physician's pamphlet on the control of
venereal disease, for example, aroused intense anger in the *Kazan
Medical Journal* (1931, No. 4-5). The pamphlet did not sufficiently
extol Soviet accomplishments in this field or sufficiently berate bourgeois failures.

In our time [the reviewer lectured] the time of the socialist offensive,
when all hostile class forces are resisting desperately, the pen is obliged
to shoot just as accurately and truly as the revolver. Paper, the printed
word, speech—all are weapons that must guard our life, our construction,
our philosophy from all sides. . . . We say loud and clear: it is not only
useless to write such "scientific" works [as the pamphlet under review],
but also harmful and criminal.

It may be that the "criminal" physician survived this rhetorical
fusillade, but more than verbal guns seem to have been used against
some statisticians in the State Planning Commission. Apparently they
did not satisfy the Party's insistence that the goals of the Plan must
be the scientific prediction of mathematicians no less than the passionate desire of "shock-brigaders" (*udarniki*). To be sure, such
statisticians, like the physician writing on public health or the fictional professor in *Fear*, were on the dangerous frontier between the
natural and the social sciences, but one finds an attempted crusade
against wrecking in the mathematical theory of statistics, too. B. S.
Iastremskii, a 53-year-old insurance specialist who had vainly criticized the established authorities in statistical theory before the Revolution, won a following at the time of the great break. He helped
"unmask the wreckers" in the Planning Commission, and then teamed
up with two young Bolshevik mathematicians to produce an allegedly
revolutionary *Theory of Mathematical Statistics* in 1930. If other
mathematicians were obliged to support this book in a milieu where
the distinction between pistols and pens was lost, then it might seem
reasonable to suppose that "the proletariat on the front of the cultural
revolution," to quote a young Bolshevik mathematician in 1930, was
indeed "storming heaven itself," forcing the mature scientist "to
place not only himself as citizen [*obshchestvennik*] but also his
science in the service of socialist construction, to reconstruct it."

Yet there is evidence that requires major amendments to these
simple conclusions. Mathematicians apparently were *not* forced to
accept the new theory of statistics; at the end of 1930 a supporter of
the theory complained that O. Iu. Shmidt, the most important Bolshevik "on the scientific front" and a mathematician himself, was

indifferent to the new theory, and within a few years it appears to have died altogether. Lysenko's program for boosting yields did not turn into an attack on geneticists until 1936. The pistol-waving review cited above was not at all typical of the journals on natural science; throughout the great break they continued to print specialized articles, and showed the influence of the times only by occasional editorial declarations of Soviet loyalty and by considerable transformations of their editorial staffs. Looking through such journals, one begins to understand why Radek reported that "the broad mass of specialists" had responded to the clamorous demands for positive proofs of patriotism in a "Philistine" *(obyvatel'skii)* way, with little more than correct declarations of loyalty, or silence. In fact this conclusion is suggested by the Bolsheviks' exasperated repetition of the warning that such a flaccid response was not enough, that "Philistine" specialists could not escape history, or, to use Radek's industrial paraphrase of Lincoln, that they would be "cast aside by the flywheel of history." Perhaps the "Philistine" specialist had a firmer grip on the dizzily spinning Russian flywheel—than Radek himself? To ask this in sneering malice is to take sides, and not with the liberal opponents of regimentation, but with the type whose only cause was self-preservation, who would not sacrifice himself in any cause.

Direct evidence of the extent and geological force of this "swamp" *(boloto)*—if the metaphor may be shifted to the standard Bolshevik pejorative for the passive, adaptive, self-centered type—is provided by the scientific conventions of 1930. They were the highpoints of a drive to capture the scientific societies, whose virtually complete autonomy had aroused only headshakes and grumblings before 1930. Now, the Bolsheviks proclaimed, this autonomy was to be destroyed. But for all such loud talk the conventions of 1930 were much the same as those of previous years: a great mass of special papers were read, most of them trivial or repetitive, as in scholarly conventions the world around. The great break at each convention was a keynote speech, with a corresponding resolution, on the role of science in the construction of socialism, and, when the convention broke up into its many sections, perhaps two or three papers on the dialectical materialist reconstruction of science.

The pettiness both of the victories claimed and of the rebuffs lamented is the most striking characteristic of the Bolshevik reports of these conventions. The Congress of Physiologists, for example, was pictured as making history in its handling of the Pavlov *affaire*. He stayed away from it, as he consistently did from all but foreign conventions, to demonstrate his disapproval of the Soviet regime. Pre-

131

vious congresses of physiologists had elected him honorary chairman *in absentia*, but the Congress of 1930 passed him by, and elected to its "honorary presidium"—the entire Political Bureau of the Communist Party. As against this victory, a defeat: the famous Professor A. F. Samoilov, whose report on electrical methods in physiological research was the most memorable event at the convention, dismissed dialectical materialism "with genial irony." In Baku, to take another example, a Congress of Pathologists adopted the proper resolutions and elected to its presidium the 36-year-old Dr. S. G. Levit, one of the leaders of the drive for a dialectical-materialist reconstruction of science. But then a foreign professor who told the convention that science should be free both of religion and of Marxism was duly applauded at the end of his speech. Perhaps, the Bolshevik reporter noted hopefully, the audience did not understand him, for he spoke in German.[4] In Odessa, where the physicists held a pleasant August meeting, there seem to have been no such contretemps. The 50-year-old Academician A. F. Ioffe, a universally respected physicist and a genuinely enthusiastic supporter of the Soviet cause (though not of dialectical-materialist reconstructions of physics) gave a keynote speech appealing for planned research to aid industrial expansion. Clearly, Ioffe and Levit belonged to a tiny band of prophets in a heathen land, where principled and outspoken opponents were even rarer, and certainly much hardier. Reading through the reports of the conventions, one senses a vast flaccidity silently, perhaps indifferently, absorbing a few brave Bolshevik speeches.

There was one illuminating exception to this rule, the rebellion of the Congress of Mathematicians in June 1930 and the related trouble of the Moscow Mathematical Society in December. The turmoil in statistics had nothing to do with these events, and other substantive issues relating to mathematics were only slightly involved. The "Moscow school" was famous for its otherworldly absorption in pure theory, and D. F. Egorov, the 61-year-old chief of the "school," would not criticize this tradition or declare his interest in serving the Five Year Plan. As this fact suggests, the main source of trouble seems to have been a general stiff-necked nonconformity in Egorov and an equally stiff-necked liberalism in his colleagues. He scandalized the Bolsheviks by refusing to join the Union of Scientific Workers, while remaining an elder of the Orthodox Church, and the Moscow Mathematical Society not only kept him on as president but listed émigrés in its membership. Already in the "reelections" of 1929, Bolshevik graduate students at the University of Moscow singled him out for attack, and it seems that he was removed from control of the Mathematical Institute. Still, he was a leading figure at the All-Union Congress of Mathematicians in June, 1930, and it may well be that his example was a contributing cause of the rebellion in the Congress. It refused to send greetings to the Sixteenth Congress of the Communist Party, which was then in session. A complete revolution was not attempted; the mathematicians did resolve to aid socialist construction, though cautioning that theoretical work should not be neglected in the interests of immediate practicality. But 1930, the year of savage class warfare in the villages and "shock brigades" in the towns, was hardly a time even for a limited rebellion, which was continued, moreover, by the refusal of the Moscow Mathematical Society to expel Egorov.

The climax was reached at the end of 1930, when Egorov told a meeting of the Society that "nothing else but the binding of a uniform *Weltanschauung* on scientists is genuine wrecking." It is significant that the Bolsheviks present could not agree on the appropriate reaction. The one who took the floor tried to smooth over the clash with talk of a misunderstanding, for which he was subsequently accused of "rotten liberalism" and "Maecenasism." Bolsheviks with the proper "irreconcilability" *(neprimirimost')* took action after the meeting was over. Egorov was arrested. But his colleagues in the Society, including a member of the Communist Youth, silently defied the terror by holding a regular business meeting. (They were expected to condemn the arrested man and engage in "self-criticism" for resisting Bolshevization so long.) Thereupon five mathematicians, styling themselves an "Initiating Group for the Reorganization of the Mathematical Society," published a denunciation of the Society's belief that " 'one can be a Egorov by conviction yet work honorably with the Soviet regime.' " They could hardly have given a better characterization of the government's policy toward "bourgeois" scientists during NEP, but they lashed this belief as "Philistinism [*obyvatel'shchina*], hiding in its corner from the class struggle, and decorating this corner with scientific aestheticism instead of the canary of the rank-and-file Philistine." The other mathematicians, however, would not yield to revolutionary appeals any more than to terror. The wretched affair had reached a climax without issue. The Society was not reorganized but simply ceased functioning for more than a year, in the course of which Egorov died. The place and cause of his death are not in the public record, nor are the steps leading to the revival of the Society in 1932. One supposes that the locked opposition of the intransigent Bolshevizers and unyielding liberals gave way to some such complex adjustment of principle and reality as had already made the functioning of the other scientific societies possible.[5]

Until 1932 it was still not clear that an adjustment would be made even with the complaisant majority of the old specialists. The Bolshevizers kept up the struggle for something more than complaisance, and looked beyond the scientific societies to the places where scientific work was done. A young Bolshevik biologist told a meeting of the Communist Academy in January 1931:

> However strange it may be, in the fourteenth year of the Revolution, though we have at our disposal a colossal apparatus of scientific establishments, museums, laboratories, observatories, etc., in essence we do not possess them at all. It would seem to me . . . that the Association of Natural Science [of the Communist Academy] should set itself the organizational and ideological task of entering, of penetrating these institutes, these observatories and laboratories, through the cells of atheists that exist there, the sections of VARNITSO that exist there, all the circles of political or other character that exist there, so that we will have at each institute some cells on which we can rely in our work.

As if in response to this suggestion, the Party's Central Committee decreed on March 15, 1931, that the Communist Academy should establish its "methodological control" over the most important *vedomstvennye* (ordinary state) scientific research establishments. They were to submit their research plans for approval by the Academy and admit the representatives of the Academy to the drawing up of future plans.

The old distinction between the special network of Marxist-Leninist establishments and that of *vedomstvennye* (ordinary state) scientific establishments was thus to be erased; the Communist Academy, which had previously been the directing center only for the former, was now apparently to become the center for all. Clearly, there was a conflict here with the competence of the Academy that Peter the Great had founded, the Academy of Sciences of the USSR; and one wonders what dreams of supreme power may have come to the young Bolsheviks in the Communist Academy during 1931, as they began their work of establishing "methodological control." Their victory over the societies must have had a paradoxically sobering influence, for it had been too easy. Under the aegis of the same decree, they launched a new drive against the scientific societies. VARNITSO and the Union of Scientific Workers called a public meeting, where, we are told (in the journal VARNITSO, 1931, No. 3, p. 59) various speakers "completely exposed the protective colors in which the societies have redecorated themselves, using Marxist terminology for this and also some change of leadership." Forcibly converted, Russia's mature scientists were coming under the entirely logical suspicion of hypocrisy, and Soviet Marxists seemed about to follow the depressing example of Spanish Christians: forcefully ridding themselves of Moors and Jews, they felt a natural compulsion to know the hidden thoughts of Moriscos and Marranos.

In 1932, however, the frenzy of Stalin's first Five Year Plan was at last spent. Everywhere Lenin's famous slogan in an earlier lull was revived: "Better less, but better." Criticisms and cautions that had formerly been denounced as deviations now came from the Central Committee itself. In June A. I. Stetskii, the head of the Central Committee's Propaganda and Agitation Department, called off the ardent young Bolsheviks who had been establishing the Party's "methodological control" even in engineering and ichthyology. In *Pravda* (4 June 1932) he voiced the familiar complaint of "a purely verbal, formal, declaratory" endorsement of Marxism, but he did not conclude, as he had a year before (in the journal of the Communist Academy), that the pressure on the old specialists must be increased, the struggle intensified. He concluded that arduous, prolonged work at the specific material of the sciences was necessary, so that the non-Party specialist might be convinced of Marxism in terms of his own specialty. And foreshadowing the fate of the Communist Academy itself, Stetskii called on Communist scientists to leave their special societies at the Academy and dissolve into the broad societies of non-Party scientists. Three months later the Central Executive Committee of the Soviet Union called for an end to "shock brigade" methods of effecting the cultural revolution in higher education. The intervention of student and Party organizations in the management of the higher schools was to stop, in part— we may suppose—because the political reliability of the rectors had been tested in the fire of the past few years. The overemphasis on "continuous productive practice" was to end, for this practice had been producing technicians rather than engineers. Of course, the professors who had been called reactionary for predicting as much were not explicitly vindicated, very likely because the Soviet economy needed technicians anyhow, and because professors needed to learn respect for the Party's decrees. The "brigade" methods of teaching and grading were to be dropped, and the individual responsibility of students to individual teachers was firmly re-established. Professional competence was to be the only basis for filling vacancies and giving promotions in faculties, and graduate students were to be appointed only by the faculties concerned, and only from graduates of higher schools. Evidently the day of the *vydvizhentsy*, the "pushed up" ones, had passed.

In 1933, indeed, the tables seemed to be turned altogether: Communists in fields of higher learning were subjected to "re-elections" at the hands of professors. More precisely, the Party organizations in institutions of higher learning examined their members at public meetings, to which non-Party specialists were urgently invited in order to help weed out unworthy Communists. The actual results were hardly revolutionary. Many of the professors at these meetings were discreetly silent, and only a few Party members suffered expulsion (e.g., a laboratory assistant for having his son circumcised with religious rites, a graduate student for giving flippant answers to questions on Leninist theory). Most, including the leading Bolshevizers of higher learning, were merely given a forum in which to tell the story of their lives as model Communists. (I. I. Prezent, for example, who had abandoned the Deborinites and the Mendelian biologists when they lost favor, and was now becoming Lysenko's chief advocate, was the star of the meeting that expelled the religious laboratory assistant and the flippant graduate student.[6]) But, however trifling the actual purge of the new "red specialists" may have been, its staging gave ceremonial recognition to the continuing importance of the old non-Party specialists.

Of course, it would be quite wrong to imagine that the great break had passed without trace. The older generation of scientists, still the possessor of essential knowledge, was still in charge of many university faculties and scientific research institutes; and most were still felt to be ideologically alien, though all but a very few indomitable spirits now refrained from the expression of any but the correct ideology. What was new was a fundamental transformation in the intellectual autonomy of these old specialists. In principle, they had lost it altogether; to use a favorite expression of the day, they had "disarmed themselves" (*razoruzhilis'*) before the Party's Central Committee. In practice they still enjoyed an almost unimpaired autonomy in their subject matter, and an immeasurable autonomy in ideology—immeasurable because of the mask of silence and possible hypocrisy that covered it. How long this incongruity of principle and practice would continue depended on the Central Committee's assessment of changing necessities and possibilities. Aside from the "disarming" of the old specialists (at least in principle), the Committee had gained an enormous number of new scientists in training, most of them from social classes that it hoped would produce great specialists who would be genuinely Bolshevik in ideology.[7]

The reader may feel inclined to conclude that the Bolsheviks had become fatally embroiled with the law of enforced belief, as we may call the truism that hypocrisy and unthinking zealotry spring up where heresy and freethinking are cut down. Ultimately, it would seem, one of the two would have to die, either creative thought or thought control. But we cannot rest with this generality, for the silence of the Central Committee on the substantive issues of natural science was one of the most striking characteristics of the great break. They had razed the walls of academic autonomy, but one senses a moat of irrelevance still lying between their ideology and the natural sciences, bridgeable, perhaps, but hardly by the primitive zealots who assumed control of the Bolshevik ideology during the great break. Moreover, on the scientists' side, enforced belief might become genuine in time; the Church that Egorov refused to quit had been forced on his ancestors by an earlier state.[8] General considerations tell us little; to assess the meaning of the great break for Soviet scientists, we must examine the further history of relations between Soviet scientists and Soviet ideologists.

Almost thirty years have passed since the great break. To what extent has the conversion of Soviet natural scientists become genuine? And how has this conversion—in part, enforced appearance, in part, inward reality—affected the Soviet Marxist philosophy of science and the natural sciences themselves? A reliable answer to these questions depends on research that has only been started. What follows, accordingly, is a tentative sketch, a series of hypotheses, to be modified or destroyed by further research.

The general philosophy that triumphed during the great break was a congeries of rather vague formulas that enjoyed little refinement or change as long as Stalin monopolized the right to "develop Marxism further." But scientists were expected to prove the genuineness of their conversion to this philosophy by helping the Party's philosophers apply it to the special sciences. In fact there seems to have been more conflict than co-operation between scientists and philosophers, a conflict that has fluctuated with the alternating waves of Communist confidence and mistrust in the population at large, scientists included. The mistrust that characterized the great break burst out again (probably with greater violence) during the great purges and the treason trials of 1936-1939, and again at the culmination of Stalinism in the period 1947-1953. At such times crusading ideologists have been ascendant, angrily charging scientists with subservience to bourgeois theories and with resistance to the Bolshevization of science. In the alternating periods of comparative Communist trust in scientists as in the population at large, scientists have been ascendant, reproaching the ideologists for discrediting Marxism by illiterate attacks on proven theories. And in such periods of relative trust, most of the ideologists have hastened to forget or forswear illiterate attacks, echoing the scientists' insistence on technical competence in the philosophical analysis of the natural sciences.

This pattern can be most clearly and completely established in the case of physics. Ideological attacks on relativity and quantum mechanics—and on the eminent physicists who stood up for their science—flared up during the great break, during the purges, and again in the late 'forties and early 'fifties. In the intervals such attacks nearly disappeared, and eminent physicists set the tone of philosophical discussion of their subject. Indeed, the pattern can be illustrated by tracing the double and triple tergiversations of individual ideologists (e.g., A. A. Maksimov or V. E. L'vov) as one period has given way to another. The only men who were consistently hostile to the new physics, regardless of the Party's fluctuating attitudes toward scientists, were not ideologists but a tiny group of old physicists, now deceased.

To the extent that other natural sciences have caught the ideologist's eye (a small extent for most fields during most of Soviet history), much the same pattern can be established. Genetics and its allied disciplines are the great exception. To be sure, there have been zigzags in the ideologists' evaluation of this science too, and they can be correlated with the major fluctuations in the Party's willingness to trust scientists. But this correlation is of secondary importance in genetics. Cutting through such zigzags and fluctuations, the long-run curve of Lysenko's "Michurinism" rose steadily until 1953 and has declined only slightly since.

The great break enabled Lysenko to emerge from obscurity as the Commissar of Agriculture's "revolutionizer" of agricultural science, but the end of the great break did not hurl him back into obscurity as it did many other "revolutionizers." Within the agricultural field he continued to build his reputation and his following until 1936, when a new spasm of mistrust seized the Communist Party, and Lysenko began his full-scale assault on genetics. (At the same time he appropriated the reputation of the recently deceased Michurin, who, while he lived, seems to have been cold to Lysenko's advances.) By 1940 Lysenko was on the verge of complete triumph, but in the preceding year Stalin had signaled a *détente* by expressing confidence in the loyalty of Soviet specialists, and an uneasy truce ensued between Lysenko and the geneticists. In 1948, after Zhdanov had called Bolshevik ideologists once more to battle against bourgeois culture, Lysenko rushed the geneticists with a weapon that no other Bolshevizer of natural science has ever wielded: the explicit approval of the Party's Central Committee, in the face of which nearly all public opposition to "Michurinism" collapsed. The thaw following Stalin's death revived public opposition to Lysenko, but the thaw has not caused "Michurinism" to melt away. In the present period of comparative calm for other natural sciences, conflict continues between the geneticists, who have recruited some allies from other fields of academic natural science, and the "Michurinists," who are deeply entrenched in the agricultural schools and experiment stations, and seem still to enjoy the favor of practical politicians as well as ideologists.

It is the present writer's hypothesis that the Soviet Union's chronic agricultural crisis has given Lysenko's crusade its lasting seriousness, in contrast to the intermittent vaporings of would-be Bolshevizers in other fields of natural science. Bolshevik efforts to increase agricultural productivity have been partly a struggle with technical backwardness, and partly a struggle with traditional peasant notions of proper social organization. Lysenko, by enlisting seedmen and stockbreeders in the holy cause of scientific socialist agriculture, has offered help on both levels of the chronic agricultural crisis. He has come forward as the mobilizer of agricultural science against poor varieties of plants and animals, the recruiter of peasant scientists en masse for the improvement of socialist agriculture. He has recruited them by elevating their traditional lore to the status of a comprehensive theory of life, and by exploiting their rough contempt for the subtleties of the academic scientist.

The most serious objection to this hypothesis is that the practical successes of "Michurinism" could not have won agriculturists and Party chiefs to support Lysenko, since these practical successes have been incorrectly explained, vastly overrated, or altogether illusory. Though serious, this objection is not unaswerable. As long as Lysenko's opponents have been unable to consign all his claims to the third category, he has had ground for rebuttal. Moreover, as the point was reached where nearly every seedman or stockbreeder, when offering an improved variety, did so in the name of "Michurinism" and in defiance of the geneticists, it became impossible for the *latter* to claim practical successes for themselves.

If this hypothesis concerning "Michurinism" proves true, then the

139

turmoil in Soviet biology can be little affected by trends in the philosophy of science. It can die down as (or if) Soviet agriculture approaches Khrushchev's goal: to "overtake and surpass" American levels of productivity. For the rest, answers to the questions raised on page 137 above must be even more conjectural. It may be that the cyclical interaction of natural science and Soviet Marxism is doomed to continue. But there are other possibilities. If the present rapprochement of Soviet ideologists and natural scientists is the result of mutual trust that will prove permanent, then the atmosphere that nourishes primitive Bolshevizers will be steadily dissipated, and Soviet Marxism will begin to face its supreme test as a philosophy of natural science. Losing its past function as a crude faith for bellicose ideologists and a scourge for suspect scientists, it will have to speak ever more rationally, subtly, meaningfully about natural science, or develop into a philosophy that can.

REFERENCES

1 See M. N. Pokrovskii, "O podgotovke nauchnoi smeny," *Kommunisticheskaia revoliutsiia*, 1929, No. 13, pp. 62-64.
2 See the articles by K. V. Ostrovitianov, I. K. Luppol, and A. Ia. Vyshinskii, in *Nauchnyi rabotnik*, 1929, No. 7-8; *Antireligioznik*, 1929, No. 6; and *Nauchnyi rabotnik*, 1930, No. 1.
3 See the reports in *Izvestiia*, 13 January, 10 September and 16 November 1929. See also the reports in *Nauchnyi rabotnik*, 1929, Nos. 1, 2, 3, 4, and 1930, No. 1.
4 See B. M. Zavadovskii, "Itogi IV vsesoiuznogo s'ezda fiziologov," and S. Vail', "II vsesoiuznyi s'ezd patologov," *Estestvoznanie i marksizm*, 1930, No. 2-3, pp. 142-165.
5 The most detailed account of the Egorov affair is in the declaration of the Initiating Group for the Reorganization of the Mathematical Society. See *Nauchnyi rabotnik*, 1930, No. 11-12. Cf. also the report in *VARNITSO*, 1930, No. 11-12, and E. Kol'man, "Vreditel'stvo v nauke," *Bol'shevik*, 1931, No. 2. See also *Uspekhi matematicheskikh nauk, Novaia seriia*, 1946, Vol. I, No. 1 (11), p. 236.
6 See *Front nauki i tekhniki*, 1933, No. 12, pp. 115-122. For convenient evidence of Prezent's Deborinite and Mendelian past, see M. L. Levin's speech in O. Iu. Shmidt (ed.), *Zadachi marksistov v oblasti estestvoznaniia* (Moscow, 1929), pp. 88-89.
7 This has been the main stress in Soviet comments on the great break in the cultural revolution. See, e.g., E. Iaroslavskii (Yaroslavsky), *O roli intelligentsii v SSSR* (Moscow, 1939), pp. 25 *et seq.*
8 In Russia, as in the rest of Europe, Christianity was a minority faith until it was established by royal edict. Vladimir, the Primary Chronicle tells us, ordered the chief heathen idol flogged through the streets and thrown in the Dnieper. "And then through the whole town Vladimir sent these words: 'If anyone does not come to the river tomorrow morning [for baptism], be he rich or poor, or beggar or slave, he will be my enemy.'"

GUSTAV WETTER, S. J.

Ideology and Science in the Soviet Union
Recent Developments

AMONG THE CHIEF TRAITS of the Russian revolutionary intelligentsia, Nikolai Berdyaev cites a kind of obsession with certain ideas (usually social), the ability to devote oneself entirely to these ideas, even to the extent of placing life itself at their service, and finally an extreme dogmatism related to this attitude. Their interest did not center on how true some new doctrine was but on how effective it might be in the fight against absolutism and the existing social order. In this context certain ideas imported from the West that were adaptable as a theoretical foundation for socialism underwent a peculiar reformulation. A doctrine that in its country of origin might have been regarded as no more than a theory, a hypothesis, or a partial truth was immediately reforged in Russia into a kind of new revelation.

In this connection the observation Berdyaev makes concerning the attitude of the old Russian intelligentsia to positive science is particularly revealing and important to the present topic. Berdyaev distinguishes between scientific and philosophical positivism. In contrast to philosophical positivism, scientific positivism by no means excludes metaphysics and religious faith. Although some scientists, even in the West, have turned science into a weapon against metaphysics and religion, it cannot be denied that the West has created a science that is religiously and philosophically neutral. The Russian intelligentsia assimilated scientific positivism, however, in an entirely different manner. They fell into a virtual idolatry of science, and interpreted "science" as materialistic dogma, and scientism as a new faith—a dogma and a faith that expose the injustice of the present social order and that lead the people (the proletariat) toward their liberation.[1]

This situation raises some questions relevant to the subject of

141

our investigation, for it cannot be denied that the majority of early Russian Marxists developed in the intellectual climate created by the Russian intelligentsia. What is the present situation in Russia? Does the attitude of the old Russian intelligentsia prevail today? If this is the case, in which cultural strata? Does it survive underground, as it did under tsarism, or has it decisively altered the face of the new culture? Does a conflict still exist between a doctrine that is propagated by the state and an intelligentsia that protests against that doctrine in the name of science? If so, is this simply a repetition of the protest that arose during the second half of the past century, or is the relationship to science of those who protest today essentially different from the one held by the previous objectors? Finally, what are the prospects for future intellectual development in the Soviet Union?

In the following pages we shall attempt an answer to these questions by analyzing several discussions held in the Soviet Union concerning problems on the borderline between philosophy and the natural sciences. These discussions are particularly concerned with quantum physics, the theory of relativity, cosmology, and biology. The discussions held in October 1958 at the All-Union Conference on the Philosophic Problems of Modern Natural Science are especially informative in this connection. This was an impressively planned conference of philosophers and leading natural scientists, organized by the Academy of Sciences of the USSR in cooperation with the Ministry for Higher Education, for the purpose of establishing and strengthening the "alliance" between philosophers and natural scientists, on the basis of Marxist-Leninist theory. (See below, pp. 192-207.)

Before we deal with these discussions, however, some brief remarks are necessary concerning the manner in which the fundamental relationship between philosophy and the individual sciences is viewed in the Soviet Union. According to the doctrine of Soviet philosophy, it is the object of the individual sciences to determine the laws applying to each individual area of reality. On the other hand, it is the task of dialectical materialism to determine those general laws that govern the totality of reality. Contrary to the interpretation of philosophical positivism, this task is not merely restricted to a summation of the knowledge brought to light by the positive sciences. Dialectical materialism decisively rejects positivism, according to which the individual sciences are self-sufficient and require no philosophy. Instead, the general laws that are valid for total reality must be formed by generalizing the special laws obtained by all the individual sciences, by raising the results of the individual sciences to a higher level of abstraction.

Therefore, the relationship between philosophy and an individual science, to begin with, consists in the fact that philosophy represents a generalization of results from the individual sciences. In this sense, dialectical materialism likes to boast that it represents none other than "the scientific world view," the ultimate summation of the natural sciences, and it constantly claims that it finds "brilliant corroboration" of its doctrines in the modern natural sciences. This claim is connected with a second aspect of the relationship between dialectical materialism and the modern natural sciences: if dialectical materialism originates in science and represents its higher stage of generalization, thereby it becomes a valuable heuristic principle of scientific research as well. Consequently, natural scientists ever since Lenin's time have been required to use dialectical materialism as their method of research—and only those scientists whose research is based on dialectical materialism are considered capable of fruitful work, even in their specialty. The Soviet philosophical periodical, *Voprosy filosofii* (Questions of philosophy), stated in an editorial article devoted to this All-Union Conference: "For its fruitful and healthy development, science requires equipment consisting not merely of material means—laboratories, experimental installations, instruments, etc., but also an equipment of ideas that will guide the thinking of scientists along the correct path."[2]

No one could seriously object to the role of philosophy as a heuristic principle for the individual sciences so long as he is at all willing to accept the possibility of a philosophy that does not originate from within the individual sciences. It is essential, of course, that no logical errors be committed during the process of philosophic generalization, and that the assistance philosophy offers the individual sciences remain within this framework of a heuristic principle. To what extent these conditions are borne out will be shown by the following analysis of the boundaries between the work of philosophy and that of the individual sciences in the Soviet Union.

In physics, quantum physics is the area in which most differences of opinion between Soviet physicists and philosophers occur. There is a unanimity among them, however, as to the fundamental problems of the philosophical interpretation of quantum physics. Their primary concern is to oppose certain positivistic and idealistic interpretations advanced by some Western physicists, in particular, by the so-called "Copenhagen School" of Niels Bohr, Werner Heisenberg, and others. At the same time, Soviet scientists consider that this area provides one of the best opportunities for demonstrating dialectical materialism as an effective working tool.

The first point of controversy between Soviet natural philosophy and the Copenhagen School concerns the principle of complementarity advocated by the latter. It is well known that to describe the physical behavior of a micro-object, such as an electron, it is necessary in some cases to use the model of a corpuscle, while in others it is necessary to use the model of a wave. These two models are mutually exclusive, yet they also complement one another, since both are required for a complete description of a micro-object. This peculiar relationship of mutual exclusion and "complementation" is one aspect of what Bohr designated as complementarity. Internal contradictions arise, however, if one attempts to ascribe both properties to a micro-object simultaneously. Therefore, theoretical physics accomplishes this description in the following manner: it first interprets the object as a particle and assigns it a function such as is ordinarily used to describe a real wave, the so-called wave function. According to the Copenhagen interpretation, however, the meaning of this wave function does not imply that the micro-particle itself "is" a wave; the wave has the character of a probability wave, that is, it merely expresses the possibility of finding the particle, regarded as a corpuscle, at a certain place when one is performing a position measurement.

This interpretation is now rejected by Soviet physicists and philosophers. The interpretation of the wave as a probability wave is regarded as a form of idealism, because in such an interpretation the wave is not regarded as a real property of the micro-object but only as an expression of the observer's knowledge.

A further point of controversy between the Soviet physicists and the Copenhagen School is the concept of physical reality introduced by that school. It is not possible to ascribe two mutually exclusive situations simultaneously to a particle that exists independently of the observing subject. The Copenhagen School, therefore, is inclined to limit the reality concept entirely to the so-called "physical reality," i.e., to the micro-object just subjected to measurement in the instrument and simultaneously modified. The question of the inherent nature of the micro-object is rejected by these positivistically inclined physicists as meaningless. Contrary to this doctrine, which views reality as a constituent part of the observer (the perceiving subject), Soviet physicists unequivocally insist that the question of the "inherent" micro-object is not at all meaningless, and that the latter is to an extent recognizable.

A third criticism the Soviet physicists and philosophers direct against the Copenhagen School is aimed at the latter's denial of the validity of the principle of causality in the domain of micro-physics. The wave-particle dualism of micro-objects just described also represents the foundation of Heisenberg's uncertainty relation. In classical physics, by determining the position and momentum of a macrophysical body, it is possible to predict its further course without ambiguity. Causality is often interpreted as implying no more than this predictability of the future behavior of objects and their uniform sequence. In the domain of microphysics it has now been found that a simultaneous measurement of the position and momentum of a micro-object is impossible in principle: the more uncertain one of these quantities remains, the more accurately the other can be determined. The mathematical expression for this mutual relation was formulated by Heisenberg in the uncertainty relation mentioned above. Thus it is impossible to predict the behavior of a micro-object without ambiguity, and if causality is interpreted to mean no more than the predictable sequence of phenomena, one deduces that the law of causality is no longer valid in the microphysical domain.

In contrast, Soviet physicists and philosophers insist on the universal validity of the principle of causality, and defend philosophic determinism, despite the quantum-physical indeterminacy of the Heisenberg uncertainty relation. In order to avoid misunderstanding, they emphasize that the determinism they defend must not be interpreted as a rigid Laplacian determinism that excludes chance. In dealing with chance, Soviet physicists and philosophers refer to the doctrine of dialectical materialism, according to which necessity and chance do not represent two mutually exclusive categories: on the contrary, the way of necessity is paved by a multitude of coincidences. This idea is not further developed philosophically, however.

On the other hand, Soviet physicists are not unanimous in interpreting quantum physics philosophically. Three trends are distinguishable: (a), the concept of quantum ensembles, defended mainly by D. I. Blochintsev; (b), the concept of the reality of the quantum states, defended mainly by V. A. Fok and A. D. Aleksandrov, both of the University of Leningrad; (c), the so-called causal interpretation of the quantum theory; this resembles the interpretation recently advanced by Louis de Broglie, David Bohm, and Jean-Pierre Vigier.[3]

Despite the fact that the only review of quantum mechanics at the All-Union Conference was presented by Fok, the most authoritative position in the Soviet Union is apparently the interpretation advanced by D. I. Blochintsev, the director of the United Nuclear Research Institute at Dubna, near Moscow. He begins with the concept that the wave function does not directly refer to the behavior of an *individual* micro-object, but primarily characterizes the behavior of a so-called "totality" (ensemble). Only via the detour of totality does the physicist obtain fundamental access to knowledge of the behavior of the individual particles. Thus Blochintsev believes he can make several valid statements as to the properties of micro-objects, and that the chief of these properties ascribes to micro-objects not only properties of real particles, but equally properties of a real wave. Consequently, he regards the concept of motion along a trajectory as inapplicable with respect to the micro-object.[4]

The theory of ensembles is also defended by the acting director of the Institute for Philosophy of the Academy of Sciences of the USSR, N. E. Omel'anovskii, in his work, Philosophic Problems of Quantum Mechanics (Moscow, 1956). Omel'anovskii also claims that micro-objects possess real corpuscle-wave properties; he regards this as the fundamental idea in his book, though on a number of other questions he does not agree with Blochintsev. Omel'anovskii also finds it essential to distinguish between Heisenberg's uncertainty relation and the philosophical "principle of uncertainty," which he understands as the principle of complementarity, with its doctrine of the fundamental "indeterminability" of the effect of the measuring instrument on the micro-object.[5]

Fok objects to Blochintsev's ensembles that they represent "speculative structures."[6] Fok recognizes the reality of the quantum states of the micro-object, and defends the view that the wave function represents the real state of an *individual* micro-object. The quantum state of the object contains "potential possibilities" for various external interactions that are realized, depending on whether it is exposed to one or another external condition.[7] Similarly, according to his Leningrad colleague, A. D. Aleksandrov, the electron inherently contains a certain position and velocity merely "in the possibility" realized under certain macroscopic conditions, either of position or of velocity.[8]

Each school invokes dialectical materialism as authority for its position, and accuses its opponent of violating some aspect of that philosophy. Fok accuses Blochintsev's ensemble theory because, contrary to the doctrine of dialectical materialism, it does not begin with the micro-object and its states, but with the observations; thus his position resembles that of Bohr, who also denies that the wave function belongs to the micro-object.[9] Conversely, Blochintsev regards Fok's interpretation (that the wave function characterizes the individual particle) as a violation of dialectical materialism likewise, since it implies the unrecognizability of the state of the individual particle preceding the experiment, and assumes the possibility that a change in its states will follow without cause.[10]

It is true that today Fok seems less concerned with approaching the Copenhagen School too closely. In his communication at the All-Union Conference, he remarked that in his recent book, *Atomic Physics and Human Knowledge*,[11] Bohr modified his previous philosophical outlook at a number of points, and Fok permitted himself the observation that "it is now possible to declare oneself in substantial agreement with Bohr."[12] In dealing with the categories of causality and determinism, Fok stated, "We physicists employ these concepts as we ourselves have worked them out, independently of philosophy," and he even granted the possibility that his interpretation of these categories might contradict the views of the philosophers. These views received critical comment in the report of his lecture, and also in the discussion that followed it, when J. P. Terletskii objected that Fok's lecture merely represented a semantic modification of the Copenhagen interpretation of quantum mechanics.[13]

Fok's and Aleksandrov's interpretations are widely held at the University of Leningrad, as was shown during the discussion of Omel'anovskii's book in the physicists' seminar on philosophy at that university, when the ensemble theory was universally rejected. It is interesting that during this discussion Aleksandrov defended several theories of the Copenhagen School, related to the principle of complementarity, and that the opinion was expressed that quantum mechanics must be accepted as it is, without any subjective additions or wishful thinking. In no sense, however, did this discussion represent a departure from dialectical materialism, to which allegiance was reaffirmed; it merely expressed a desire to do justice to physical facts and to oppose certain oversimplifying positions. Objection was raised to relying on ensembles as a means of overcoming philosophical opposition, by asserting that the act of referring the wave function to an individual micro-object represents idealism, while the act of referring it to the ensemble represents materialism.[14]

Today the differences of opinion between Soviet philosophers and physicists as regards the theory of relativity are much less significant. The varying interpretations in this field, in fact, concern only certain secondary questions, and even such differences are much less drastic. Nearly a decade has now passed since the theory of relativity met with great mistrust in the Soviet Union, since it brought to light certain facts that then seemed irreconcilable with dialectical materialism. According to the theory of relativity, length, time, and even simultaneity are relative concepts, that is, they are determined by the choice of systems of reference—for example, the relative velocity of the observer. This situation appeared irreconcilable with the objective character of reality and its independence from the observing object, required by dialectical materialism. In rejecting the theory of relativity, some went so far as to speak of "reactionary Einsteinism." The arguments thus leveled against the theory of relativity were on a somewhat simple level. During Stalin's lifetime this attitude evoked a violent reaction among Soviet physicists. The periodical *Voprosy filosofii* in 1951 opened a discussion of relativity that lasted until 1955. The result was victory for the school that tried to be fairer to the theory and to prove it acceptable to dialectical materialism. Fok and Aleksandrov were the leading proponents of this school, and it was they, in fact, who wrote the article on relativity in the new edition of the *Bol'shaia sovetskaia entsiklopediia*.

Aleksandrov ascribes the confusion in many Soviet writers as to the problems of the theory of relativity to the fact that they fail to differentiate between the "relative" and the "nonobjective," that is, subjective. Although length and time intervals are found to be relative (i.e., dependent on the choice of a system of reference), this does not imply that they are dependent on an observing *consciousness*. Relativity is a part of objective reality, and is quite independent of any observing subject. A reference object serving as the origin of a reference system may be any arbitrary object, not necessarily a human observer.

Aleksandrov emphatically refuses to declare the theory of relativity to be reactionary and idealistic. On the other hand, he does consider it necessary to take a critical position toward it. As he declared at the All-Union Conference, this critical position refers not only to its philosophical assumptions and conclusions, but also to a certain extent to its physical content. The principles of dialectical materialism are always aimed at objective reality as it exists independently of the observing subject. Accordingly, Aleksandrov regards the theory of relativity as primarily a physical rather than a mathematical theory. He sees its essence not as the development of the *principle* of relativity already established in Galileo's work, or as proof of the relativity of length and time; he sees its essence, rather, in its discovery of the unity of space-time—i.e., in the fact that space and time do not represent two independent "modes of the existence of matter" (to employ a concept of dialectical materialism) but do represent a single common mode of existence: space-time. Taken separately, space and time are only components of the unity, space-time, depending on the choice of the system of reference.

Similarly, Aleksandrov does not regard the essence of the general theory of relativity to be the transfer of the principle of relativity from systems undergoing uniform and rectilinear motion (as in the special theory of relativity) to systems undergoing accelerated and rotary motion with respect to one another—usually considered as the essence of the general theory of relativity. Instead, Aleksandrov regards the essence of the general theory of relativity in the proof that the unity of space-time is not homogeneous, and therefore not necessarily subject to a Euclidian metric: rather, its metric depends on the distribution of matter.

The critical reformulation of the theory of relativity demanded by Aleksandrov primarily concerns the over-all structure of the theory. In the conventional structure of this theory one proceeds from the relative to the absolute. Aleksandrov insists on the opposite procedure. The starting point must be the material (real) connection between phenomena (i.e., the "actions"), and from these connections the general laws and concepts of space-time relations that arise from them are to be derived. According to Aleksandrov, the general space-time structure of the world is a manifestation of its cause-effect structure: the causal relations determine the space-time relations.

Aleksandrov's program met with enthusiastic approval, not only at the Conference, but also, and especially so, in the report of the Conference in *Voprosy filosofii*. The only objection raised was that Aleksandrov himself does not adhere consistently to his own fundamental approach. M. F. Shirokov advanced basic reasons for hesitation. The wish was expressed that in future there should be separate discussions of the philosophical questions of the general theory of relativity, in which it would be necessary, to begin with, to deepen philosophically the categories of dialectical materialism: absolute and relative, abstract and concrete, property and relation, content and form.[15]

On the whole, the discussion of the theory of relativity showed distinct evidence of a desire to work out a formulation of the theory that would correspond with the basic character of dialectical materialism. In addition, Soviet thinkers in dealing philosophically with questions related to the theory of relativity, devote particular attention to two individual problems that also involve a world view. The first concerns the problem of the geocentric versus a heliocentric world view. The fact that in the general theory of relativity Einstein extended the principle of relativity to include reference systems undergoing accelerated and rotational motion implies that all reference systems in the universe would be equally justifiable. In a certain sense, though in a considerably limited one, it might be said that the controversy between the Ptolemaists and the Copernicans was pointless, and that both were "equally correct." Soviet philosophers, however, defend the anachronistic view that religion stands or falls with the geocentric system, and therefore they violently attack this particular implication of the theory of relativity.[16]

The second problem has the same ideological background. With the aid of a supplementary hypothesis, Einstein also deduced from the general theory of relativity that the universe is unbounded but not infinite, analogous to a spherical surface, which is also unbounded but nevertheless finite. To Soviet philosophers, however, a spatial finiteness of the universe appears to imply also a specific origin in time, and with it a need for an act of world creation. Yet this would violate one of the principal theories of dialectical materialism, according to which the material world is infinite in space as well as time. Therefore, these philosophers constantly oppose Einstein on this point.

In the field of cosmology, Soviet thinkers look for a verification of dialectical materialism in the work of the great Soviet-Armenian astrophysicist, Ambartsumian. According to his theory, the stars originate in groups, so-called associations, and this process is still in progress. This view is now taken to imply a proof that the world was not created, but, so to speak, "arises" continuously. At the Conference Ambartsumian defended the view that the metagalaxy is not homogeneous. For Soviet cosmologists, this is a disproof of the "idealistic" interpretation held by some physicists and philosophers of a finite and expanding universe, since that interpretation requires a homogeneous metagalaxy.

In the field of biology, the controversies among Soviet scientists and philosophers are far more violent than those in the field of physics. In biology the disputes center on two problems: that of the origin of life, and to an even greater extent, that of heredity.

Regarding the origin of life, the theory advanced by A. I. Oparin, the director of the Institute for Biochemistry for the Academy of Sciences of the Soviet Union, still enjoys the highest respect. It was he, in fact, who presented the lecture on this topic at the All-Union Conference. Oparin divides the evolutionary path of lifeless matter up to the point of life into three main periods: the first, which took place in the lithosphere of the earth, involves the formation of simple hydrocarbon molecules and their derivatives, such as methane, ammonia, etc. After these substances had escaped from the interior of the earth into the atmosphere (still without oxygen) they found by means of electrical discharges, ultraviolet light, etc., the sources of energy that were necessary for their upward development along the path of polymerization to increasingly higher molecular structures, up to the formation of the giant molecules of albumin-like polypeptides, polynucleotides, etc.

Then follows the second principal period. These complex compounds are now washed by precipitation into the primordial ocean where the third period begins. It is precisely the idea of this period that constitutes the main difference between Oparin's theory and other Soviet interpretations. In the process of the formation of life, Oparin attributes a decisive importance to the so-called coazervate droplet. These are minute clusters arising from the coagulation of numerous albumin-like giant molecules of polypeptides. They are separated from the surrounding fluid by a distinct boundary, and they possess the ability of capturing certain substances from their surroundings. Oparin regards them as the initial systems, which perfect themselves progressively by the method of natural selection until one can speak of genuine living organisms. Oparin regards the characteristic quality of life (and in this he again differs from many other Soviet biologists) as the purposefulness by which a multitude of individual chemical reactions are aimed at achieving a very specific goal through a unique and complicated interaction—the continuous self-renewal and self-preservation of the organism. The progressive perfecting of the originally purely chemical exchange reactions between the coazervate and the fluid surrounding it, up to the most complicated reaction networks and constant reaction cycles, where the dialectical "jump" into a new "quality" takes place, occurs within the range of pre-biology by natural selection. The act of moving this category downward into the pre-biological domain represents a fundamental idea characteristic of Oparin's theory.[17]

Many discussants arose after Oparin's communication, all of whom recognized his great achievements in dealing with this problem, but all of whom criticized his theory. Konikova opposed Oparin's interpretation, that the physico-chemical processes can lead only to the formation of albumin-like structures but not to genuine albumins, which in Oparin's theory are formed only within the higher system unit of the coazervate, under the action of natural selection. Konikova regards this as a disagreement with Engels' teaching concerning the role of chemistry in the formation of life.[18]

The controversy between the proponents of the classical theory of heredity and the defenders of Michurinism has revived with great agitation during recent years. The early history of this controversy is probably well known, since it elicited international argument only a decade ago. The chief point of conflict refers to the inheritance of the characteristics an organism acquires during its lifetime. According to the Mendel-Morgan theory of heredity, the carriers of inheritance are the genes within the chromosomes of the cell nucleus. Genuine alterations in inheritance (so-called mutations) are possible only (according to this theory) if some cause effects a change in the nature of the gene. Such changes may be accomplished artificially, as by X-rays. As yet, however, it is not possible to induce any one desired change by artificial means.

This theory and its prerequisite, the assumption of genes, are violently opposed by the followers of Michurin and Lysenko. They base their theory on the principle of the unity of an organism with its environment. It is said to be possible, accordingly, to induce certain changes in an organism by changing the conditions of its environment. Such changes may then be passed on by heredity. Thus it is believed possible for man to guide the evolution of nature in the direction desired, and to breed new species at will. Since this doctrine accommodates a basic requirement of Marxist philosophy (Marx had put forward this requirement to Feuerbach: hitherto, the philosophers have merely offered varying interpretations of the world; the problem now is to change the world), it has enjoyed the highest approval of the Party. At the historic "August meeting" of the Lenin Academy of Agricultural Sciences in 1948, the opposing school was silenced. It was branded as "reactionary," and "idealistic," and the "progressive," "materialistic" school of Michurin thereafter dominated the field.

Even before Stalin's death, Lysenko's doctrine had been contradicted on one point: the problem of the formation of species.[19] After Stalin's death, the opposition to Lysenko assumed such proportions that in April, 1956, Lysenko felt obliged to resign his office as president of the Lenin Academy of Agricultural Sciences. The opposition to him concentrated in the pages of the *Botanical Journal* and the *Bulletin of the Moscow Society for Research in the Natural Sciences.* Dubinin, who in 1948 had fallen into disfavor, became director of the Moscow Institute of Genetics. This does not imply, however, that Michurinism has again been rejected and that Lysenko has lost all significance. Khrushchev has often acknowledged his work, has protected him from the enmity of his colleagues, and has recommended the Lysenko method of nest seeding in the corn plantations so important to him.[20]

The controversy has gradually returned to the central issue in the Michurin-Lysenko theory, the inheritance of acquired characteristics. In recent years discussion of this point has been conducted in *Voprosy filosofii*, with a violence far exceeding that on any comparable argument. The followers of Michurin have particularly distinguished themselves by their vehemence. Lysenko himself entered the fray in 1958 with an article reminiscent of those publications which appeared immediately after 1948, in which he praises the Party, its Central Committee, Lenin, and dialectical materialism, and refers to Michurin's genetics as the only genuinely materialistic and practically fruitful theory speaking of "progressive science" and even of "progressive experience," calling his opponents "reactionary."[21]

In contrast, the contributions to this discussion by the proponents of the classical theory of heredity are set forth with restraint. They point to the great success achieved by the chromosome theory in recent years, particularly as a result of the application of the use of mathematical, physical, and chemical methods. In this connection, certain errors in the interpretation of genes, which at the time and with justification had evoked hostility from Michurin's camp, had been overcome. Not so long ago, they asserted, the genes were conceived of as high-grade stable molecules of specific albumins. Recent research had shown, however, that the leading role in the material basis of heredity was played by desoxyribonucleic acid (DNA), with its capacity for increasing by reproducing identical molecules, and its capacity for controlling albumin synthesis. They alleged that this substance of heredity is not to be interpreted as a self-sufficient factor isolated from the metabolic process, but as depending on the metabolism both of the individual cell and of the total organism.

Evidently, this view represents an attempt to satisfy Michurin's principle of the unity of organism and environment. Moreover, the stability of DNA must not be interpreted in too absolute a manner, but as depending on the effect of natural selection, which produces and maintains this relative stability of DNA. This view, too, is intended to satisfy Michurin's requirement of a possibility of influencing the evolution of nature.[22] Another attempt to meet Michurinism halfway was made by vehemently rejecting the exploitation of the gene theory for purposes of eugenics.[23] This new formulation of the gene theory was represented as being purely materialistic. The problem, it was claimed by proponents of this view, is to avoid two extremes: one is too mechanistic, and fails to do justice to the peculiarity of biological systems; the other is that of idealism or vitalism, which separates the biological processes from the physical and chemical laws on which they are based. With reference to Engels, however, it is asserted that not every connection of genetics with physics and chemistry can be labeled as mechanistic.[24] The accusation that classical genetics has been proved fruitless in practice (one of the principal arguments of Michurin's school) is skillfully parried: the practical success achieved by American geneticists in corn breeding was cited—an argument that perhaps reflects Khrushchev's weakness for corn plantations.[25]

All these precautions appear to have been necessary in order to permit the opponents of Michurin to say a few bitter truths. They accuse the Michurinists, after their victory in 1948, of having looked on the modern gene theory in its novel formulation as not worthy of serious analysis, and of having rejected all experimental material presented by the proponents of this theory, lock, stock and barrel, as being irreconcilable with the methodological requirements of Soviet science, and that they did this without any critical analysis. Lysenko is accused of being impervious to experiments, since he simply rejects all experiments that do not corroborate his own prejudices, so that his errors increase with time.[26] For a theory to be true, it is not enough that it should be a new one, it must also be susceptible of experimental verification.[27] Altogether, so the claim goes, it would be absurd to interpret the fight between Michurinism and the proponents of the classical theory of heredity as anything but a simple contest of opinions, such as is common in all science; it is not a battle between the "scientific," the "materialistic" school, and the "unscientific," the "idealistic" one. They observe that a strange and unique situation has arisen in the field of genetics, one that does not exist in any other scientific discipline: there are not two kinds of physics or chemistry, yet genetics is supposed to be different, in that the philosophical outlook of proletarian scientists is presumed to make them entirely incapable of recognizing the objective laws of nature, and that they are supposedly required (consciously or unconsciously) to distort these laws according to the class interests of the bourgeoisie and to create a pseudo-scientific, reactionary genetics—the gene theory. How can such a situation be explained?[28]

The followers of Michurin often react violently to these carefully edited articles by the proponents of the gene theory, and they make liberal use of philosophical arguments. Ol'shanskii accuses Morgan's theory of heredity of having nothing in common with dialectical materialism, and in particular of being guilty of being "metaphysical," "mechanistic," and "idealistic": "metaphysical," inasmuch as this theory assumes the existence within the body of an "absolutely autonomous" principle, independent of the body and its conditions of life; "mechanistic," inasmuch as the theory bases all biology on chemistry; "idealistic," since this "hereditary material," the gene, which is enclosed in the body as in an envelope, controls the body without being controlled by it, which causes it to resemble "the soul."[29] Ol'shanskii also objects angrily that the followers of Morgan try to insert certain ideas of Michurin's theory into their own system, although they do not follow from the premises of the gene theory.

In studying these attitudes, one cannot avoid the impression that this battle between the followers of Michurin and the proponents of the gene theory often resembles the quarrel over the emperor's beard, since the opposing parties actually do not substantially differ in their evaluation of the concrete scientific material. On the one hand, the followers of the gene theory tend increasingly to assume that the metabolic process affects heredity, and thus to acknowledge the possibility of a controlled change in heredity.[30] On the other hand, the followers of Michurin by no means deny the major role played by DNA in heredity.[31] As stated by a representative of the gene theory, the difference between the two schools of thought (in so far as the controversy is conducted within the framework of scientific data) often consists in this: Michurin's school of genetics approaches the problem more from the ecological-physiological point of view, and considers the organism as part of its environment; whereas the proponents of the gene theory focus attention on the mechanism of heredity, and put special emphasis on research into the structure and function of those elements within the cell that are involved in heredity.[32]

No special lecture at the Conference of 1958 was devoted to the problem of heredity. In the summary of the Conference, only a very general reference was made to the "successes of the Michurin theory," but in his concluding remarks Fedoseev emphasized "the role of physics and chemistry in the investigation of biological problems,"[33] and in the report of the Conference in *Voprosy filosofii* it is stated that the Conference "once again exhibited the great achievements made by applying physico-chemical methods to the most important problems of heredity."[34] This indicates that no attempt was made to settle the controversy between the two schools.

Michurin's followers, however, received strong protection from the highest Party authorities. As early as 27 September 1958 Academician Lysenko was awarded the highest government distinction, the Order of Lenin, on the occasion of his sixtieth birthday.[35] On 14 December 1958 *Pravda* violently attacked the opponents of Lysenko and their publications, particularly the *Botanical Journal* and the *Bulletin of the Moscow Society for Research in the Natural Sciences*. Three days later Lysenko, addressing the Plenary Session of the Central Committee of the Communist Party of the USSR, leveled sharp criticism at the Biological Department of the Academy of Sciences of the USSR and at the activities of its director, Engelgart, and the president of the Academy, Nesmeianov. This criticism was echoed in the resolution of the Plenary Session charging that "several scientific institutions and several scientists conduct their work without contact with the state farms and the collective farms," declaring that Party organizations are charged with "inspecting daily, with specialized competence, the work of scientific research institutes and of aiding them in the execution of their task"; in addition, the need was expressed for developing a system of financing scientific institutes and individual scientific workers employed in research aimed at promoting effectively the productivity of the state farms and collective farms and leading to scientific progress. [36]

Although the resolution referred only very generally to "several scientific institutions," Lysenko's speech leaves no doubt as to the intent. The Presidium and the Biological Department of the Academy of Sciences acted accordingly. On 20 January 1959 it organized a joint session for the purpose of assessing the new developments in the situation. The relation between chemistry and biology was discussed both by representatives of the gene theory and the followers of Michurin, and the consequences of the reprimand by the Plenary Session were evaluated. By way of self-criticism, it was acknowledged that the Bureau of the Biological Department failed sufficiently to direct the work of the institutes toward useful goals. The criticism voiced by *Pravda* on 14 December 1958 concerning the editorial work of the *Botanical Journal* was also acknowledged and extended, again by way of self-criticism, to the work of the office of the Biological Department, and even to the Presidium of the Academy. As a result, the journal received a new editorial committee. On the basis of these concessions, however, the meeting dared to emphasize the necessity for a "broadly conceived, courageous and creative use of the newest achievements in physics and chemistry as applied to biology," and even to urge that a previous resolution of the Presidium (in 1957) concerning the establishment of an institute for physical, chemical, and radiation biology be carried out. [37] Publication of the report of the Conference in the Proceedings of the Academy of Sciences was deferred, however, until after the impending XXIst Congress of the Communist Party of the Soviet Union.

The XXIst Congress brought a substantial success to the opponents of Michurinism. Their main concern (the utilization of physics and chemistry in biology) was even entered in the "Controlling Figures for the Development of the People's Economy in the USSR for the Years 1959-1965," which forms part of the resolution of the Congress. In discussing the development of science, this document states: "The whole complex of biological science will gain in importance to the extent to which the achievements of physics and chemistry are put to use in biology. For this purpose, such branches as biochemistry, agrochemistry, biophysics, microbiology, virology, selection, and genetics will play a leading role."[38] Nesmeianov, the president of the Academy of Sciences, outlined the contribution of the sciences to the fulfillment of the Seven Year Plan. When he came to the field of biology, he first mentioned in general terms the criticism of the Plenary Session in December 1958 as to the work of the biologists, and then reported that the Presidium of the Academy had taken corresponding measures. His remaining remarks on the biological sciences, however, were devoted to the great importance of physics and chemistry in clarifying the life processes, not only the metabolic process, biosynthesis, and others, but explicitly heredity. He then gave several examples of the immense practical usefulness for agriculture that the influence of chemical effects on the life processes might have.[39]

The annual general meeting of the Academy of Sciences took place the end of March 1959. The vice-president of the Academy, Topchiev, spoke on the topic of the significance of the congress for the tasks of science. In discussing the biological sciences, he repeated the criticism voiced by *Pravda* and the December Plenary Session, and also an extensive analysis of the role of chemistry in biology. At the annual general meeting of the Biological Department of the Academy, held at approximately the same time, a similar discussion occurred.

In subsequent months, however, the situation again changed, this time to the disadvantage of the opponents of Michurinism. The June 1959 Plenary Session of the Central Committee of the Communist Party of the Soviet Union again gave extensive consideration to the problems of the organization of science. The inadequate contacts of many research institutes and universities with practical application and economic production were once more criticized, while Khrushchev requested the Presidium of the Academy of Sciences to submit proposals for the reorganization of the Academy. In particular, he recommended the creation of scientific centers and laboratories

157

in individual plants, state farms, etc., as well as the removal of certain scientific fields from the control of the Academy (e.g., mining, the coal industry, etc.). From his speech it was learned that Dubinin, the principal opponent of Lysenko, had been transferred from Moscow to the newly erected University of Novosibirsk (in Siberia), where he was to take over the direction of the Institute for Psychology and Genetics. Khrushchev objected to this, accusing Dubinin of having contributed little to either theoretical or applied science, saying that he owed his renown entirely to his attacks on Lysenko, and that if his work in Moscow had been fruitless, it would be no less so in Novosibirsk or Vladivostok. Khrushchev did add that he did not wish to be in the position of umpire in the controversy between the two scientists, that the best judges are experience and life, and that these had decided in favor of the theory of Michurin and Lysenko.

In *Voprosy filosofii* for October 1959, the discussion of Michurinism was resumed. In it appeared an article by Academician Semenov expressing great hopes for the success of the practical application of physics and chemistry to investigations of heredity, and taking a critical position with respect to Lysenko. Semenov's article was followed by one by Lysenko expressing his regrets that for more than ten years the Biological Department of the Academy had been directed by biochemists. Both these articles represent a record of reports read at the expanded meeting of the Presidium of the Biological Department of the Academy at the end of January 1959.

A third article follows, clearly representing the views of Michurinism; from its typographical appearance (differing from that of the two preceding articles) it conveys the impression that it delivers the editor's own verdict on this discussion. At the end of the article, the author (a Bulgarian named Panchev) cites a statement by Criqui claiming that Michurin's doctrine deserves the serious attention and respect of Western scientists, and then concludes crisply, "This proves that Michurin's doctrine has won a victory in its duel with the idealistic doctrine of Weismann-Mendel-Morgan. At present there is absolutely no cause for bringing metaphysics in biology back to life among us."[40]

In order to respond to the question we posed at the beginning of this essay, we must first tackle the last one concerning the fundamental relationship between dialectical materialism and individual science. We do not wish to deny that in the Soviet philosophical treatment some aspects of the problems raised by modern natural science are well treated—in particular, the philosophical dispute regarding the theory of relativity and quantum physics. Nor do we wish to deny that some *individual* theories of dialectical materialism (for example, the retention of causality, and of an "inherence" independent of the observer and measuring process, even within the domain of the microphysical) are definitely reconcilable with modern physics, or that they might even prove fruitful for scientific research. This statement by no means carries the implications Soviet philosophers like to deduce from it, however: that it provides a corroboration of dialectical materialism *as such*, and in particular, a corroboration of its fundamental theory, that there exists nothing but matter in the world, and that material reality is the *only* reality. The arguments derived from the natural sciences in support of this thesis usually represent philosophical misunderstandings.

We consider in particular that dialectical materialism does not remain consistently faithful to its program of representing the ultimate generalization of scientific knowledge, but that it is unwilling on the other hand to allow certain fundamental features of its system to be contradicted by scientific research. More specifically, this involves the concept that reality contains nothing but matter, and that consciousness—in so far as it is acknowledged to be nonmaterial—arose from matter by purely evolutionary means. These ideas are presented, not in the sense of heuristic principles, but definitely in the sense of irrefutable statements of truth. The presence of such theses in Marxist philosophy can be historically explained by the fact that Engels prematurely and in a philosophically uncritical manner imparted an absolute validity to certain scientific theories current in the nineteenth century. These theories were subsequently disproved by scientific experiments; nevertheless they had acquired an obligatory character for modern dialectical materialism because of Engels' authority.

It is this uncritical philosophic generalization and the premature "absolutization" of certain preliminary scientific theories that in our opinion has caused interference in scientific work because of Soviet ideology, rather than any attempt to create accord between scientific and philosophical knowledge. Such an attempt would appear to me to be entirely legitimate, providing philosophy or metaphysics is assumed to be at all possible.[41] No ultimate disagreement can possibly exist between secure scientific knowledge and secure philosophical knowledge. Therefore, if occasional conflicts do arise between philosophy and science, the only conceivable solution is to let the conflict provide the stimulus for finding a solution to the controversy by deepening philosophical as well as scientific knowledge.

Just as it is basically impossible that science should be hampered by philosophy, so long as both disciplines remain within the boundaries of their competence, so is it impossible that philosophy should be compromised by science. This is fundamentally applicable to religion as well. In this sense, we definitely agree with Berdyaev when he designates science as being neutral with respect to metaphysics and religion. If today dialectical materialism takes up arms against religion in the name of "science," then it cannot have genuine science in mind, but only its pseudo-scientific dogma. The battle between dialectical materialism and religion is not decided on the scientific plane, but on the philosophical. In this respect, it is of particular interest that precisely those doctrines to which Soviet philosophy clings because of its hostility to religion provide it with an opportunity to assume a critical position with respect to certain scientific theories as well. [42]

Such misunderstandings, however, are to be found not only in the Soviet philosophy of today: they date back to Engels himself. This is significant in answering the initial question: to what extent does the spirit of the Russian intelligentsia of the past century survive in the Soviet Union today. If Berdyaev cites faith in science as a primary characteristic of the Russian intelligentsia of the nineteenth century, then it would follow from the material presented above that this faith in science is not only present today, but virtually dominates the intellectual climate. Let us ignore the question as to whether this officially endorsed attitude is actually the one shared by the majority of Soviet scientists. Faith in science manifests itself primarily in that preliminary (often outdated) scientific hypotheses, theories, or partial truths are labeled absolute and raised to the status of a pseudo-religious revelation. However, if this process of making absolute truths out of preliminary scientific theories goes back to Engels, it would seem that faith in science is not exclusively a characteristic of the Russian intelligentsia, even though they may have assimilated this faith with unique devotion and enthusiasm. Moreover, it was not in Russia that this appeal to "science" first acquired the status of a weapon against social exploitation, absolutism, and a religion that had been abused to support these ills. All these attitudes are also encountered in Engels—and it remains an open question as to who deserves more credit, Engels or the Russian intelligentsia, for the fact that this position has today become the official opinion in the Soviet Union. For our purposes, it suffices to observe that this is the case.

In contemporary Russia we observe yet another result of the attitude of the old Russian intelligentsia to science: the subordination of science to practical goals. The material presented above shows that in recent months the application of science to immediate practical purposes has been given new impetus.

If the cultural life of the Soviet Union today is decisively influenced by the intellectual climate of the nineteenth-century intelligentsia, the question arises as to whether there may not again exist a stratum of intellectuals and scientists who oppose this climate, much as the nineteenth-century intelligentsia protested against the climate of their times. The fact that such opposing currents are present today is clearly indicated by the frequent complaints in the Soviet press that some scientists, even leading ones, take too little interest in philosophical problems and exhibit a certain "positivistic" inclination. The All-Union Conference, as well as the great efforts in recent months to organize seminars in philosophy for natural scientists at the various universities, might have the primary purpose of overcoming this indifference to philosophy on the part of many leading natural scientists. The reorientation in the theory of relativity, as well as the revival of the Michurin controversy, undoubtedly represents a protest by science against its abuse in the name of ideology. To be sure, in these controversies, both sides appeal to dialectical materialism. It is difficult to decide, however, to what extent the individuals involved are actually concerned with dialectical materialism, and whether their references to it may not have been made simply in order to be able to defend a point of view that deviates from the previous official doctrine.

It is further noteworthy that in Russia today protest against ideology in the name of science takes a form different from the protest of the nineteenth-century Russian intelligentsia. Then one said "science," referring in fact to a pseudo-philosophical dogma. Moreover, this dogma was presented, not in the name of truth, but in the name of social utility. On the other hand, if Soviet scientists defend themselves today against the coercion of ideology and the regime, they are actually concerned primarily with the question of scientific truth.

It is difficult to decide what prospects this situation implies today. In this respect perhaps the Michurin controversy is the most revealing. From the pertinent material cited above, we may deduce that the regime is determined again to subject science to the control of the Party in even stronger terms than before. Recent measures along such lines appear to approach the severity of 1948. Nevertheless, it is suggestive that these measures have not succeeded in liquidating the controversy. It also appears to follow from the material we have presented that not only the followers of Michurin but their opponents as well possess powerful patrons within the Party. Perhaps we can deduce from this that even within the Party it is gradually being recognized that scientific controversies cannot be solved by ideological means, much less by Party decree.

REFERENCES

1 N. A. Berdyaev, "Filosofskaia istina i intelligentskaia pravda," *Vekhi* (Moscow, 1909), pp. 3 ff., especially pp. 6-12; the same essay, *Sinn und Schicksal des russischen Kommunismus* (Lucerne, 1937), pp. 24 f.

2 *Voprosy filosofii,* 1959, No. 3, p. 13.

3 *Ibid.,* 1959, No. 2, p. 74.

4 D. I. Blochintsev, "Kritika filosofskikh vozzrenii tak nazyvaemoi Kopengagenskoi shkoly v fizike" (Criticism of the philosophical views of the so-called Copenhagen School of physics), in *Filosofskie voprosy sovremennoi fiziki* (Philosophical problems in modern physics; Moscow, 1952, pp. 358-395), p. 389.

5 *Voprosy filosofii,* 1959, No. 10, p. 120.

6 *Ibid.,* 1952, No. 4, p. 170.

7 *Ibid.,* p. 174.

8 *Vestnik Leningradskogo Universiteta,* 1949, No. 4, p. 65; and *Voprosy filosofii,* 1953, No. 2, p. 207.

9 *Voprosy filosofii,* 1952, No. 4, p. 173.

10 *Ibid.,* 1952, No. 6, p. 175.

11 Niels Bohr, *Atomic Physics and Human Knowledge,* New York, John Wiley and Sons, Inc., 1958.

12 *Voprosy filosofii,* 1959, No. 2, p. 72.

13 *Ibid.,* 1959, No. 2, p. 75.

14 *Ibid.,* 1957, No. 6, p. 185.

15 *Ibid.,* 1953, No. 5, pp. 225-245; *ibid.,* 1959, No. 2, pp. 77-82.

16 See for example: A. I. Uemov, "Geliotsentricheskaia sistema Kopernika i teoriia otnositel'nosti" (The heliocentric system of Copernicus and the theory of relativity), in *Filosofskie voprosy sovremennoi fiziki* (Philosophic problems of modern physics; Moscow, 1952, pp. 299-331), p. 310.

17 See A. I. Oparin: *The Origin of Life,* Edinburgh, 1957.

18 F. Engels: *Die Dialektik der Natur,* Berlin, 1952, p. 273. "All chemical investigations of the organic world lead . . . backward in the last instance to an object which, though resulting from ordinary chemical processes, differs from all others in that it represents a self-executing, permanent chemical process—the albumin."

19 Lysenko teaches that the fight for existence prevails only between individuals of different species, not between individuals of the same species, who support one another for the sake of preserving the species. This doctrine also forms the basis of the method of nest sowing propagated by Lysenko.

20 See for example *Pravda,* 1, 5, and 10, April 1957.

21 *Voprosy filosofii,* 1958, No. 2, pp. 102 ff.

22 *Ibid.,* 1958, No. 7, pp. 102 ff.

23 *Ibid.,* 1958, No. 2, p. 115.

24 *Ibid.,* 1958, No. 7, p. 110.

25 *Ibid.,* 1958, No. 2, p. 113.

26 *Ibid.,* 1958, No. 2, p. 116; No. 7, p. 105.

27 This evidently represents a reference to the law formulated by dialectical materialism as the fundamental law of all development, the law concerning unity and the battle of opposites, in particular the opposition between old and new.

28 *Voprosy filosofii,* 1958, No. 2, p. 113.

29 *Ibid.,* 1958, No. 6, p. 123.

30 *Ibid.,* 1958, No. 2, pp. 123 f.

31 *Ibid.,* 1958, No. 8, p. 95; 1959, No. 10, p. 114.

32 *Ibid.,* 1958, No. 2, p. 125.

33 *Ibid.,* 1959, No. 2, pp. 69, 61.

34 *Ibid.,* p. 84.

35 *Vedomosti Verkhovnogo Soveta SSSR,* 2 October 1958, p. 794.

36 *Pravda,* 20 December 1958.

37 *Vestnik Akademii Nauk SSSR,* 1959, No. 3, pp. 3 ff.

38 *Vneocherednoi XXI S'ezd Kommunisticheskoi Partii Sovetskogo Soiuza. Stenograficheskii otchet* (The Extraordinary XXIst Congress of the Communist Party of the Soviet Union. Stenographic report) Vol. 2, Moscow, 1959, p. 534.

39 *Ibid.,* p. 214.

40 *Voprosy filosofii,* 1959, No. 10, p. 114.

41 The word metaphysics is here used in a sense different from the one it has in Soviet literature. In the present sense, dialectical materialism is also "metaphysics."

42 In the field of genetics we have encountered such a case in the rejection of the gene, with the justification that the gene is to a certain extent equivalent to a soul. The fact that this involves misunderstandings of religious doctrine is irrelevant in this connection. The statement that the world was created is not equivalent to the statement that it had a temporal beginning; to equate geocentrism with a religious philosophy of life represents an anachronism; and it is ununderstandable how the gene and the soul could be regarded as identical.

BENJAMIN SCHWARTZ

The Intelligentsia in Communist China
A Tentative Comparison

THE WORD INTELLIGENTSIA, while Russian in origin, has frequently been used with reference to Asian and other non-Western societies. Behind this usage there lurks the suggestion of some peculiar resemblance between groups in these societies and those to whom this word has been applied in Russia. Suggestive notions of this type generally are eagerly accepted and often achieve the status of journalistic clichés before being subjected to any sustained examination.

It is my own feeling that meaningful comparisons can indeed be drawn between the Russian intelligentsia and the various "intelligentsias" of Asia, but that comparison here as elsewhere involves an awareness of significant differences as well as of identities. It is precisely the juxtaposition of identity and difference which gives the comparative approach its value as a critique of generally accepted notions.

In the following pages I should like to make certain tentative comparisons between the Russian intelligentsia of the mid-nineteenth century and the Chinese intelligentsia of the twentieth century, with concluding reflections on the post-Communist situation in both countries.

Like all words of this type, the word intelligentsia has hardly been reduced to a crystalline precision, even as applied to the Russian scene. A survey of the literature on this subject indicates that the word is used with a wide range of meaning and that the outer limits of this range are by no means sharply defined. Often it seems to mean no more than the cultured stratum. All that can be said is that within this range there are certain characteristics and motifs which are generally conceded by all to fit clearly within the category.

164

Beyond this, the word refers to precisely those strata of the population in which individuality tends to be particularly well marked, so that any generalization about the "intelligentsia" as a whole, whether in Russia or China, can have no more validity than any generalization of a crude statistical type.

Finally, before we can attempt to transpose this term to China we must ask ourselves: what distinguishes the Russian intelligentsia in the narrow sense from those called intellectuals in the West? Probably it is precisely in its distinguishing features that the Russian intelligentsia is most comparable to the intelligentsias of Asia.

It is by no means easy to find these distinguishing characteristics. In the West, as in the case of the mid-nineteenth-century Russian intelligentsia, the word "intellectuals" is generally applied to that part of the educated class which claims to concern itself actively with what are considered the important issues of the age. In the West, also, the intellectuals tend to distinguish themselves from the common run of educated careerists and strictly professional men. Even the sense of alienation, which is often thought to distinguish the Russian intelligentsia, is of course an important part of the sensibility of the intellectuals in the West during the nineteenth and twentieth centuries. Finally, as has often been pointed out, the substantive ideas of the Russian intelligentsia are to a large extent the ideas of nineteenth-century Europe.

One of the obvious and most striking differences is the difference in the surrounding environment. The image of Russian society in the nineteenth century, as reflected in the writings of the *intelligenty* themselves (as here defined) is one of stark, almost melodramatic simplicity. On the one side, there is the anonymous and uniform peasant mass; on the other, the despotic state with its supporting nobility. Occasionally we find in the writings of the intelligentsia the idea of using the Tsar against the nobles or the nobles against the Tsar, or an occasional tendency to distinguish the various religious sectarian groups from the peasant mass as a whole. From the layman's point of view, however, Berdyaev's statement that "the intelligentsia was placed in a tragic position between the state and the people" holds generally true. Whether of noble, petty noble, or humble origin, the *intelligent* need not strive to achieve a stance of critical opposition—of "alienation"—from society: alienation is thrust upon him by an oppressive state and by a peasant mass which inhabits a different spiritual world. On the other hand, the Western intellectual operates in a much more complex, variegated and morally ambiguous environment. He may be vastly discontented, but he must struggle to locate the target of his animus, and he is likely to attack the status quo from many different vantage points—political, social, aesthetic, and religious.[1] Furthermore, those "conservatives" who defend the social order cannot be denied the quality of intellectuals. But in France, where the French revolutionary tradition had itself become part of the status quo, one could defend parts of the status quo in the very name of revolution.

One of the characteristics associated with this more clear-cut alienation is a tendency to "totalistic" attitudes. The nineteenth-century West, to be sure, was rich in monistic philosophic systems and totalistic socio-political theories which envisaged the total destruction of the social order and the utopian resolution of all human difficulties. As a matter of fact, the totalism of the Russian intelligentsia is set almost completely within a framework of current Western ideas, whatever may be its roots in Russian "national character" or the nature of Russian religion. Yet the Western advocates of a totalistic outlook have had considerable difficulty in relating their outlook in any clear-cut way to current social and political realities. In nineteenth-century Russia, where the "establishment" could be regarded without an excess of imagination as almost the incarnation of evil, where one could assume on Rousseauist grounds the essential goodness of the vast, silent, suffering peasantry, the expectation that a "root and branch" destruction of the establishment might lead to a total transformation of the conditions of human life recommended itself with particular force.

Such totalism is even to be found in a man like Herzen, whose major tendency, at least in the latter part of his life, seems to have been to regard all forms of authority as inherently vicious. In spite of his concern with individual liberty, he cannot easily be identified with Western "liberalism." Martin Malia draws an instructive parallel between Herzen and John Stuart Mill.[2] As Mr. Malia points out, both had an overriding concern with individual liberty, and both were concerned with the relations between liberty and social harmony. Yet Mill does not choose between a total acceptance or rejection of the whole complex socio-political machinery of Great Britain—a machinery which certainly embodied the principle of authority in various forms. Instead, he engages in a detailed and prosaic study of how the machinery of law, parliament, industrialism, etc., can be shaped to promote his ends. The pathos of Herzen, living in the same England, is quite different. To him, the whole social machinery, even in the "liberal" states of the West, is deeply interwoven with the hated authoritarianism of the past, albeit in mitigated form.

The machinery of parliaments, bureaucracy, law courts and industrial enterprise embodied the same mechanism of external authority as the hated machinery of the Petrine state.[3] Herzen would have swept away the whole evil incubus of the past. The very polarization of the Russian situation was an advantage, since one could see evil in all its stark nakedness without the disguises, mitigations and ambiguities of modern Western society.

Linked to this totalism, we find an aversion, not only for specialized, professional careers, but even for specialized and departmentalized modes of thinking. In a somewhat narrow way, the *intelligenty* of the nineteenth century (in sharp contrast to the specializing intellectuals of the twentieth) are nonprofessional universal men. If the generation of the 'sixties and 'seventies become specialists, it is mainly in the strategy and tactics of revolution. Here again, the repressive policies of the regime may have played as much of a role as did the subjective inclinations of the intelligentsia. Whatever the cause, an aversion to the demarcation of autonomous "pure" spheres of science and art seems to be one of the distinguishing characteristics of the nineteenth-century Russian intelligentsia, both in its earlier "philosophic" phase and its later social revolutionary phase.

Turning to the sphere of the "content of thought," one is struck by the dominance of certain strands of thought. (Again, this does not mean, either in the case of Russia or of China, that other ideas and other motifs are not to be found.) Mr. Karpovich, commenting on a discussion of nineteenth-century Russian thought, asks at one point, "To what extent are the ideas treated in the present discussion unique to Russia or even particularly characteristic of Russia?"[4] The same question might be asked with even greater emphasis concerning twentieth-century China. However, beyond this question there lurks another. Why are certain Western ideas received with greater enthusiasm than are others? The intellectual scene in nineteenth-century Europe is extremely complex and variegated. It abounds in mutually contradictory tendencies. One finds, however, that by some principle of selectivity certain strands of this thought find a much more fertile soil than do others. To the intellectual historian, the question, why do certain ideas enjoy more favor than others, may be just as significant as the question, is there anything uniquely Russian or Chinese in these ideas. For, behind this principle of selectivity, one may discern certain specific Russian and Chinese preoccupations. One may also legitimately speculate on the degree to which habits of thought derived from the past may have influenced the pattern of choice.

One of the dominant motifs of the thought of the nineteenth-century Russian intelligentsia is a chiliastic historicism. History was leading to a final apocalyptic event. The concept of a redemptive history, of course, is one of the most characteristic strands of nineteenth-century Western thought. In mid-nineteenth-century Russia, however, totalistic cataclysmic conceptions of history culminating in a redemptive revolution tend to dominate over gradualistic evolutionary views of historic "progress." Herzen and Belinsky, it is true, seem to have turned against their early Hegelianism, and to have rejected the authority of the "forces of history," along with other forms of authority, and to have reverted to something like the tradition of enlightenment. Yet Herzen continues to contemplate the total liberation of men from the whole social and cultural order of past and present. When one believes that a totally evil past and present can be replaced by a totally good future by means of some cataclysmic convulsion, the difference between "enlightenment" and "historicism" is somewhat reduced. In the one case, one believes in the working-out of historic forces; in the other, in the good will of enlightened men; but the mystique of the utopian revolution is shared by both.

Another dominant theme in the thought of the mid-nineteenth-century Russian intelligentsia is, of course, the theme of Populism. In Russia the peasant masses who make up the people are an entity apart from both the ruling classes and the intelligentsia, and it is easy to conceive of the people as a monolithic unity with a potential "general will" of its own. The Rousseauist conception of the people as a sort of collective whole recommends itself more than does any concept of the people as a sum total of widely differing individuals or of a plurality of varying groups. It is the people who are the victims of the present order, and it is the people who will be the object of historic redemption. There is, to be sure, a wide range of opinion as to whether the people themselves are the instrument of their own redemption. Anarchists like Bakunin would simply set loose the protean forces latent in the people. Those who participate in the movement "to the people" are also convinced that a modest educational stimulus will release such creative forces. At the other pole we have the Jacobinists, who believe that the general will of the people or the aspirations of the people must become incarnate in a guiding elite drawn from the intelligentsia itself.

The Marxism of the 'nineties, of course, rejects the concept of the united people in favor of class struggle. Instead of the "people," the urban proletariat becomes the agent of historic redemption. Yet, as has often been pointed out, the Marxist intelligentsia continues to manifest many of the tendencies we find among the Populists. As Mr. Haimson demonstrates in his *Russian Marxism and the Origins of Bolshevism,* many of the same divisions and polarities which existed in the Populist movement crop up again in Marxist guise. The two movements share a chiliastic view of history, a common espousal of "socialism" and a rejection of "capitalism." The notion of a collective general will is now attributed to the proletariat, rather than to the people as a whole, but in the Leninist transformation of Marxism we have again the Jacobinist notion of the general will incarnate in a vanguard elite. The concern of Marxism with the role of economic production would suggest a greater concern with economic development on the part of the Marxists than on the part of the Populists. (In Marxism, after all, it is the forces of production which bear the hopes of the future.) Alexander Gerschenkron[5] suggests that this was still not true of most of the pre-Soviet Marxists (with the exception of the Legal Marxists) who were much more concerned with overcoming capitalism than with economic development per se. Even if Russia did have to pass through the whole dirty work of capitalist industrialization, there was no reason for the Marxist *intelligent* to involve himself in the mess directly.

Common to most nineteenth-century intelligentsia, as already indicated, is an orientation toward socialism and a rejection of nineteenth-century economic liberalism in theory, and capitalism in practice. This is even true, as we have indicated, of the "individualist" Herzen. It is not easy to define the positive content of the word "socialism" as used by various individuals and groups. The very tendency of Populism to think of the people as a collective entity somehow places the collectivity on a higher plane than the individual. In general, collective forms of economic and social activity are associated with altruism, with social equality and humanity, and with other values. In nineteenth-century Russia this proclivity for collectivism comes, of course, to be linked with the idealization of the *obshchina.* Negatively, socialism implies a rejection of the capitalist ethic with its frank commitment to individual economic gain. Mr. Gerschenkron explains this bias toward "socialism" in terms of the confrontation of Russian "backwardness" with the humanitarian ideas of nineteenth-century Europe. Yet since the aversion to the "capitalist ethic" seems to be such a ubiquitous phenomenon, one wonders whether Weber's view that it is the emergence of the "capitalist ethic" in the West rather than its absence elsewhere which requires explanation, is not more cogent. In most cultures, ruling classes have tended to justify their existence in terms of some non-economic "service" ideal. In most cultures the systematic and rationalized pursuit of wealth has never achieved ethical respectability. Whether in addition a bias toward the "collective" exists in historic Russian culture is something the layman can hardly judge. One would hardly expect the *intelligenty*, who regarded themselves as men dedicated to universal human goals and ideal tasks, to turn their attention to industrial and mercantile activities, particularly since the emerging industrialism of nineteenth-century Russia was in their view closely linked to and supported by the whole "establishment." It is only slowly, and in the teeth of fierce opposition, that the notion of an automatic link between sheer economic growth and general cultural and political "progress" takes hold among twentieth-century liberals and Mensheviks.

In sum then, a messianic historicism, a Populism which later is channeled by some in a Marxist direction, and a general commitment to "socialism" are among the prominent strands of thought which make the outlook of the mid-nineteenth-century Russian intelligentsia eminently comparable to that of the twentieth-century Chinese intelligentsia.

Another feature of the development of the Russian intelligentsia which may be of some relevance in considering the modern intelligentsia in China is the concept of the "new man" which begins to emerge in Russia in the 'sixties. Here we have, in addition to certain general emotional attitudes and certain characteristic patterns of thought, a certain image of the ideal individual. The new man is the man who consciously converts himself into an instrument of his social and political goals, who allows no personal aims, no scruple, no sentiment or whims to deflect him from his historic role. He also has an unflagging faith in the purity of his own motives, in the rightness of his own ideas. As has often been pointed out, this image of the "new man" is probably the direct ancestor of the image of "Bolshevik man."

These, in short, are some of the characteristics of the Russian intelligentsia which strike the student of modern China as relevant for purposes of comparison.

Something must be said at the outset about the entirely different cultural backgrounds of the two "intelligentsias." Terms such as "backward" and "traditional" may be used to describe both cultures by those who judge everything by the yardstick of economic development. It flatters our "modernist" chauvinism to assume that the only important fact about premodern cultures is the fact of their non-modernity. Yet the differences in the concrete historic antecedents of the two intelligentsias are enormous. Whether the Russian intelligentsia has no tradition or is deeply rooted in Russia's religious tradition, it is certainly a new social fact in the nineteenth century (or, at the earliest, the late eighteenth century).

In China the twentieth-century intelligentsia is to a considerable extent spiritual as well as biological heir of the scholar-official class that has dominated the political and intellectual life of China for centuries. When one attempts to summarize some of the characteristics of the traditional Chinese elite, one finds some traits that remind us, curiously enough, of the Russian intelligentsia, as well as some significant differences. First of all, one notes that this elite is a small group hovering above a huge peasant mass—a group which very self-consciously distinguishes itself from the mass and tends to regard the "people" as a sort of monolithic entity. In sharp contrast to the Russian intelligentsia, the elite is also the state-service class. Its Confucian ideology inculcates an exaltation of public service, so that the class bears within itself centuries of bureaucratic experience.

Yet before one hastens to a too facile definition of the twentieth-century Chinese intelligentsia as simply a temporarily displaced bureaucratic class, it should also be noted that within the millennial history of China strong strands of alienation, withdrawal, and protest are evident. The image of Confucius himself is that of a man who cannot be "used" by any of the prevailing regimes of his time, in spite of his eminent qualifications for public vocation. The tradition of protest, withdrawal, and even of martyrdom is an integral part of the Confucian tradition. Furthermore, beyond the Confucian tradition, there lies the Taoist tradition with its derisively anarchistic contempt for the state and all its *Wichtigtuerei*, and its tradition of Buddhist withdrawal. None of this implies "democracy." However, it also does not necessarily imply a predisposition to modern totalitarianism.

Again it should be noted that within the Confucian tradition there is something like a concern for the minimal economic welfare of the masses—a certain idea of noblesse oblige vis-à-vis the "people" (*min*). This principle of obligation was, of course, unaccompanied by any concept of "popular sovereignty" or of the latent wisdom of the unenlightened masses. Political initiative could come only from the enlightened superior men. Nevertheless, the idea of obligation to the people provided a sort of traditional nucleus around which certain types of modern populism could grow.

171

Deeply engrained in the tradition we find an emphatic anti-mercantile orientation and an exaltation of the public service career over all private wealth-gathering activities. One even finds an equivalent to the dream of the *mir*. In spite of the fact that the organization of land tenure in China has been for centuries more or less "private," there has been a persistent tradition within the heart of Confucianism that this situation represented a falling away from the primeval communal organization of agriculture represented by the so-called "well-field"[6] system. The Confucian dream of utopia is of a docile peasant commune benignly supervised by the sage official. One must add that the "well-field" utopia had no anti-authoritarian or antihierarchic implications. On the contrary, it was an integral part of the idealization of the ancient Chou feudal order. None of this, however, implied a very favorable disposition toward any "capitalist ethic."

We are not attempting to suggest here any fundamental affinity between the scholar-official class of traditional China and the Russian intelligentsia of the nineteenth century. I am merely suggesting that there existed in the tradition of this class certain dispositions which may have favored the emergence in the Chinese intelligentsia of tendencies not unlike those of the Russian intelligentsia. Of course, many of the characteristics of the twentieth-century intelligentsia must be explained in terms of discontinuity with the past—in terms of the tragic situation within which this intelligentsia now finds itself.

For convenience, we may divide the twentieth-century Chinese intelligentsia into three generations. There is the transitional generation of the late nineteenth and early twentieth century—men whose roots lie deep in the old culture, who have undergone the regimen of a traditional education, but who are already deeply shaken by the desperate plight of their state and society. They are already prepared to consider new institutions and foreign ideas, and yet are in many ways still part of the older literati.[7] The crucial break comes with the student generation of the beginning of the twentieth century, many of whose members must be considered as the first truly "alienated" intellectuals of modern China. The third significant generation is the student generation of the May 4th period (1919), men now in their fifties and sixties. It is in this generation that the basic intellectual tendencies of recent decades crystallize.

The first generation is not yet alienated from the state. It still yearns to be "used," and still hopes to save the state from ruin. It is in the next generation that we see the emergence of the mystique of revolution. Only with this generation can we begin to speak with any assurance of a modern intelligentsia. It is also this generation which faces the enormous frustrations of the post-1911 period. There are many who enter political life in the sordid "warlord" period, but a clear cleavage appears between the "political opportunists" (*cheng k'o*) who serve, and the alienated intelligentsia who remain outside. The May 4th generation does become involved in the revolutionary activities of the Kuomintang-Communist alliance. Some of its members, in fact, become the bureaucracy of the Nationalist government. Yet many remain an alienated intelligentsia. The reasons for this are complex. The bulk of the intelligentsia had become committed in the period between 1919 and 1927 to a generally "left" and antitraditional stance. There were, to be sure, individuals like Liang Sou-ming, Feng Yu-Lan and others who may be considered the Chinese equivalents of the Russian Slavophiles. They continued to stress the validity, even the superiority, of certain Chinese values and often used Western conceptions to support their views. Like many of the Slavophiles, however, they carefully dissociated themselves from the official neo-traditionalism of the established regime and remained on the outside. The Nationalist government under Chiang K'ai-shek attempted to create a neo-traditional underpinning for its nationalism and regarded the stance of the intelligentsia with profound mistrust. With the growth of the Maoist phase of Chinese Communism, we have a small segment of the intelligentsia who, as it were, simultaneously became professional revolutionaries and acting functionaries of a Communist state within a state.

In this light one does not feel that the alienation of the Chinese intelligentsia from the state is as decisive or as profound as that of the mid-nineteenth-century Russian intelligentsia. During the period between the 1911 revolution and the rise of the Nationalist government, the intelligentsia does not confront the massive power of a state from which it feels alienated. It rather confronts the disintegration of the state. Under the Nationalist government it is indeed alienated, yet the officialdom of that government is drawn from a background identical with its own, and there are many elements who live in a twilight world between government and intelligentsia, in spite of their mutual hostility. With the rise of the Communist state many of the intelligentsia were prepared to serve without undergoing the enormous adjustment from the life of "professional revolutionary" to bureaucratic functionary which we find among the old Bolsheviks in Russia. One can speak of the alienation of the twentieth-century Chinese intelligentsia from the state. It is, however, a much more ambiguous and less decisive alienation than that of its Russian nineteenth-century counterpart.

Nevertheless, it is interesting to note that, as in the case of the Russian intelligentsia, the best of the Chinese intelligentsia do not turn their attention to the "practical" professions, in spite of a concerted effort on the part of the late Ch'ing government and later of the Nationalist government to channel it in this direction. A "bureaucratic" career, academic life or writing seem to be the major alternatives, and the choice determines one's future alignment as a conformist or as an alienated intellectual. To a considerable extent one must bear in mind the persistence of traditional habits of thought and behavior. Beyond this, we find, as in the Russian case, a reluctance among the more sensitive to commit themselves to specialized professions while the major agonizing problems of their society remain unsolved.

It is in terms of emotional attitudes and certain dominant strains of thought that the resemblance between the two intelligentsias becomes most striking. Thus the major general drift in the long run is toward "totalistic" attitudes. It is curious to note in this connection that the first important Western influences in China were preponderantly an Anglo-American liberalism running up through the philosophy of John Dewey, whose current Chinese spokesman, Hu Shih, has become in the Chinese view almost the embodiment of American liberalism. It is important to note that even Western liberalism, particularly if one includes certain French variants of that vague concept, can assume in a Chinese environment a totalistic coloration, and that this aspect is completely compatible with a total negation of the past. Some "Liberals" like the early Ch'en Tu-hsiu remind us more of Russian nihilists of the Pisarev variety than of Western liberals. To Ch'en, "democracy" and "science" were corrosives for dissolving the traditional culture. Again, the mystique of the redemptive revolution is not incompatible with all forms of liberalism, and it is very much a part of Sun Yat-sen's early "liberalism." The very fact that the 1911 revolution in itself actually solved so little created a bias toward total solutions. In the early 'twenties, we find the famous controversy on "isms" and "problems," which deals most explicitly with the issue of total versus "pluralistic" solutions of China's difficulties. On the one side we have Hu Shih's espousal of Dewey's insistence on attention to concrete, discrete problems and on rejection of all-embracing nostrums. On the other side we have the new converts to Marxism-Leninism, who insist that the social order is a whole and who ardently look for an all-embracing solu-

tion. In the long run, the Marxist-Leninist claim to a monistic interpretation of the world and a monistic resolution of China's difficulties
weighed heavily in its favor during the 'twenties and 'thirties. The
widespread acceptance of a Marxist-Leninist world image, it must
be added, however, did not imply a necessary commitment to the
Communist party. To the very brink of 1949 a large part of the
Chinese intelligentsia remained apart from the Communist movement
itself. In China, however, as in Russia, the chiliastic view of "progress" was to dominate gradualistic, evolutionary views.

Something like a populist strain emerges quite early in China,
although it is speedily overwhelmed by the influence of the Russian
Revolution. The young nationalists of the early twentieth century
were quick to add the rhetoric of Rousseau to the rhetoric of Mencius. At first this populism assumes a Western liberal coloration and
is closely linked to political democracy. Later, in the case of Sun
Yat-sen himself, this gives way to the notion of a "general will," which
becomes embodied in a party elite. That anarchistic variety of populism which insists on the spontaneous initiative of the people itself
does not become deeply entrenched in China. In seeking Chinese
equivalents to the movement "to the people," one can only point to
isolated instances such as T'ao Hsing-chih, Liang Sou-ming, James
Yen, etc. These men, however, are basically gradualistic and wedded
to an educationalist approach. One can perhaps discern something
like a movement "to the people" within the framework of Chinese
Communism during the Yenan period. Yet this takes place within a
bureaucratized and institutionalized framework which makes the
analogy quite specious. Whatever may be their subjective attitudes,
the young cadres approach the peasants as functionaries of a regime.
In general, it is the elitist rather than the anarchist brand of populism
which wins in China. The notion that popular energies are to be
tapped is certainly present, but it is linked to the conviction that
their energies must be guided by those who know.

Although Marxism-Leninism after 1919 cuts short the emergence
of a full-blown Populism, it would appear that Lenin's successes
in China owe as much to those attitudes he shares with the Russian
elitist Populists (e.g., Tkachev) as to those which divide him from
them. In the long run, the notion of a vanguard elite embodying a
general will is of more importance than the notion of the messianic
role of the urban proletariat, although the dogma is retained. The
Leninist theory of imperialism and the Leninist commitment to industrialism do indeed add something which is very relevant to the
deep nationalist and social resentments of the Chinese intelligentsia,

but the whole Maoist development of Chinese Communism might well have dispensed with Marxist class assumptions were it not for the international aspects of the movement.

The word "socialism" also won speedy approval in China. Sun Yat-sen begins to equate "socialism" with "the people's livelihood" at a very early point in his career, in spite of his Anglo-American background. At the same time he begins to turn his attention to the problem of "skipping the capitalist stage." Socialism had won general approval in the most diverse circles long before the October Revolution. One may assume that the same factors are operative here as in the Russian case, perhaps reinforced by the implicit anti-capitalism of the traditional culture.[8]

All of these similarities tend to support the thesis that the phenomenon of the intelligentsia is a universal concomitant of the confrontation of a "traditional" society with the modern West. There are, however, certain overriding differences which seem to me to loom quite as large as the similarities.

Viewed from the vantage point of China, Russian culture, even in its earliest form, must be viewed as an "affiliate" of the West. The Orthodox religion draws on the same Judaic and Hellenic sources as does the Christianity of the West.

Furthermore, the Russian enlightened nobility of the eighteenth century was in sustained contact with Western ideas, while the Petrine state had taken on many of the aspects of contemporary Western states. The language itself with its Indo-European structure and its heritage of Judeo-Hellenic concepts lends itself easily to the transposition of Western ideas. Thus, in spite of the gloomy social and political scene, the nineteenth-century Russian intellectual and literary development seem to mark the culmination of a slow growth, rather than a complete traumatic break. The intelligentsia may be in revolt, but it is in revolt within a continuous historic process. This feeling of culmination is most spectacularly manifest in the magnificent literature of the nineteenth century, with its universal appeal. Yet even the literature of ideas, whatever its lack of originality, is forceful, eloquent and self-assured. The Russian intelligentsia is reasonably at home in its intellectual and spiritual world.

In twentieth-century China we have not only a profound social and political crisis but also the seeming collapse of a culture and a whole system of values. The twentieth-century intelligentsia feverishly seeks Western values to fill the vacuum, and it must attempt to convey its ideas in a linguistic medium which is saturated with the categories of thought of an entirely different culture. It is no wonder that the writings of this intelligentsia frequently seem naïve and awkward to the Western eye. The Chinese *intelligent* is much less self-assured than his Russian counterpart, much less at home in the world of ideas he has come to embrace, much more in need of a new orientation.

One aspect of this cultural crisis is the burning need for a sense of national dignity. One of the striking aspects of the mid-nineteenth-century Russian intelligentsia is its disassociation from nationalistic aspirations. This intelligentsia may be nationalistic in certain senses of the word, but it is entirely divorced[9] from the aspirations and ambitions of the Russian state. On the contrary, it deplores the success of Russian arms and the oppressive extension of the influence of the Tsarist state abroad. (The sense of deprivation of dignity deriving from the loss of a sense of identification with state power does not exist for this intelligentsia.) In China, the preoccupation with the weakness and decay of the state is a common denominator uniting the last generation of the literati with the "alienated" generations of the twentieth century. To use the old Chinese phrase, "enriching the state and strengthening the military"[10] is an aim shared by the most diverse ideological commitments. The deep resentment and sense of deprivation of dignity which accompany China's political humiliation become the personal resentments of the whole articulate class.

This difference reflects an enormous difference in the objective situation of the two societies. In spite of Russian backwardness, the Petrine reforms had made Russia one of the great powers of nineteenth-century Europe. The economic bases of this power may have been woefully weak, but this did not prevent the chancelleries of Europe from dreading the expansion of Russia's might. At the very end of the nineteenth century, the Chinese reformer K'ang Yu-wei could still offer Peter the Great as a model for his emperor. Not until the rise of Stalin in the twentieth century did a new sense of Russia's weakness as a world power become felt, and this sense was closely associated with a consciousness of her economic backwardness. The spokesmen of Stalinism are acutely and morbidly concerned with building up the power and prestige of the Russian state. In this light, the new ruling class hardly resemble the spiritual descendants of the nineteenth-century intelligentsia. Even Lenin, in spite of his strategic use of nationalism, in this respect still seems to belong to the older intelligentsia.

In China, the growing success of Marxism-Leninism owed much

to the appeal of the Leninist theory of imperialism, particularly those parts that are related most directly to national resentments. While Marxism had been accepted in Russia in its original cosmopolitan garb, Marxism-Leninism was widely received in China only after it had already been bent to the uses of a resentful nationalism.

Most of the factors discussed above would seem to argue for a more compliant attitude toward totalitarianism on the part of the Chinese intelligentsia. The ardent cravings for a sense of national dignity, the deep spiritual insecurity, the long tradition of authoritarianism, the orientation toward state service, the rejection of "capitalist" values, etc., would all appear to have created preconditions for a complaisant attitude toward the Communist state.

While such a conclusion would provide a neat ending to this paper and conform to our usual expectations concerning "Asia," life continues to be richer than gray theory, and the intelligentsia in China tends to betray the unpredictable qualities of the intelligentsia elsewhere.

It is true that a considerable portion of this intelligentsia either actively welcomed the Communist assumption of power in 1949 or acquiesced in it. This is in striking contrast to the situation in Russia during the October Revolution. There, a large part of the political intelligentsia was anti-Bolshevik, and a considerable body of non-political intellectuals was also anti-Bolshevik. These facts, of course, reflect the enormous changes in the intellectual evolution of Russia during the late nineteenth and early twentieth centuries, which are discussed by Mr. Pipes in this volume. In twentieth-century Russia, the intelligentsia as here defined had become only one strand in a variegated intellectual stratum that included nonpolitical intellectuals, professionals who certainly considered themselves *intelligenty*, and groups advocating a wide gamut of opinion among the more politically minded intelligentsia. There was certainly no automatic polarization toward Leninism. Whatever similar tendencies existed in twentieth-century China, they were inhibited by the dire conditions created by the Japanese War and by the polarization of power toward the two political forces which enjoyed a military base. Efforts on the part of intellectuals to create "third force" groups were rendered ineffectual by this situation.

It must also be emphasized that in committing itself to the new regime the Chinese intelligentsia as a whole had not necessarily committed itself to the type of totalitarianism which subsequently emerged. It had committed itself to the acceptance of certain Marxist-

Leninist premises. Many hoped that the totalism of the new regime would remain within a more moderate "new democratic" framework. It is doubtful whether they anticipated the whole fantastic "thought reform" experience.

The regime itself directed some of its most concentrated efforts to the psychological transformation of the intelligentsia. The whole "thought reform" experiment would seem to reflect an ambition to achieve by new methods a form of monolithic "internalized" consensus such as the Soviet Union has never achieved. On the other hand, the fact that much of this effort has been focused on the intelligentsia would indicate a deep and abiding suspicion of that stratum in spite of its complaisant attitude.

In certain respects the present situations in Russia and China cannot be compared. In the forty years since the October Revolution there has emerged in the Soviet Union a new professional and managerial class that hardly remembers the past. The Soviet Union has attempted with some success to appropriate the word intelligentsia to designate this class. A similar attempt is taking place in China, but as of the present, the word intelligentsia still refers to the older intelligentsia, and whatever professional class exists is still drawn from "older cadres," who, in the view of the regime, share many of the shortcomings of the intelligentsia as a whole.

It has perhaps not been sufficiently noted that the redefinition of the term intelligentsia has not solved all problems even in the Soviet Union. The professional classes may be acquiescent but they nevertheless lay claim to private preserves of specialized knowledge which, in some sense, place them beyond the pale of party omniscience. There is, of course, a long history of efforts to "bolshevize" the professionals in the Soviet Union. At the moment, the regime would seem to have made a tacit surrender to the expertise of those professions it regards as essential, in return for unquestioning political loyalty.

In China, on the other hand, the renewed attack on the intelligentsia since 1957 has involved an attack on the pretensions of experts and professionals as one of its integral ingredients. At the moment, the Chinese regime is rather more impressed with the "defects" common to the literary and academic intelligentsia and the professionals than with the differences between them. Both groups have dared to pit their judgments against the judgments of the Party on the basis of criteria external to the Party line. At the moment a concerted effort is under way to reduce the stature of both the professional and the nonprofessional intelligentsia.

The particular animus of the regime toward the intelligentsia, however defined, reflects of course the shocking revelations of the "Hundred Flowers" episode of 1956-1957. This is hardly the place to consider the reasons behind this episode or the intentions of the Communist Party leadership. For our purposes it is sufficient to note that the official slogan, "Let the hundred flowers bloom, let the hundred schools contend," was meant to suggest to the intelligentsia that a certain undefined area of free discussion was now open to them. What emerged was highly revealing. Not only were the literary and cultural policies of the regime attacked; not only did professionals challenge the authority of the Party within their areas of competence; but there were even those who raised the dread question of power itself. The very grounds on which the Communist Party claimed political infallibility were challenged. In raising the question of political power, the "civism" of the Chinese intelligentsia went beyond anything that has occurred in the Soviet Union since the inauguration of the "Khrushchev era." The numbers involved were, of course, small. One may surmise, however, that those who had the courage to speak represented many more who were silent. It is also true that this is still the older pre-1949 intelligentsia.[11] Yet it was also the intelligentsia who had embraced the new regime and gone through all the ardors of "thought reform." Any notion of a natural proclivity on their part for limitless dosages of totalitarianism must certainly be rejected after this episode. The regime may ultimately reduce this older intelligentsia to complete silence and create a completely conditioned "new intelligentsia." One can no longer speak, however, of any unlimited receptivity on its part to totalitarian control.

In the end, the intelligentsia in China as in Russia remains an incalculable and unknown quantity. Chinese totalitarianism, like Russian totalitarianism, may have had one of its roots in the past propensities of the intelligentsia of these countries.[12] In China, in fact, the top leadership of the Communist party itself derives from that stratum. Yet the relations of the intelligentsia as a whole to the regime remain a problem. A rejection of Western liberalism does not necessarily imply a willing acceptance of totalitarian extremism in all its forms. Between the two lies a whole spectrum of possibilities. If the intelligentsia in twentieth-century China dreamed of "totalistic" solutions, this does not mean that the form of totalism that actually emerged has proven completely palatable. If it rejected Western liberalism, its exposure to certain habits of thought derived from liberalism has made a certain impression on it.

Finally, as to the extent that the traditional culture of China has shaped the present scene, it must be pointed out that this culture contained many conflicting tendencies. It is easy enough to draw up a list of such predispositions as may have facilitated the acceptance of totalitarianism, yet within the older culture one can also discern predispositions that run in quite another direction. These tendencies were not "liberal," or "democratic," or "individualistic," and it would be wrong to romanticize them. They did involve, however, the concept of moral norms that transcend the arbitrary will of the ruler, and even the concept of what might be called the civic obligation of the literati to defend these norms. In China, as elsewhere, the intelligentsia remains an unpredictable variable.

REFERENCES

1 One may say that the "alienation" of Kafka and Kierkegaard is essentially more radical than anything one can find among the Russian intelligentsia. It is, however, different in kind.

2 Martin E. Malia, "Herzen and the Peasant Commune," in *Continuity and Change in Russian and Soviet Thought* (Cambridge: The Harvard University Press, 1955), pp. 214-215.

3 The unenthusiastic attitude of many of the intelligentsia toward modern Western political, economic and social development may spring in part from their implicit awareness that, in a sense, the Petrine state with its bureaucratic, military, and police machine was the most "modern" and "rationalized" sector of Russian society.

4 Michael Karpovich, "Review," in *Continuity and Change*, p. 279.

5 Alexander Gerschenkron, "Nineteenth Century Intellectual History," in *Continuity and Change*, p. 33.

6 The "well-field" in the idealized schematic account of Mencius consists of eight plots of land assigned to eight families surrounding a ninth plot, the yield of which sustained the lord. Presumably the plots were cultivated collectively.

7 Men such as K'ang Yu-wei, Yen Fu, Liang Ch'i-ch'ao, Chang Ping-lin, etc.

8 This account of trends in China is extremely crude. Economic liberalism, Chinese equivalents of Slavophilism, and all sorts of other tendencies are to be found. We are here simply isolating certain major tendencies.

9 Here again we are excluding such men as Aksakov and Katkov from our definition of intelligentsia.

10 An aim, incidentally, rejected by the main line of Confucian orthodoxy. This intelligentsia does not suffer from the sense of loss of dignity that marks the Chinese intelligentsia after the collapse of the Chinese Imperial State.

11 Actually, however, an astonishing number of students became deeply involved in these criticisms.

12 I continue to believe that this was one of the roots of totalitarianism, and to reject the currently fashionable theory that totalitarianism is merely a "function" of the "industrialization process."

JULIÁN MARÍAS

The Situation of the Intelligentsia in Spain Today

To DEPICT THE PRESENT POSITION of the intelligentsia in Spain in a manner that would be both truthful and comprehensible is difficult for many reasons: first, because of its complexity; second, because of the profound variations the Spanish intelligentsia have experienced within a few decades; third, because the function of this group in Spanish life and its objective content differ appreciably from those of the intelligentsia in the United States or in other European countries. It is necessary, therefore, to refer constantly to the changes that have occurred since the end of the nineteenth century, and to certain characteristics peculiar to contemporary life in Spain. Furthermore, one must treat separately the politico-social position of the intellectual minorities within the life of the country, on the one hand, and the results they have achieved, their most important creations, their physiognomy, their present possibilities and risks, on the other.

The year 1898 is a decisive date in the history of contemporary Spain. This was the year of the war with the United States, that meant the loss of what remained of the Spanish empire overseas, Cuba, Puerto Rico, and the Philippines. This was also the moment when Spain came to realize how false and insufficient had been the principles on which its life had been based since the restoration of the monarchy in 1874. All this experience was called in those days, "the national disaster." At the same time, however, this date signaled the beginning of the intellectual resurgence known as "The Generation of 1898," that produced what has been called "the golden half-century" of Spanish culture.

This generation (that of Unamuno, Ganivet, Baroja, Azorín, Valle-Inclán, Benavente, Machado, Maeztu, Menéndez Pidal) bridged the

182

fifteen-year gap that Spanish *intellectual* life had suffered as compared with Europe, even as compared with Spain's general mentality, since the beginning of the nineteenth century. It restored Spanish intellectual life to a position "at the height of the times." Aside from the extremely high quality of their work, these writers achieved this distinction through the authenticity of their intellectual vocation, and this single trait, common to them all, enabled them to function with a kind of dedication and total surrender, a compelling motivation, that had not been witnessed in Spain for a long time and one not often seen in other countries. The force driving these men was their need for clarifying their position in relation to their own country, their preoccupation with Spain, and their conviction that only a strong creative effort could throw light on their own destinies and integrate Spain, with all its original personality, into Europe. Above all, they were great writers, a literary generation, it has been said. In Spain, I believe, the vital significance of theory as such had been lost—indeed, theory had become foreign, and the only way of recapturing it, of giving it a rebirth (an authentic, not an imitative one) was through the literary temperament. Herein lies one of the most notable characteristics of contemporary Spanish thought, which incidentally was perhaps the first to discover the literary requisites of true theory and the cognitive value of certain literary forms.

Shortly after 1898 Spain enjoyed a period of relative prosperity. Spanish political life made it possible for intellectuals of varying tendencies and shades of thinking to get along. Until 1917, at least, the intellectual group remained, if not united, associated. The intellectual, who had enjoyed little influence until then, began to acquire prestige and increasing popularity, derived partly from the fact that the major writers usually published articles in the daily newspapers. At that time books had a relatively small circulation, but some publishing houses such as Renacimiento, or the publications of the Residencia de Estudiantes, Espasa-Calpe, and after 1923 the *Revista de Occidente* especially, presented a series of distinguished books by Spanish authors, along with translations of first-rate foreign works, that gained a growing minority audience. Within twenty or twenty-five years Spain emerged from its peripheral, isolated position as one of the least "provincial" countries of Europe.

The subsequent generation, which shared in the same resurgence, numbered Ortega y Gasset, Marañón, Eugenio d'Ors, Gabriel Miró, Pérez de Ayala, Juan Ramón Jiménez, Ramón Gómez de la Serna, Picasso, and Solana. The social influence of the intellectuals increased, they were no longer solely or even primarily "writers," but exponents of doctrine, in some instances university professors. Gradually an "intellectual minority" was being constituted, and though its "social effectiveness" was incomparably less than that of the *écrivain* or *homme de lettres* in France or the *Gelehrte* in Germany, it began to make its weight felt in the life of the country. The universities, which had begun to decline in the seventeenth century, and at the beginning of the twentieth had reached a low level of almost no creativity, within a few decades achieved a repute that represented a considerable progress. In 1936, the Spanish universities were on the whole inferior to those of the great European nations, but certain departments, such as the Faculty of Philosophy and Letters at Madrid, had reached a level that in some aspects equaled the highest anywhere, while the general perspective was extraordinarily encouraging. The names of men like Ortega, Morente, Zubiri, Menéndez Pidal, Américo Castro, Montesinos, Salinas, Navarro Tomás, Gómez Moreno, Obermaier, Asín Palacios, Sánchez Albornoz, Lapesa, Lafuente, and Zulueta are sufficient proof.

At the same time there had come about a progressive politicizing of Spanish life, begun, if I am not mistaken, about 1917, coincident with the cleavage produced by World War I. With but few exceptions, Spanish intellectuals were very moderate, politically speaking, and generally were little prone to political activity, but with rare exceptions they were unequivocally liberal, convinced of man's duty and responsibility to orient his own life and to take part in the destiny of his country. The dictatorship of Primo de Rivera (1923-1930), with its interference in every aspect of national life, caused the intellectual minorities, especially in the universities, to assert an attitude of opposition, translated into the desire to face up to the problem of reconstructing the state and improving social conditions. On the establishment of the Republic in 1931, most intellectuals, like the majority of the population, welcomed it with hope and enthusiasm, and at first exerted some influence on it. It must be confessed, however, that their participation in government was minimal and that their influence almost immediately evaporated, to be replaced by other forces, alternately yet more extreme or reactionary but strictly political, and in general hostile to the intellectual class.

The Civil War of 1936-1939 signaled the deepest rupture in Spain's experience (at any rate since Napoleon's invasion in 1808-1814) and simultaneously the dispersal of the fragile intellectual world. During the war years and immediately thereafter, cultural institutions were suspended or destroyed, the spirit of belligerency pervaded everything, free speech was abolished, and intellectuals as such, in so far as they attempted to maintain their status as not mere citizens, had little to do. As is well known, a considerable part of the intellectual element emigrated. This statement should be qualified, however: usually it is taken for granted that the emigration of the intellectuals took place *at the end* of the Civil War, yet it is a fact that many writers, professors, artists, etc., left Spain *at the beginning* of the war because of the situation prevalent since its outbreak. After 1936 there were many who felt that the world for which they had struggled had vanished in any case, whatever the outcome of the war. To some degree this basic attitude was blurred by a variety of interests. Some intellectuals who decided to remain émigrés tried to forget that their emigration had begun years before the end of the conflict. Others who returned to Spain had preferred to emphasize their residence there rather than their earlier disengagement, as mentioned above, from both belligerent sectors. Some have remained in retrospect faithful to political principles they had considered dead even in 1936, or personally to their fellow intellectuals who emigrated in 1939. In others the dominant motive has been their decision to live in Spain, to share the destiny of those who in any case wished to remain with the thirty million Spaniards who of course were not going to emigrate.

For about five years (from 1936 to 1940, approximately) there was nothing but dispersal and silence in the strictly intellectual area. What was to be heard could not be called "intellectual," but rather the result of various substitutes for the intellectual. Later on, efforts toward a reconstruction began, slowly and painfully. Although I am not going to speak here of those who have remained émigrés, since my subject is the situation in Spain itself, I must say one word in this regard: the intellectual émigrés worthy of the name (i.e., those who are not merely political) have long maintained close fellowship with those residing in Spain: they read and know one another's work, in reciprocal esteem. This applies not only to those in Spain who may be considered dissidents, but also to many who, even though they unequivocally allied themselves to the other side, have preserved their qualifications as men of letters or of thought. It may be said that *among the intellectuals the Civil War has been overcome.*

The reconstruction of an intellectual life for Spain has met with great difficulties. I shall try to enumerate briefly some of them. The first difficulty, a consequence of the enormous moral trauma caused by the Civil War—above all, because it was *civil*, breaking morale and sundering the social unity of a people, and second, because it was a war, a combat—was what I would call the abdication of a good part of the intellectuals, who renounced the requisites of their function, abandoned their rights, and surrendered to pressures. This consequence seems to me to have been the paramount one, the thing that permitted those pressures (even when they were not strong or had ceased to be strong) to have been more than ample, since with but minor exceptions they have been rarely resisted. On the other hand, such pressures have been correspondingly the less intense, and, *once the premise of a general pressure was accepted,* a considerable margin of *de facto* intellectual action was possible, provided the intellectuals attempted no formal revindication of their rights. This alone explains the apparent contradiction that, despite the state's absolute control of public and private education on every level, as well as of all publications (books, magazines, and newspapers) by means of a previous censorship without appeal, the naming of university chairs and appointments to all teaching positions—despite this control, in the last twenty years a considerable amount of intellectual activity, often of a very high quality and in many cases *free and independent,* has taken place. This is true to such an extent that I am convinced that an impartial and intelligent inventory of Spanish intellectual production in the last two decades would show, surprisingly enough, that on the whole it is not inferior to that of an equivalent period before the Civil War.

Something quite different would have to be said as to its *effects,* for the second difficulty in the reconstruction of Spanish intellectual life has consisted (and still does) in the anomaly of the *communication* between intellectuals and the public. It is difficult to understand what the real situation is: censorship is universal, omnipotent, and without public norms to regulate it—that is, the writer has no rights, he cannot count on the possibility of publishing anything. This automatically produces in many writers an "internal censorship" that frequently exceeds that of the state, so that an author or a newspaper editor does not even "attempt" to say anything. Conversely, the writer who really does "attempt" to do so, and is willing to face a few difficulties, discovers that he can *in fact* say innumerable things that would have seemed impossible *a priori.* Of course, since publicity cannot be counted on, such attempts are rarely noticed, commented on, continued and articulated in a coherent intellectual action, but remain isolated, "exceptions," although they may be very numerous or comprise almost all the writings of some authors.

This is why there exists in Spain an *individual,* limited prestige attached to certain intellectuals known to say what they think, not what they supposedly should think. These are the men whose intellectual publications go through many editions, whose philosophical lectures draw audiences of five hundred or a thousand, even in the provincial cities. On the other hand, the men with "false prestige," promoted with all the powerful means at the disposal of government or political or apparently religious organizations, despite all their advantages, have not managed in a single case to gain national esteem.

Yet not only has the danger not passed—it is increasing. The third great difficulty for the Spanish intelligentsia is what I would call the "as if," or the false intellectual activities which are not entirely false. The official institutions (universities, research centers, literary and scientific awards conferred by the state, etc.) are subjected to a constant and intense pressure, and often they operate in a meaningless, fictitious fashion. Yet there are very few intellectuals who refuse to participate in these institutions, and many of the most valuable and personally independent intellectuals appear to be associated with them and actually project their prestige through institutions which are not really in their hands and which do not fulfill their own criteria. Such intermingling produces a dangerous confusion, especially when viewed from abroad: the foreign observer focuses on a few illustrious names, those he knows, and he supposes the others are analogous, although the merchandise itself may be very different from the flag it flies. There are many reasons—primarily economic, but also the desire for an official rating, which indeed has repercussions beyond the national frontier, even in unexpected places —that explain, if they do not justify, such participation.

Such participation entails a twofold consequence, however. In the first place, when times are difficult, the intellectual has to maintain a kind of incorruptible rectitude if he hopes to avoid a chain reaction; the slightest deviation automatically leads to others, and he finally discovers that certain "innocent" compliances have taken him where he did not want to go. In the second place, the public becomes confused, and does not know what to believe. Those over forty, who know "who is who," and have experienced another state of affairs, can still orient themselves and make the correct subtractions. The younger generation, however, seem not to know how to distinguish, and although the majority may be "nonconformists," even at times with extremist tendencies, they are impregnated with the ideas and slogans prevalent throughout their lives, and profoundly affected by them. Indeed, this is precisely the explanation for their frequent and automatic "extremism."

The significance of these facts is that in its creative capacity, Spanish intellectual life has been saved, despite countless risks and at the cost of efforts ranging from asceticism to heroism. Now, however, begins the greatest danger, which can jeopardize the future of that life for the next twenty years. What solution can there be? Undoubtedly, the only effective one would be a transformation of the present conditions of Spanish life, one both profound and salutary, moderate and intelligent. It would help immeasurably, too, if Spanish intellectuals might have the intelligent and well-oriented aid of their colleagues abroad. None of these possibilities, however, is in the hands of the writers, thinkers, and professors in Spain. All they can do is to intensify the rigor of their demands upon themselves and affirm their solidarity, to constitute a "corporate" spirit, and to be prepared to uphold in so far as possible the rights of the intelligentsia.

Now we must inquire into the *internal* characteristics of Spanish intellectual life. What are its forms, its principal creations, and its problems, and finally, what is its true value, and to what extent does it correspond to its reputation?

The twentieth century witnessed an achievement in Spanish culture unequaled since the Golden Age, since the mid-seventeenth century. From then on, Spain stood apart from European intellectual activity—certainly in the fields of philosophy and the sciences, while even literature lost the innovating power that had persisted from the time of La Celestina through that of Calderón. In subsequent centuries the exceptional people dedicated their efforts toward "Europeanizing" Spain and bringing it again abreast of the times. Yet when we speak of "Europeanizing," and compare the "enlightened" men of the eighteenth century with the Generation of 1898, we fall into error. The former tried to Europeanize Spain by *accepting*, by translating and adapting what was being done in France, England, Italy and Germany, while the latter genuinely realized their aim by means of *creating*, by forming of themselves a new philosophy, a new literature and art.

It is noteworthy that the forms of this intellectual endeavor have been both distinguished and popular. The most disciplined Spanish thought has achieved a literary form that assured communication and a marked impact on the life of the country. Only this explains the fact that it is easier to publish a theoretical work in Spain than almost anywhere else, that the intellectual wins social renown and esteem, and that there exists a substantial minority familiar with the themes of contemporary thought and profoundly concerned with them.

Nevertheless, within only sixty years, and considering the difficulties, one could not expect Spanish intellectual life to have attained a homogeneous level or an adequate scope. It remains very much a concern of the minority, it lacks an adequate personnel, while the bibliographies on many subjects are either poor or nonexistent, and the most original, fecund ideas often remain undeveloped or neglected. The summits in thought, in literature and art compare with those of any other nation, but the totality of the Spanish intellectual scene when viewed in profile is decidedly inadequate. Further, there are obvious discrepancies between one field and another. The literature of this last half-century is splendid, the poetry, especially that of the first thirty years, of an extremely high level. Works of genius, though perhaps fragmentary, may be found in various areas of the humanities, such as philology and the literary studies of the school of Menéndez Pidal, Arabic studies, under Asín Palacios and his pupils, studies in the fine arts, spear-headed by Gómez Moreno, and above all, philosophy, which under the stimulus of Ortega y Gasset has created the so-called Madrid School. In addition, there are those "islands" of science in the fields of biology and physics, under the leadership of Ramón y Cajal, Cabrera, Marañón and others, that promise a scientific movement as yet unfulfilled and that flourishes chiefly among those Spanish scientists who are working in research centers in the United States and certain European countries. Severo Ochoa, awarded the Nobel Prize for Medicine in 1959, symbolizes this group.

An original and decisive characteristic of all such intellectual production is the fact that its organizing center, so to speak, is philosophy. It should be grasped that authentic philosophy in Spain today is pursued with originality and intensity, but in very small volume—if one discounts what amid general indifference is officially proffered as "philosophy." The interesting thing is that philosophers have applied their point of view and their method to the study of other subjects—sociological, historical, literary, artistic and scientific—and that after some years the men who cultivate these disciplines have come to utilize constantly in their own fields the perspectives and methods of philosophy, especially those of contemporary Spanish philosophy. This is a phenomenon, I believe, unique to Spain (to some extent it has spread to Hispanic America), and one that may have far-reaching results in renovating the humanities, even the natural sciences.

One unexpected consequence of the "central" position held by philosophy in Spain is that it has become a topic of exceptional interest, indeed, it has hardly any rivals. No other sphere of intellectual life has had to face so many pressures and so much hostility, no other has elicited greater attempts at "simulation," none has aroused a like enthusiasm.

The present situation of the Spanish intelligentsia may be summarized thus: a splendid sixty-year-long tradition of uninterrupted creativity exists, though fragmentary and unconsolidated. This represents a tremendous possibility if it becomes stabilized and if its original ideas receive an ardent application, but it is assailed from many sides and runs the risk of being dissipated and lost. One urgent need is the formation of working groups trained in rigorous work. It is also necessary to ensure the free communication (both among themselves and with the public) of those who are re-establishing criticism, nonexistent today, and concomitantly the assertion of just and justified hierarchies. None of these things is easy if the young intellectuals with a real vocation lack the proper stimulus, if political or economic pressures interfere with the continuity of production, if contact with the outside world and international attention are absent. The general rating of the Spanish intelligentsia today is assessed at far below its true value, for obvious reasons. For more than two centuries first-rate Spanish creative works were very scarce; at the beginning of this century they became astoundingly numerous, but it took time for this to become known, especially abroad. When the world began to be aware of such work, the difficulties in Spain, the deliberate distortion of the reality of the country, the belief on the part of many that "all was finished," the superficial acceptance of false values, and the consequent disillusionment—all these things resulted not only in checking this incipient recognition but nullifying it. Apart from fortunate exceptions or very limited circles of perceptive observers, the Spanish intelligentsia today is *either unknown or improperly evaluated.*

For the Spanish intellectuals this can be not only painful but dangerous. I think it also a misfortune for the intellectual destiny of the West, since, if my hopes do not deceive me (I do not believe I am subject to wishful thinking), the Spanish contribution to the thought of our century is an essential one, well worth preserving.

BIBLIOGRAPHY

1 Pedro Laín Entralgo, *España como problema.* 2 vols. Madrid: Aguilar, 1956.
2 Dolores Franco, *La preocupación de España en su literatura.* Madrid: Adán, 1944. (Revised edition: *España como preocupación,* Madrid: Guadarrama, 1960.)
3 José Ortega y Gasset, *España invertebrada.* (*Invertebrate Spain.* New York: Norton, 1937.)

4 Ramón Menéndez Pidal, *España y su historia*. 2 vols. Madrid: Minotauro, 1957.

5 Gregorio Marañón, *Ensayos liberales*. Buenos Aires: Espasa-Calpe, 1946.

6 Julián Marías, *Introducción a la Filosofía* (*Reason and Life: The Introduction to Philosophy*. New Haven: Yale University Press, 1956).

7 Julián Marías, *Los Estados Unidos en escorzo*. 3rd edn. (*Obras*, vol. III). Madrid: Revista de Occidente, 1959.

8 Julián Marías, *Ensayos de convivencia*. 2nd edn. *El intelectual y su mundo*. 2nd edn. (*Obras*, vols. III-IV). Madrid: Revista de Occidente, 1959.

9 José Ferrater Mora, *Cuestiones españolas*. (Jornadas—53.) México: El Colegio de México, 1945.

10 José Luis L. Aranguren, *Catolicismo día tras día*. 2nd edn. Barcelona: Noguer, 1956.

I. Philosophy and the Natural Sciences in the USSR

THE SIGNIFICANCE OF THE DOCUMENT below requires no extended explanation. It reflects (if often obliquely) the genuine controversies that are carried on among Soviet scientists and philosophers, despite the external appearance of unanimity and the acceptance of dialectical materialism demanded by the authorities. The present discussion was originally published in the *Vestnik istorii mirovoi kul'tury* (Moscow: No. 1, January-February 1959). This text is a complete translation of the original Russian version, based on the slightly abridged translation first published in the *Soviet Survey* (London: No. 29, July-September 1959). We would like to express our thanks to the editors of the *Soviet Survey* for allowing us to use their translation, and to Gabriella Azrael for her rendering of the passages not included in that journal.—Ed.

A CONFERENCE on the philosophical problems of science, called by the Academy of Sciences and the Ministry of Education, took place in Moscow on 21-25 October 1958, with 620 philosophers and scientists from the Soviet Union and several other countries participating. The conference heard and discussed the following papers:

(1) "Lenin's Materialism and Empiriocriticism," Academician M. B. Mitin; (2) "Lenin and the Philosophical Problems of Modern Physics," N. E. Omel'anovskii, Member of the Ukrainian Academy of Sciences; (3) "The Correlation of Forms of the Movement of Matter in Nature," B. M. Kedrov, Doctor of Philosophy; (4) "The Philosophical Content and Significance of the Theory of Relativity," A. D. Aleksandrov, Corresponding Member of the Academy of Sciences; (5) "On the Interpretation of Quantum Mechanics," Academician V. A. Fok; (6) "Cybernetics and Science," Academician S. L. Sobolev and Professor A. A. Liapunov; (7) "Some Methodological Problems of Cosmogony," Academician V. A. Ambartsumian; (8) "On the Role of Physics and Chemistry in the Investigation of Biological Problems," Academician V. A. Engelgart and G. M. Frank, Corresponding Member of the Academy of Sciences; (9) "The Problem of the Origin of Life in the Light of the Discoveries of Modern Science," Academician A. I. Oparin; (10) "The Leninist Theory of Re-

flection and Modern Physiology of the Sense Organs," N. I. Grashchenkov, Corresponding Member of the Academy of Sciences.

The conference opened with an introductory speech by A. M. Nesmeianov, President of the Academy of Sciences. He pointed out two special features in the development of natural science today—the profound differentiation and specialization of the sciences, and at the same time their contact and mutual interpenetration. These tendencies give special urgency to the philosophical generalization of scientific discoveries. Some scientists adopt the positivist slogan that "science is a philosophy in itself," and surrender to the illusion that they can do without philosophy in their scientific work; in reality they become prisoners of the very worst philosophy. Scientists must make efforts to obtain a thorough creative mastery of dialectical materialism. The main task of the conference was to reinforce the creative unity of philosophers and scientists, which would make it possible to raise the theoretical level of science and facilitate the speedy solution of its most important problems.

(1) Academician Mitin emphasized in his report that Lenin's *Materialism and Empiriocriticism* is a basic work on the relationship of Marxist philosophy and the philosophy of natural sciences. Not only a valuable party document, it is a fresh contribution to the further development of dialectical materialism. During the past fifty years this book's development of Marxist philosophy has been borne out by the achievements of science. The work reveals the revolutionary essence of natural science at the end of the nineteenth and the beginning of the twentieth centuries. Under the pressure of the new discoveries in physics of that period, the old mechanical picture of the universe was destroyed.

In the last few decades the representatives of idealistic philosophy have made great efforts to prove that the concepts of physics are merely symbols and have no connection with physical objects. A very typical example is the speech made at the XIIth International Philosophical Congress in Venice by the neo-positivist Philipp Frank, who declared that "all attempts to maintain materialistic or idealistic systems in connection with twentieth-century science have failed." Though he tried to hide behind a mask of neutrality towards the main philosophical trends, Frank developed a typically idealistic conception of the philosophy of science, reducing the whole question to the semantic analysis of scientific concepts. Thus, impotence in solving the philosophical problems of science is just as characteristic of modern idealist philosophers as it was of Machism.

A characteristic of some foreign scientists is their desire to stand aloof from the struggle between philosophical trends. Thus the physicist Wolfgang Pauli, who in 1927 published an article on "Phenomena and Physical Reality" in the Swiss journal *Dialectica*, stated that he adhered neither to materialism nor to idealism. But in associating himself with Niels Bohr's definition of objectivity, and asserting that the objective method is "that on which one can reach agreement with others," he took up a Machist position. In his study of quantum mechanical processes, Wolfgang Pauli drew conclusions about the indeterminism which, he thought, prevails in micro-processes. Like many foreign scientists, Wolfgang Pauli does not understand dialectical materialism.

The objective character of atomic phenomena has been proved by the application of atomic energy. If science has learned the laws of the microcosm and compelled the electron to "work" for man's practical needs, then there can obviously be no talk of "the free will of the electron." The idea of indeterminism also falls to the ground.

In quantum mechanics the apparatus changes the object in the experimental process. For this reason, some scientists have deduced that "there exists no object without an apparatus," that "the apparatus creates the object," etc. In actual fact, the fundamentally new role of the apparatus in quantum mechanics by no means cancels out the question of the objective reality of micro-particles. All that is necessary is to allow for the influence of the apparatus on the object. This naturally requires new and very subtle methods of analysis and experiment, and correspondingly new concepts.

Foreign scientists have recently shown a growing interest in dialectical materialism. A highly significant fact in this context is Louis de Broglie's renunciation of the neo-positivist views which he held for twenty-five years. In conclusion, the speaker said that Lenin's *Materialism and Empiriocriticism* is an important ideological weapon for combating the philosophic position of the revisionists. The success with which socialism has been built in the U.S.S.R. and the countries of the people's democracies proves the falsity of the ideas advanced by the revisionists.

(2) M. E. Omel'ianovskii dealt in detail with the solution offered by modern idealist philosophy to the problem of objective reality. While the positivist philosophers are openly trying to banish the concept of objective reality from science, the physicists, on the contrary, strive to preserve it. Werner Heisenberg, for instance, has said that the concept of the "real" plays just as vital a part in quantum mechanics as in classical physics. At the same time, he wrongly separates the concepts "objective" and "real." "Objective," in Heisenberg's view, means that which is described mathematically, while the real can be described only in the concepts of classical physics. Still Heisenberg often comes close to a correct understanding of certain philosophical problems. For instance, he has written that "elementary particles, colliding with a great exchange of energy, can be converted one into another. This state of affairs can be most simply described by saying that basically all particles consist of an identical substance; essentially, they are different stationary states of one and the same material. . . . There is only one matter but it can exist in different discrete states." If we disregard certain terminological inexactitudes, the formulation quoted here may be accepted as correct.

The physicist Max Born asserts that the scientist in his sensory impressions "must see more than hallucinations, and that something more is information about the real world." For Born, electrons, atoms, and fields are part of the external world which exists independently. To those philosophical doctrines which deny this he gave the name, "physical solipsism." He sees the key to the rational understanding of reality in the idea of invariance. What ordinary people call "real things" are "invariants of perception" which reason constructs by means of an unconscious process. In Born's views we discern a recognition of the dialectical character of physical reality, but the assertion that invariants are constructed by reason is wrong.

Quantum mechanics testifies to the enormous importance of dialectical materialism for modern physics. Referring to three ways of dealing with the problem of synthesising the corpuscular and the wave pictures of the behavior of micro-particles, and analyzing each of these three views, Omel'ianovskii said that they express the connection between corpuscular and wave properties in a form inadequate to the identity of opposites, which is one good reason for their shortcomings.

In conclusion, the speaker criticized the neo-Thomist Wetter's book, *Dialectical Materialism*. Omel'ianovskii emphasized in particular that there were no grounds for Wetter's assertions as to the compatibility of the dialectical-materialist and the neo-positivist interpretations of quantum physics.

(3) B. M. Kedrov observed that the most characteristic feature of modern science is the intertwining of the sciences and the appearance of several borderline areas of knowledge. This makes necessary a more thorough study of the correlation of the forms of the movement of matter in nature. There are two main approaches to this problem: the structural and the genetic. Correct results can be obtained only if both aspects are simultaneously taken into account. As science advances we observe two deviations from this path. The first consists in divorcing the higher forms from the lower, and regarding the higher forms of movement as absolute. Such modern idealist trends as neo-vitalism, holism, etc., are shot through with this tendency. The metaphysical separation of the higher and lower forms of motion is a gnoseological source of idealism.

The second deviation is the attempted mechanistic reduction from higher to lower forms of motion, from the complex to the simple. Only the study of dialectical method (particularly as regards the correlation of the forms of movement) would help avoid mistakes of the first as well as of the second kind. Kedrov pointed out that mistakes have been made in the critique of resonance theory. The positive significance of the theory lies in its revelation of the quantum-mechanical aspect of chemical phenomena. This, however, has given rise to the mistaken idea that the essence and specific nature of chemical and biological processes is fully exhibited in their quantum-mechanical characteristics. But this is only the debit side of those great successes in chemistry which quantum mechanics has already brought and promises to bring in the future. Consequently, the essential problem lies in the elucidation of the proper correlation among the different forms of the movement of matter. It is therefore necessary to combine the structural with the genetic approach.

Kedrov gave the following as the main forms of the movement of matter in nature: the quantum-mechanical, the macro-mechanical, the sub-atomic physical, the chemical, the molecular-physical, the geological, and the biological. The geological form of the movement of matter is a new concept, introduced by Kedrov.

(4) A. D. Aleksandrov, Corresponding Member of the Academy of Sciences, emphasized that the theory of relativity is a physical theory of space and time. The principle of relativity expresses the uniformity of the structure of space-time. On the basis of this assumption, and with certain mathematical transformations, it is possible to prove that there exists in space-time a system of coordinates in which these transformations from

one totality to another preserve the ratio of effect and have the appearance of ordinary Lorentz transformations. Thus, since the structure of space and time is endowed with transformation invariance, both the inner laws and the interactions which determine that structure also have the same property.

Aleksandrov formulated the concept of space-time as follows: space-time is the multiformity (plurality) of all events, considered only from the point of view of its structure, which is determined by a system of relationships of precedence (or subsequence), apart from all other properties. Space-time is four-dimensional multiformity. He emphasized that it is impossible to consider the general principle of relativity, which asserts the equal validity of all systems of coordinates, in the same sense as the special principle, which asserts the equal validity of inertial systems of coordinates. Einstein's attempts to discover a general principle of relativity, and the confusion of this general principle with "covariance," are a purely mathematical error, arising from an exaggeration of the role of the principle of relativity, which obscures the true nature of the theory of relativity as a theory of absolute space-time. Aleksandrov reduced the general theory of relativity to a theory of gravitation.

(5) Academician V. A. Fok pointed out that the fundamental distinctive characteristic of the objects with which quantum mechanics is concerned is found in the specific nature of the method used to describe them. The limitations of this method are the result of the existence in these objects of both wave and corpuscular properties. The limitations set upon the classical description of atomic objects are formulated with the help of what is known as Heisenberg's inequality. By taking this into account one may avoid the paradoxes implicit in the classical method of description. The formulation of the conditions which make possible the avoidance of such paradoxes is the work of Niels Bohr, who calls it "complementarity." Complementarity is related to the limitations imposed on the classic methods of description. The quantum method of description essentially involves a concept of probability. But it does not follow from this that it refuses to describe the individual properties of an object. Probability is introduced into quantum mechanics as a primary concept, serving to characterize the potential possibilities inherent in an object, whereas in classical physics, in the kinetic theory of gases, for instance, probabilities are arrived at as a result of averaging.

As for the question of determinism in quantum mechanics, Fok pointed out that in quantum mechanics, as in modern physics generally, causality is preserved, but there is no room for determinism, in the Laplacian sense.

Bohr's original formulations of his quantum theory are not quite precise. He did not, for instance, draw a distinction between the concepts of causality and determinism. This gives grounds for accusing Bohr of positivism. The incorrect, positivist interpretation of Bohr's ideas by some of his pupils has become known as the Copenhagen interpretation of quantum mechanics, or the Copenhagen school, but it is better not to use this term, since what matters is not Bohr's mistakes, but the rational nucleus which his ideas contain. Fok related that a year and a half ago in a talk with Bohr in Copenhagen, he pointed out to Bohr the imprecision of his formulations. Not long ago he received Bohr's new work, *Atomic*

Physics and Human Knowledge, which stresses the objectivity of quantum-mechanical description and its independence of the perceiving subject, accepts causality, and rejects only Laplacian determinism. There was no mention in this work of uncontrolled interaction between apparatus and object. It is therefore possible to agree completely with Bohr after this correction of his formulations, and the term "Copenhagen School" should not be used in a pejorative sense.

In conclusion, Fok criticized de Broglie's point of view, which he felt to be old-fashioned, essentially incorrect, and powerless to contribute anything to science, as practical experience has shown.

(6) Academician S. L. Sobolev gave the participants in the discussion a thorough exposition of the subject of cybernetics. He dealt with the principles on which electronic machines work, and the questions of programing. Sobolev made the point that in living organisms we also have to do with regulating systems, with the transmission, processing, and storage of information. Since cybernetics studies processes without regard to the concrete or biological means by which they are carried on, processes in living organisms are also a proper subject for its investigations. Attempts are being made to imitate certain features of animal behavior, even conditioned reflexes, by means of machines. Experiments of this kind make it possible to verify the completeness of the description of any biological process.

Cybernetics has a great importance for the study of the problem of heredity. Heredity is a sort of transmission of information by parents, a stream of information from the parent organisms to the organisms of their progeny. The development of the living organism starts from the embryo cells, where the information transmitted to them by the parent organisms is stored. This information must be utilized to regulate the subsequent development of the living organism. It has been suggested that there may be also a return influence from the embryo cell to the parent organism, which can then correct the disposition of information, to help the embryo cell select only elements favorable to it. But it is difficult to imagine how this can take place. Perhaps such a mechanism will be discovered, but for the moment it seems unlikely.

Sobolev stated that cybernetics provides a stimulus to the construction of regulating machines, and greatly influences mathematical logic, as well as the mathematics of computation. The solution of a number of problems would have been impossible without the creation of mathematical machines. In conclusion, he said that the views expressed by some writers, to the effect that cybernetics is a pseudo-science, idealistic, mechanistic, etc., are the result of a misconception, and originate only from a total ignorance of the actual content of cybernetics.

(7) Academician V. A. Ambartsumian in his paper, "Some Methodological Questions of Cosmogony," said that the creation of artificial earth satellites is of enormous practical and philosophical importance. We have now begun to look at the world from a broader viewpoint, abandoning geocentrism, not only in theory but also in practice. Touching on the question of the structure of the greater universe, he said that the phenomenon of the red shift in the spectrum of the galaxies and the nebulae, and

the Doppler effect, are of fundamental importance. Some scientists who try to interpret this phenomenon and who are tolerant of the ungovernability of extrapolations, which lead to the most extreme idealistic deductions, arrive at what they call the theory of the expanding universe. Others, refusing to accept what lies behind this phenomenon, forget its fundamental significance. In that region of the universe which we observe, the separation of galaxies from one another and their dispersal really does happen.

The universe we observe is not uniform in the macroscopic sense. The creation of matter in space, as we observe it, is extremely heterogeneous, not only quantitatively but also qualitatively. Astronomical observation destroys the oversimplified model of a homogeneous universe, and also the supposition on which it is based, that there is a linear dependence between the recession velocity and distance. The discovery that in some systems there is a great dispersion of velocities is a new development. Accumulations have been discovered that consist of galaxies with such high velocities that they part from one another because the force of Newtonian gravity does not suffice to hold them together. In conclusion, Ambartsumian called for the abandonment of the dogmatic approach to the problems of science on the part of some philosophers.

Discussion. Several scientists took part in the discussion of these papers. M. V. Shirokov criticized A. D. Aleksandrov's views on the theory of relativity. He did not agree with the rejection of the general theory of relativity and its reduction to a theory of gravitation, and argued that such a presentation amounts to a denial of the objective reality of a field of inertial forces and the effects they produce, such as the change in the acceleration of the force of gravity with a change of latitude, the phenomena of trade winds, the change in the frequency of light as it goes past a round object, etc. The rejection of the general principle of relativity as a general law of nature takes us back to the Newtonian conception of the forces of inertia as unreal. Passing on to the question of the Copernican and Ptolomaic systems, Shirokov said that in so far as the theory of relativity for isolated systems by virtue of the law of conservation and the new theory of gravitation bears out the theorem of the center of energy, the Copernican system is superior, not only in Newtonian mechanics but in the theory of relativity as well.

D. D. Ivanenko, in pointing to the great successes of the theory of elementary particles, advanced the hypothesis that since there exist definite connections between these particles, there may exist some "proto-matter," the search for which is becoming an immediate task for science. The only possible attempt along these lines, it seems, is the construction of a nonlinear spinor theory of matter.

An important question of the quantum theory today is the problem of gravitation. In a quantum theory of gravitation, it appears that the gravitational field can change into other forms of matter. Dirac, especially, subscribes to this point of view.

In constructing our picture of the world as a whole, it is necessary to probe not only into the origin of the stars but also into the origin of elementary particles. In this connection the question of anti-particles is very important. These questions are closely bound up with cosmogony.

Roughly speaking, the problem is that of the possibility of observing anti-worlds, and also of possible relations between the signs of charges that predominate in our universe and its other physical features.

E. Kolman noted that philosophical thought is seriously lagging behind physics. The theory of elementary particles needs especially careful attention. He expounded in detail the new theory of matter, the content of which has been formulated by Heisenberg. An important feature of the new theory is that it regards the field not only as continuous but as discrete. Heisenberg's theory may be considered the result of a 2000-year development of scientific theorizing about matter, proceeding from undifferentiated first matter to the multiplicity of elemental substances. In Kolman's view, Heisenberg's theory represents the final break with "stupid mechanistic determinism" and puts dialectic determinism in its rightful place. But Heisenberg's own philosophical views have proceeded from positivism to objective idealism. The same transition from subjective-idealistic views to objective idealism is characteristic of other modern physicists, in particular Niels Bohr and Max Born. Kolman criticized the philosophical positions taken by mathematicians as regards contemporary mathematics. He showed that the majority of contemporary mathematicians proceed to a constructivist point of view, which has made possible great advances in mathematics. However, the gnoseological initial point of view of constructivism leads to subjective idealism.

Ia. P. Terletskii criticized Fok for defending the Copenhagen interpretation of quantum mechanics, and for ignoring other points of view. Terletskii thought it an immediate necessity to develop the trends which give an interpretation of quantum mechanics different from that of the Copenhagen school. Defining the different interpretations of the quantum theory, he paid particular attention to the theory of de Broglie and his pupils, and drew the conclusion that on the general philosophical plane this theory does not go beyond the framework of dialectical materialism; in his opinion, this makes it superior to the Copenhagen interpretation of quantum mechanics.

P. K. Anokhin dealt with the links between physiology and cybernetics. He sees an example of the great significance of cybernetics for the physiology of the nervous system in its establishing the significance of feedback. With the introduction of precise mathematical calculation, cybernetics can inform the physiologist of regularities he could not discover for himself. It is very important in turn that specialists in cybernetics should have a knowledge of physiology. Every external agent which acts on the nervous system of an organism not only causes a current of nervous impulses but also indicates the material apparatus necessary for future action. The study of this process can be very useful in the construction of calculating machines.

Academician Naan, of the Estonian Academy of Sciences, said that the application of the relativistic theory of gravitation to the problem of the structure of the universe has been a great scientific success. Yet the metaphysical raising to absolutes of the results obtained and the idealistic fantasies built round them have seriously obscured the meaning of these results and damaged the credit of relativisitic cosmology. From the end of the 'twenties, the view was gradually established in the West that the metagalaxy, and indeed the whole universe, has had a catastrophic origin. This view provides a favorable soil for various idealistic speculations.

Unfortunately, we often find, instead of an analysis of the problems of modern cosmology and a criticism of unfounded conclusions, that our philosophical literature asserts that particular theories are untenable because they contradict the tenets of dialectical materialism. But modern cosmological theories do not in themselves contradict either dialectical materialism or the basic laws of physics. In this context the need has arisen for solving a number of problems, such as that of the origin of matter in its prestellar state. The hypothesis of a collision between matter and anti-matter, with the formation of highly concentrated radiation, may prove acceptable. Despite its swift accumulation, the material under observation is for the moment insufficient for the construction of a satisfactory model of a metagalaxy, but it is sufficient to prove that the catastrophic hypothesis in cosmology is unnecessary. Naan also showed that the facts on astronomy accumulated in our time do not allow us to draw a simple conclusion as to either the metrics of space or the properties of space in general.

D. I. Blochintsev, Corresponding Member of the Academy of Sciences, noted three different conceptions in the interpretation of quantum mechanics, and emphasized that he considers Bohm's and de Broglie's conceptions untenable, a view which Terletskii supported. A fundamental step which will radically change our ideas about particles and space is needed; we need a completely new idea, totally different from the classical conceptions.

Docent M. N. Rutkevich disagreed with Kedrov, who thinks that in the construction of matter we must consider the subordination of forms of movements, as well as their coordination. If we take the types of elementary particles and the corresponding fields, there is no subordination. There is only coordination, interrelation, and reciprocal conversion. Therefore, one must construct a system of the forms of movement, starting with these better-known kinds of physical movement. Rutkevich criticized Kolman because Kolman considers Heisenberg's theory of matter a form of return to the principles of Anaximander. It is incorrect to assert that from the point of view of contemporary physics all bodies are made of some sort of matter that has no properties. He also criticized Kedrov's assertions of the existence of a geological form of movement. Other scientists participated in the discussion of the papers, commenting on various questions.

The conference then heard the papers in the Biological Section.

(8) In the paper given by Academician V. A. Engelgart and G. M. Frank, Corresponding Member of the Academy of Medical Sciences, it was emphasized that the exploitation of methods offered by physics and chemistry opens up great prospects for the penetration into the material substance of the phenomena of life. Engels' definition of life as the form of existence of albuminous bodies existing in continual self-perpetuation of their chemical components has not only withstood the test of time but has received even more concrete elaboration.

The application of isotope tracers has made possible the discovery of fundamentally new regularities in metabolic processes beyond the reach of ordinary chemical methods. It has been found that in the process of metabolism, a speed of transition previously unsuspected develops quite unexpectedly. Complicated organic complexes, forming part of biological structures undiscoverable by ordinary chemical methods, are formed, break down, and are recreated.

There has been a fundamental change in our conception of the ways in which matter moves. It used to be thought that the disintegration in the metabolic process continues up to the appearance of the end products, but it has now been found that large molecular fragments may be used over and again to form complex structures, so that there may occur a repeated reconversion in the process of disintegration, and, as it were, a repetition of the synthesis with the ultilization of the same products of partial decompensation.

Electronic optics, electronic microscopy, and the diffraction of X-rays have opened a new era in the study of the structure of living matter in the submicroscopic molecular sphere. A new field which may be called molecular morphology is emerging. A continuous ladder of structural relationships in the spatial organization of living matter is being established, beginning with the structural protein molecules and ascending to the elements of the cell visible through an ordinary light microscope. The speaker also thought the cybernetic approach to the elementary life process is possible, e.g., the automatic control of chemical reactions in the organism by particular cells in the organism. This field may provisionally be called micro-cybernetics. Obviously, the role of sound is here playing the part of Brownian movement, acting uninterruptedly on the structural correlation, on the statistical distribution of speeds, and consequently on the concentration of chemical products, and on the ruptures of the half-formed links, as the result of fluctuations of mechanical tensions.

The speaker asserted that the whole sum of data at our disposal testifies to the primacy of metabolic processes as the basis of the phenomenon of life; consequently, the role played by chemistry in the investigation of biological processes is easily understandable. It is therefore justifiable to some extent to regard the physical processes and properties of a living system as merely the effects of metabolic processes. For example, the electrical activity of cells and tissues is based on a definite orientation by chemical processes.

In conclusion, the speaker criticized the simplified approach to the analysis of life phenomena that identifies an accidental aspect of the observed processes with the essence of the life phenomenon, or ascribes to an artificially present physical or chemical characteristic of the processes a decisive value as the material basis of these phenomena. There is also a danger of arguing idealistic conceptions from a strictly physical position, as is exemplified in biology by Bohr's assertion that the phenomena of life are unknowable. Contemporary science provides no justification for this assertion.

(9) Academician A. I. Oparin stressed that (as the symposium on the origin of life in Moscow 1958 had made clear), the evolutionary approach to the solution of this problem is now generally accepted. The program of that symposium was based on three stages of the development of matter;

the original appearance of the simplest organic substances, the hydro-carbons and their immediate derivatives; the conversion of these basic substances on the earth's surface into complex organic compounds, in par-ticular, into substances like the proteins; and the formation of new molec-ular systems, complexes endowed with metabolic properties.

The main disagreement at that symposium was on the question of the subsequent course of evolution. Not long ago it was widely held that in the original medium (*bouillon*) there appeared somehow or other, per-haps by pure accident, a complex molecule whose structure determined the basic properties of life. This concept of a genic molecule (at first vague) was later given concrete expression in chemical terms by the prop-osition that the molecule in question was desoxynucleoprotein. But a growing volume of biochemical data, particularly those presented at the Vienna Congress of Biochemistry in September 1958, has upset ideas that DNA has so much importance in the matter of life-determining prop-erties. One paper in particular pointed out that not only DNA but also RNA, the complex carbohydrates and the lipids—in effect, the whole cellu-lar complex—must play a part in the transmission of heredity. But the discussion of the life-defining structure of a nuclear molecule is impossible when the question is thus posed.

DNA is commonly supposed to have the property of reproducing itself in the form of an identical molecule of DNA. At the same time, it can somehow transmit information to the protein molecule, determine the structure of the proteins and their ferments, and determine the disposition of amino-acid residues. But we have absolutely no experimental data in-dicating any such transmission of information. It is often surprising that when DNA is used in practical work it undergoes great changes, under the influence of X-rays and other factors, which would bring about tremen-dous changes in the organism if that molecule were really the life-deter-mining factor. In fact, no such changes take place. If one considers that what is changing here is only some particles of the life-defining substance (naturally, important sections, all the more so in that they take form in spontaneous metabolism), the phenomenon becomes incomprehensible. These conceptions are increasingly confirmed. The idea of a living mole-cule is receding further and further into the background, constantly being refuted by facts, while the idea of an initial multi-molecular system is find-ing more and more confirmation. We must look for the beginning of life, not in the original appearance of DNA or some other molecule, but in a complex, which, in the course of its development, may be shown to include DNA also.

(10) N. I. Grashchenkov, Corresponding Member of the Academy of Sciences, said that the formation of the specific properties of the sense organs, as well as of the organs themselves, is the result of an interaction between the organism and its surroundings, e.g., the result of the formative role of the environment. In this connection he recalled Lenin's criticism (in his *Materialism and Empiriocriticism*) of the "physiologist" idealist Johannes Müller, and the work of Soviet scientists who have disproved Müller's so-called law of specific energies. Modern physiology of the sense organs has discovered in detail the formative and guiding role played by the external world in our perceptions and sense organs. The main factor

in the mechanism by which the sense organs operate is reflector activity; the interrelations between the environment and the sense organs are based on a reflex mechanism. Reflex activity is not a mere mechanical transmission of stimulus, but a more complex chemical process based on biochemical changes. Apart from the general regularities, modern physiology is studying particular regularities in the functioning of the sense organs. The phenomenon of adaptation, or adjustment to stimuli from the outside world, has become particularly important. The speaker illustrated the adjustment of the sense organs with many slides.

All the sense organs are closely interrelated. It is therefore possible, when one of the sensory systems grows tired, goes out of action, and no longer gives impulses and information to the higher nervous formations, to act upon other systems connected with it in such a way as to reactivate it. The interrelation between these systems—the connection between nervous apparati—relies on a direct contact between the peripheral and central apparati; nerve fibers run from each formation, ending at one or another group of nerve cells: if the stimulus has to be transmitted to higher levels, it is again transmitted to the nerve fibers, and so on indefinitely up to the level at which the particular stimulus being analyzed and synthesized becomes a sensation and enters our consciousness, which in turn is connected with external factors and conditioned by the external world. The speaker concluded by criticizing the idealistic works of several neurophysiologists of the capitalist countries. He also pointed out the rightful necessity of developing dialectical-materialist psychology.

In the discussion of the biological papers, Sisakian, Corresponding Member of the Academy of Sciences, showed that the profound study of the phenomena of the microcosm offers broad perspectives for the development of biology. Biochemistry leads toward the identification of the qualitative essence of the chemistry of the phenomena of life and the assertion of their materiality. Progress in the experimental techniques of biochemistry has created new and unprecedented possibilities for learning about the biochemical functions of intracellular structures. The progressive structural differentiation of the object of biochemical investigation is accompanied by the danger of segregation from our knowledge of the integral organism. The regularities established for isolated structures cannot be mechanically transferred to the cell and to the organism as a whole, although the study of those regularities brings us closer to an understanding of the organism as a whole. The biochemical interpretation of intracellular elements does not reject the idea of the integrality of the organism and of the cell as a biological unit, but on the contrary is based on this idea.

The regular process of metabolism which helps create the unity of the organism and the conditions of its life, possesses, along with an exceptional plasticity and dynamism, a clearly expressed conservatism, in which the essence of the basic contradictions in the process of metabolism is to be found. Proteins and nucleic acids play an exceptional role in determining plasticity and dynamism as well as conservatism. Plasticity is determined mainly by the quantitative changeability of the amino-acid supply of proteins, by the exceptional variability and ability of the amino acids to interact with almost all the substances they encounter. In the determination of plasticity there is a further factor created by the presence in the organism of diverse ways in which the same substance can become transmuted. Conservatism is determined by the constancy of the quality of the amino-acid composition, by the specificity of the cells themselves, by the characteristic correlation between the simple and the pyramided foundations, and the structurally defined order of the nuclear interchange of the DNA molecular chain.

S. L. Rubenstein, Corresponding Member of the Academy of Sciences, emphasized that the researches of Soviet scientists show that both extero-receptor and intero-receptor systems work according to the reflex principle. On the general methodological plane, the question of the reflex character of the activity of the sensory organs is also the question of determining the activity of that apparatus and the end product of its activity-sensation. According to the theory of reflexes, the result of an external influence is conditioned by the responsive activity of the brain. Müller's mistake results from his basing his conclusions on the internal conditions of the functioning of the organs of sense, without reference to the external conditions. Hermann Helmholtz's symbolic understanding of sensation is the result of a mechanistic understanding, in which sensation is determined by an irritant.

The key to the solution of problems connected with the activity of the sensory organs and with the theory of knowledge, as well as other important and controversial problems of modern science, is a correct understanding of the determination of phenomena, to the effect that external causes act through internal conditions. Pavlov's teachings on higher nervous activity, while conforming to the principle of determinism, have succeeded in revealing the internal conditions specific for the activity of the brain, which modify the external relations of the organism with the environment that acts upon it.

By making use of the theory of higher nervous activity, on the one hand, and gnoseology on the other, psychology has formed an essential link in the system of disciplines that study the consciousness of man. It is necessary to put an end to the negative attitude to psychology which has grown up in the Soviet Union in recent years, and which is harmful in practice and methodologically mistaken. Pavlov's teachings do not liquidate psychology, rather, they have created new and powerful instruments for its development; the development in psychology means, not a refutation of Pavlov's theory, but its creative fulfillment. The relationship between psychology and the theory of higher nervous activity is analogous to that between biology and biochemistry. The theory of higher nervous activity also studies psychic activity, but in its specific aspect. The laws of higher nervous activity play an important and essential role in explaining psychological activity, but they do not exhaust its special characteristics or define its specific regularities, that is to say, the regularities that give it its leading role.

G. Platonov said that the main defect of the papers read at the conference was the absence of any criticism of idealistic views in science and philosophy. He discerned a recent and widespread tendency among scientists to underestimate the importance of the struggle with idealism. Platonov criticized E. Kolman's preface to Norbert Wiener's *The Human Use of Human Beings*, in which Wiener says that peaceful coexistence is the only sensible relationship between scientists of opposite camps. Platonov also criticized the position of the *Botanical Journal,* which had published criticisms of the views of Academician T. Lysenko.

Professor Kostrikova criticized the representatives of the gene theory of heredity, and especially the work of Professor Dubinin. She did not agree with the views of Academician Sobolev and Professor Liapunov on cybernetics, especially their treatment of a number of successive generations as a mere stream of information. She uncompromisingly rejected their assertion that "the mechanism of the transmission of information from the parent organism to the embryo cells is unknown," and thought this view tantamount to a denial of development in living nature.

A. L. Ryzhkov, Corresponding Member of the Academy of Sciences, said that scientists often make an incorrect use of dialectical method, which is above all a method for discovering new results. Attempts to define life that use only one criterion are absolutely fruitless. In the world of viruses, for instance, fundamentally new phenomena, previously not encountered in science, have been discovered. Marxists must uncover the essence of these phenomena and not hurry with definitions. Ryzhkov criticized Oparin's conception of the origin of life as being remote from real relationships. Nucleic acid could never originate in nature in the way Oparin imagines.

Academician Gnedenko underscored the necessity for the application of the methods of mathematics to biology and criticized the negative attitude of some biologists toward the application of mathematics in biological problems.

A. A. Prokofieva-Belkovskaia (Institute of Biophysics of the Academy of Sciences) said that the work carried out at the end of the last century and in the first half of the twentieth in the fields of cytology, experimental genetics, and embryology has provided an enormous volume of facts that prove that the inheritance of concrete structural elements of the nucleus and nucleoprotein of cytoplasm lies at the basis of heredity. The capacity of these structures to reproduce themselves (connected with the presence of ribonucleic acid in them) leads to the regular and orderly transmission of these structures from one generation of cells to another, and this is the reason for the inheritance of various types of metabolism and of the forms and functions of organisms. Some of these structures are constant components of cytoplasm, such as the microsomes, the mitochondria, and the plastoids. Their behavior in a number of generations of cells lies at the basis of cytoplasmic heredity.

The structural nucleo-proteins, which enter into the cell nucleus and form chromosomes within it, display the greatest precision in self-reproduction. Precision in their distribution through daughter cells is built in by evolution in all animals and vegetables in the complex process of the mitotic division of the cell.

Over a period of about ninety years, cytologists, embryologists, and geneticists have collected a huge amount of material which confirms the hypothesis that the primary and basic function of mitosis consists in the equal distribution of hereditary factors, located along the chromosome, between two daughter cells.

The development of this field of investigation is closely bound up with the development of chemical methods of investigation, one extremely important example of which is the investigation of the cell nucleus by means of radioactive compounds. The basic regularities of mitosis are the splitting lengthwise of each chromosome and the separation of its halves at opposite poles. This ensures a high measure of constancy in the chromosome assortment of the substances of the cell nucleus in a series of cell generations. These regularities are universal, and force us to assume that such behavior on the part of the cell nucleus when the cell divides is connected with its fundamental vital properties.

Professor Maiski showed that some researchers have tried to relate all life processes to physico-chemical reactions. Some biologists, on the other hand, have dissociated biology from physics and chemistry. These extreme views are incorrect. Biological methods of research are of decisive importance in the study of biological problems, but this should not mean a lessening of attention to physico-chemical methods. At the level contemporary science has reached today, it is extremely important to apply complex methods of research so that biological methods are combined with physico-chemical ones.

Professor Panichev (head of the Department of Marxism-Leninism at the Higher Medical Institute in Sofia) criticized the statement of Frank and Engelgart as to the possibility of determining the mechanism of heredity by physico-chemical methods. He cited examples of inheritance taking place when DNA is absent. The facts force us to abandon the thesis that DNA is the sole physico-chemical substratum of heredity.

Professor Konnikova (the Academy of Medical Sciences) in criticizing Oparin's conception of the origin of life said that the weakest spot in his theory is his treatment of the transition from inanimate to animate matter, and that there is a sharp break in his account of the progressive complication of matter after the emergence of polypeptides and nucleotides, and before the appearance of protein. The more complex substances, protein in particular, do not arise in a nonbiogenic way, but are formed only in a living organism. It follows that the chemical form of the movement of matter cannot attain a level of complexity at which there can be formed a chemical substance capable of causing biological phenomena to occur and of serving as the structural material for the primary form of life: there is no immediate transition from the chemical to the biological forms of motion. One source of this conception is Oparin's belief that the essential feature of life is not the exchange of the complicated chemical substance of protein, but the harmony and perfection of the chemical reactions that are carried out by supermolecular structures for purposes of self-preservation. A logical deduction from such a view of the nature of life is the denial of chemical evolution as a stage immediately preceding the emergence of life. In denying the nonbiogenic formation of protein, Oparin's conception is opposed to reality.

Professor Kolbanovsky said that science as yet has formed no consensus as to the place of psychology among the sciences. The basis of psychology is the physiology of the higher nervous activity, which reveals the mechanism of psychological phenomena. At the same time, not all psychological phenomena can be reduced to their physiological basis. Psychology constitutes the meeting point for the natural and the social sciences.

At the end of the conference, P. N. Fedoseev, the director of the Institute of Philosophy of the Academy of Sciences, pointed out that the conference had met under the banner of the victory of the ideas of dialectical materialism. Commenting on the extraordinarily rapid tempo of progress in the contemporary natural sciences, Fedoseev called for profound and serious work on the part of Marxist philosophers and scientists on the philosophical generalization of modern scientific discoveries, and for a strengthening of the collaboration between philosophers and scientists, stressing the impropriety of importing the methods used in combating hostile ideology into scientific discussions. Fedoseev also pointed out the importance of a concrete analysis of scientific questions, observing that the absence of such an analysis could lead to mistakes, as, for example, the nihilistic rejection of cybernetics by certain philosophers.

The conference adopted a resolution noting the need for a further exploration of the philosophical problems of science and for a closer collaboration between philosophers and scientists. The resolution mentioned the desirability of founding a special journal on the philosophical problems of science, and of airing these questions in a wide variety of scientific journals.

II. "Doctor Zhivago": Letter to Boris Pasternak from the Editors of *Novyi Mir*

THE TEXT THAT FOLLOWS is a full translation of the letter the editorial board of the Soviet literary journal *Novyi Mir* sent to Boris Pasternak in September 1956 to justify their rejection of *Doctor Zhivago*. The letter was first published two years later in the *Literaturnaia Gazeta* (25 October 1958) at a time when the decision of the Nobel Committee to award the prize for literature to Pasternak created a wide stir in the Soviet Union and led to Pasternak's expulsion from the Union of Soviet Writers. In publishing this letter the Soviet authorities wished to justify the measures they had taken against the author and his work. Incidentally, however, by quoting long passages from the novel, they gave Soviet readers their first (and so far only) glimpse of the text of *Doctor Zhivago*. Despite certain obvious misconstructions (e.g., the emphasis on fear and the search for personal comfort as Zhivago's main motives), the document does provide some valuable indications of the official Soviet reaction to the problems the novel raised, in particular, to the problem of the relationship between the intellectual and society. The present translation is reprinted here by the courtesy of the *Current Digest of the Soviet Press* (3 December 1958, vol. 10, no. 43, pp. 6-11, 32), where it first appeared in English.—Ed.

Boris Leonidovich!

We, the writers of this letter, have read the manuscript of your novel *Doctor Zhivago*, submitted by you to *Novyi Mir*, and want to express openly to you all our thoughts that grew out of this reading. They are alarming and grave thoughts.

We realize that if it were simply a matter of "likes or dislikes," a matter of taste or even of radical but purely artistic differences, you might not be interested in such esthetic squabbles. "Yes, yes!" or "No, no!" you might say. "The magazine has rejected the manuscript; so much the worse for the magazine, but the artist continues to believe in its esthetic worth."

However, in this instance the question is a more complex one. The thing that alarmed us in your novel is something that neither the editors nor the author could change by partial deletions or corrections: we are concerned here with the very spirit of the novel, with its pathos and with the author's view of life as that view really is or, in any case, as it is formed in the mind of the reader. We feel it is our direct duty to speak to you about this as people to whose views you may or may not attach importance, but whose collective opinion you have no grounds for considering prejudiced and which, therefore, is at least worth hearing out.

The spirit of your novel is the spirit of nonacceptance of the socialist revolution. The pathos of your novel is the pathos of the assertion that the October Revolution and Civil War and the social changes that followed them brought the people nothing but suffering and destroyed the Russian intelligentsia either physically or morally. The author's views on our country's past and, above all, on the first decade after the October Revolution (since, if one omits the epilogue, the end of the novel coincides precisely with the end of that decade) which emerge in systematic form from the novel boil down to the statement that the October Revolution was a mistake, that participation in it by that segment of the intelligentsia that supported it was an irreparable disaster, and that everything that followed from it was evil.

For people who had read your "1905," "Lieutenant Schmidt," "Second Birth," "Waves," and "On Early Trains"—poems that, it seems to us at least, had a different spirit and a different pathos from your novel—the reading of the novel came as a grievous surprise.

We feel that we are not mistaken in saying that you conceived of the life and death of Doctor Zhivago as being, at one and the same time, a tale of the life and death of the Russian intelligentsia, of its paths to the revolution and through the revolution, and of its destruction as a result of the revolution.

The novel contains a readily discernible dividing line, which does not coincide with your own division of the novel into two books but which lies approximately between the first third and the remaining two-thirds of the work. This dividing line is the year 1917, the dividing line between the expected and what actually occurred. Prior to this dividing line your characters expected something different from what actually happened, and after this dividing line things begin to happen that they did not expect and did not want and that, to your mind, led to their physical or moral destruction.

The first third of your novel, which deals with the twenty years before the revolution, does not yet contain a clearly expressed nonacceptance of the approaching revolution. But we believe that the roots of this nonacceptance are already discernible here. Later on, when you begin to depict the already completed revolution, your views assume the character of a more orderly and more forthright system, a system more of a piece in its nonacceptance of the revolution. But initially, in the first third of the novel, those views are still contradictory. On the one hand, you admit in an abstract and declarative fashion that the world of bourgeois private property and bourgeois inequality is unjust, and you not only reject it as an ideal but also consider it unacceptable for the mankind of the future. However, when you turn from this merely general declaration to a depiction of life, to the people themselves, these people—both the masters of the unjust bourgeois life themselves and their intellectual servants who help to preserve this injustice that you recognize in general terms—all prove to be "with extremely rare exceptions, such as the blackguard Komarovsky," the finest, kindest and most refined of people, people who do good, aspire and suffer and who would not hurt a fly.

This entire world of prerevolutionary bourgeois Russia that you reject in a declarative fashion and from a general standpoint proves in actual practice—as soon as the question of depicting it in concrete terms arises—to be fully acceptable to you and, more than that, poignantly dear to your author's heart. The only unacceptable thing about it is a certain abstract injustice—always offstage—in its exploitation and inequality, while everything that happens onstage proves in the final analysis to be quite idyllic: Capitalists donate to the revolution and live honest lives; the intelligentsia enjoys complete freedom of spirit and independence of judgment from the bureaucratic machine of the Tsarist regime; poor girls find rich and selfless protectors; and the sons of factory hands and janitors have no difficulty getting an education.

On the whole, the people in your novel live well and justly; some of them want to live even better and more justly—that, in essence, is the full extent of the stake that the main characters of your novel have, at the outside, in their expectations of a revolution. The novel gives no real picture of the country or the people, nor does it show why the revolution in Russia became inevitable or the intolerable degree of suffering and social injustice that brought the people to this revolution.

The majority of those characters in the novel to whom a part of the author's spirit has been lovingly imparted are people accustomed to living in an atmosphere of discussion of the revolution, but for none of them has the revolution become a real necessity. They love to talk about it in one form or another, but they are perfectly able to live without it; not only is there nothing insufferable about their lives before the revolution, there is hardly anything that so much as sullies their lives—if only spiritually. And there are no other sorts of people in the novel (if one is speaking of the people accorded the sympathies of the author and depicted in corresponding depth and detail).

As concerns the declaratory offstage sufferings of the people, in the first third of the novel the people are something unknown, something merely assumed, and the author's true feelings toward this unknown quantity are revealed only later, when the revolution occurs and the people begin to act.

The first third of the novel is above all the story of several gifted individuals leading intellectual lives of various sorts and devoting their primary attentions to the problem of their own spiritual existence. One of these gifted individuals—Nikolai Nikolayevich—says in the beginning of the novel, "Every herd is a refuge of mediocrity, regardless of whether it claims allegiance to Solovyev, Kant or Marx. Only lone individuals seek the truth, and they break with all who do not value it highly enough. Is there anything on earth that deserves allegiance? Such things are few indeed."

In context this phrase is linked with Nikolai Nikolayevich's God-seeking, but beginning with the middle third of the novel we see it gradually become a condensed expression of the author's attitude toward both the people and the revolutionary movement.

And then the revolution comes—or, more exactly, descends with a crash. It descends unexpectedly on the characters in your novel because for all their advance talk, they did not truly expect it and its actual occurrence struck them dumb. As concerns the place of the revolution in your novel, it is difficult even to distinguish clearly between the February and the October Revolutions. In the book they appear as aspects of a single entity, the year 1917 in general, during the course of which things changed less radically at first and the former life of the "lone, truth-seeking individuals"—your heroes—is not too noticeably disrupted, while later they begin to change more and more and the changes become ever sharper and more abrupt. The characters' lives become ever more dependent on the immense and unprecedented events that are taking place in the country and as it progresses, this dependence, in turn, increasingly embitters them and makes them regret what has happened.

It is difficult to imagine in the abstract a novel that contains many chapters dealing with the year 1917 but that at the same time fails to distinguish between the February and October Revolutions as such, fails to give some appraisal—but in any case a definite appraisal—of the social difference between the one and the other.

It is difficult to imagine in the abstract, but in actual fact this is precisely what is done in your novel. It is difficult to imagine that first the February Revolution and then the October Revolution—those turning points that divided so many people into different camps—do not determine the stands taken by the characters in a novel written about this period. It is difficult to imagine that people living an intellectual life and occupying a certain position in society would not, at that time, take some definite stand or other on such events as the overthrow of the autocracy, the coming to power of Kerensky, the July events, the Kornilov revolt, the October uprising, the seizure of power by the Soviets and the dissolving of the Constituent Assembly.

But the characters in your novel do not openly express their views on any of these events; they give no frank evaluation of the events that comprised the life of the country at that time. One can, of course, say that the author simply did not wish to call things by their right names, did not want to give them a frank appraisal of his own or to appraise them frankly through the mouths of his characters, and perhaps such an assertion would contain a part of the truth, but we believe that the whole truth lies deeper than this partial explanation. And the truth, to our minds, lies in the fact that the "lone, truth-seeking individuals" in the novel gradually become increasingly embittered against the mounting revolution not because they cannot accept certain of its concrete forms, such as the October uprising or the dissolving of the Constituent Assembly, but because of the various personal discomforts to which they personally are doomed by the process of revolution.

Initially represented by the author as men of ideas, or more exactly as people living in the world of ideas, these "lone, truth-seeking individuals"—when their talk of revolution has been superseded by revolutionary events, events in which they have no part—prove, almost to a man, to be people with no desire whatsoever actually to defend any ideas, be they revolutionary or counterrevolutionary, let alone to defend such ideas with their lives.

211

To all appearances they continue to lead an intellectual life, but their attitude toward the revolution and, above all, their actions are increasingly determined by the extent of the personal discomforts that the revolution inflicts on them—hunger, cold, crowded living quarters and the destruction of the well-fed, comfortable prerevolutionary life to which they had become accustomed. It is difficult, in fact, to call to mind any work in which the characters, while laying claim to the loftiest spiritual values, are at a time of such great events so concerned with and talk so much about food, potatoes, firewood and all manner of mundane comforts and discomforts as do those in your book.

The characters in the novel, and above all Doctor Zhivago himself and his family, spend the years of the revolution and the Civil War in search of relative well-being—a full belly and tranquility amid all the vicissitudes of struggle and at a time of general national ruin. Physically, they are not cowards—you, the author, stress that point—but at the same time their sole aim is to save their own lives, and it is to this end above all that all their major actions are directed. And it is precisely the fact that in conditions of a revolution and civil war their lives might not be spared that makes them increasingly hostile toward everything that happens. They are not grabbers, epicures or excessive lovers of creature comforts; they do not need all this for its own sake, but merely as a basis for the uninterrupted and safe continuance of their intellectual life.

What life? The one that they lived before, because nothing new enters their spiritual life and nothing changes it. For them, the ability to continue this life in the accustomed way, without outside interference, is the greatest good not merely for themselves personally but for all mankind, and the extent to which the revolution stubbornly demands that they act, take a stand and declare themselves "for" or "against" determines the extent to which they turn, in self-defense, from a feeling of alienation from the revolution to a feeling of hostility toward it. During those grim years that demanded all manner of sacrifices not only from the people who made the revolution but from their enemies as well—the people who took arms against it—the "lone, truth-seeking individuals" proved themselves, when put to the test, to be nothing but "highly gifted" Philistines, and indeed it is difficult to imagine what attitude the Zhivago family, say, might subsequently have evolved toward the revolution had not that family (as happens in the novel) for one reason or another spent the winter of 1918 hungry and crowded in a Moscow apartment. But life in Moscow was cold, hungry and hard, and the "lone, truth-seeking individual" becomes an intellectual bagman, eager to prolong his own existence by any means, even to the point of forgetting the fact that he is a doctor, and of concealing this fact at a time of nationwide suffering, sickness and epidemics.

"In that new mode of existence and new form of communion conceived by the heart and called the kingdom of God, there are no nations, only individuals," Doctor Zhivago says at one place in the novel, as yet without reference to his own subsequent existence during the Civil War. But it later turns out that this remark has a profound relevancy to Zhivago himself. During the difficult years of the Civil War it is made patently clear that for him the people do not exist; there exists only himself, an individual, whose interests and suffering are paramount, an individual who feels no kinship whatsoever with the people and who feels no responsibility to the people.

Of all human values there remains for Doctor Zhivago, when he finds himself in the midst of cruel nationwide suffering, only one: the value of his own ego and—as an extension of this value, in the form of a supplementary value—of the people who are in one way or another directly involved in that ego. This ego, which is embodied in Zhivago himself and in those dear to him, is not merely the only thing worth bothering about but is in general the only value that exists in the universe. The entire past and present are embodied in this ego; if it perishes, everything perishes along with it.

It is no accident that at the height of the Civil War, Larisa Fyodorovna says, in complete accord with Zhivago's own thoughts: "You and I are like the first two people, Adam and Eve; they had nothing to cover themselves with at the beginning of the world, and we are just as naked and homeless now, at its end. And you and I are the last recollection of all the immeasurable greatness that has been wrought in the thousands of years that separate them from us, and in memory of these vanished wonders we breathe and love, and cry, and support each other and cling to each other."

A new page in the history of mankind is opening; under the impact of the Great October Revolution hundreds of millions of people throughout the world are being set into motion for decades to come, but the only value and the only recollection of all the "immeasurable greatness" of man's past proves at this moment to be Doctor Zhivago and the person with whom he is sharing his life! Doesn't it seem to you that this wellnigh pathological individualism represents the naïve pomposity of people who are unable and have no desire to see anything around them and who therefore ascribe to themselves a cosmically exaggerated importance?

On one page of the novel you say through the mouth of Doctor Zhivago that "conformity to a type is the end of a man, his condemnation." This is the reverse side of your pretense as the author that your "lone, truth-seeking individuals" are superior people, people who cannot be ranked under any sort of type, people who are above all that.

However, it is hard to agree with this opinion. We would not want to forego the right to label Doctor Zhivago, as well as the people akin to him in spirit, a quite typical phenomenon during the era of the revolution and the Civil War—yes, and in recent times as well. It is the farthest thing from our intent to maintain that there were no such people or that Doctor Zhivago's fate was far from typical.

It is our view that Doctor Zhivago is, in fact, the incarnation of a definite type of Russian intellectual of that day, a man fond of talking about the sufferings of the people and able to discuss them, but unable to cure those sufferings in either the literal or the figurative sense of the word. He is the type of man consumed with a sense of his own singularity, his intrinsic value, a man far removed from the people and ready to betray them in difficult times, to cut himself off from their sufferings and their cause. His is the type of the "highly intellectual" Philistine, tame when left alone but capable in thought as well as in deed of inflicting any wrong whatsoever on the people just as soon as he feels the slightest wrong—real or imagined—has been done to him.

There were such people, and they were not few in number; we are not contesting with you the question of whether or not such people existed, but rather that of whether they merit the unqualified vindication they are given in your book—whether they are the flower of the Russian intelligentsia, which is what you strive with all the resources of your talent to show Zhivago to be, or whether they are a disease of the Russian intelligentsia. The appearance of this disease during the era of social stagnation and reaction between the first and second Russian revolutions can readily be explained, but what point is there in representing these people, with their Philistine failure to act at critical moments, their cowardice in public life and their constant avoidance of answering the question "Which side are you on?" as superior beings who allegedly have the right to pass objective judgment on everything around them, and above all on the revolution and the people?

But it is precisely through the mouths of these people, and above all, through the mouth of Zhivago himself, that you seek to pass judgment on all that happened in our country, beginning with the October Revolution. Moreover, without exaggerating in any way, one is fully entitled to say that to no one in the novel have you, the author, accorded such unreserved sympathy as you have extended to Doctor Zhivago and to those people who so fully share his views that the majority of conversations between them and Zhivago sound more like the Doctor talking to himself.

One might add to this that nowhere in the novel have you taken such pains and exercised such talent as in expressing the thoughts and views of these people, while those who hold differing views exist in the novel only quantitatively or, to use your expression, as a "herd." They are voiceless, and are endowed with the ability neither to think nor to refute any of the allegations made at the trial that your book conducts of the revolution, a trial in which both the judge and the prosecutor are, in effect, embodied in a single person—Zhivago. He is provided by the author with several assistants who echo, with various nuances, his indictments, but there is no one at this trial to defend what Zhivago is condemning.

Meanwhile, as the discomforts and privations Zhivago suffers because of the revolution grow, his condemnation of it becomes increasingly embittered and intransigent. We feel it will not be a waste of time to trace the course of this one-sided process. This is worth doing not simply to multiply quotations but so that you yourself can see these excerpts all together, as a whole; it is possible, since they are scattered in various places among the ramblings of this immense novel, that you yourself are not fully aware of what you have written. We would like to believe that this is the case.

At one point in the novel Doctor Zhivago goes to Yuryatin; there he has an argument with Kostoyedov, who tells him that he doesn't know anything and doesn't want to know anything: "It's true, I don't want to know, and what of it? It's the honest truth. Ah, go on! Why should I want to know everything and knock myself out for everything? History takes no account of my desires; it imposes on me whatever it wishes. So let me ignore the facts too. You say 'words don't tally with reality,' but is there any reality in Russia today? To my mind, it's been so frightened that it's gone into hiding."

And here is another bit of reasoning dating from the same year (1917 or 1918—it is difficult to tell from the novel) and from the same trip to Yuryatin. This time the tirade is not Yury Andreyevich's but that of his father-in-law, Alexander Alexandrovich, with whom he lives in complete accord during the entire Civil War; in reading dialogues between the two men one has to pay sharp attention, because it is only through the punctuation that one can distinguish between what is said by Zhivago and what by Alexander Alexandrovich.

"Stop right there; I understand. I like the way you phrased the question. You found just the right words. And this is my answer. Remember the night you brought home the handbill with the first decrees—it was winter, and there was a blizzard. Remember how utterly unconditional they were. It was this straightforwardness that was overwhelming. But such things reside in their original purity only in the minds of their creators, and then only on the day they are proclaimed. The very next day the Jesuitry of politics turns them upside-down and inside-out. How should I say it? This philosophy is alien to me. This regime is against us. No one asked my permission for this upheaval. But I was trusted, and my actions—though I may have been forced to commit them—place an obligation upon me."

This is what Alexander Alexandrovich says in reply to Zhivago's question as to how they might jointly work out the most tolerable forms of mimicry, forms such that they need not blush for each other. The concluding words about forced actions are, by and large, empty words in this case: Neither Zhivago or Alexander Alexandrovich had taken any particular action in the interests of the revolution but, having found themselves under the Bolsheviks in Moscow, had simply served and received their rations for their work; later, when the ration proved insufficiently large, they had left to find a place where people were better fed. Equally empty are the words about obligation. The entire subsequent course of the novel shows that neither Alexander Alexandrovich nor Zhivago has even the slightest sense of obligation to the revolution or the people. What, then, is left? The assertion that they were betrayed, that one night they had liked the straightforwardness of the first Soviet decrees but that later, when the straightforwardness of these decrees began to be implemented and to encroach on their own way of life, they had come to feel that this regime was against them. These thoughts are explainable, but the inexplicable thing is why an attempt is made to represent the plaintiff as the judge!

But behind the revolution that has brought discomforts and privations to Doctor Zhivago there lies a definite philosophy: The revolution is wrong with respect to Doctor Zhivago; thus, he reasons, the philosophy behind it is also wrong and must, therefore, be declared bankrupt.

"Marxism and science?" Doctor Zhivago asks at the beginning of book two. "To argue about this with a stranger is at best imprudent. But be that as it may. Marxism has too little control over itself to be a science. Sciences are better balanced. Marxism and objectivity? I know of no school of thought that is more withdrawn into itself or more cut off from the facts than Marxism."

In this philippic against Marxism one already senses more than a little bitterness, but this bitterness makes itself fully felt somewhat later on, when

Zhivago meets Larisa Fyodorovna in Yuryatin (to judge by certain hints, the year is 1919).

"You have changed," she says. "You used to judge the revolution less harshly, without bitterness."

"The point is, Larisa Fyodorovna, that there is a limit to everything; in this time we should have arrived at something. But it becomes clear that the turmoil of changes and transitions is the only element in which the instigators of the revolution feel at home, that you can't feed them on bread but have to serve them up something of global scale. For them the building of worlds, the transition periods, are ends in themselves. That is all they have learned and all they are capable of. And do you know the source of all the commotion of these eternal preparations? Their source lies in a lack of any distinct, innate abilities, a lack of talent. Man is born to live, not to prepare for life. And life itself—the very phenomenon of life, the gift of life—is such an engrossingly serious matter. Then why substitute for it a childish harlequinade of immature inventions, these 'flights to America' by Chekhovian school children?"

Thus as early as 1919 Zhivago feels that it is time the revolution arrived somewhere, but that it has not arrived. Arrived at what?—that we are not told! To judge from his egocentric views of what is good and what is bad, it should at least have arrived at a point where Zhivago could resume the normal and comfortable life that he had known before the revolution. However, the revolution had not done this for him and he incites people against it and pronounces sentence both on it and on its participants: They are ungifted; they have learned nothing and are capable of nothing.

He regards the Civil War as an immature invention, a " 'flight to America' by Chekhovian school children." This is wit of a rather low order, but the malice, it must be admitted, is no trifling matter!

All about Zhivago life is breaking up and being transformed; it is a cruel, bloody and difficult process whose expediency and rightness can only be judged from the standpoint of the interests of all the people, from the standpoint of a man who values the people above everything else. But it is precisely this standpoint that is lacking in Zhivago—his position is the opposite. He judges the people and the things wrought by the people from the standpoint of his own personal physical and mental well-being; it is quite natural, then, given this stand, that in the conditions of the Civil War he should return with ever-growing frequency to the thought that the things left behind him were better than the present he now has to live in. And since his own well-being is the principal measure of all things, the transformation of life is, consequently, to no end and he would rather see a return to the old than a continuation of the transformation.

"In the first place," he says to Livery Averkiyevich, the commander of a detachment of partisans, "the idea of total perfectibility as it has come to be understood since October does not move me. In the second place, all this is still a long way from being realized, and so far such oceans of blood have been paid for nothing more than talk about it that it would almost seem the end does not justify the means. In the third place—and this is the most important—when I hear people talk about transforming life I lose all control of myself and fall into despair."

And somewhat later he returns to the same thought:

"Transformation of life! Such a notion can only be entertained by people who, while they may have seen a good deal of life, have never come to know life, have never felt its spirit, its soul. For them existence is a lump of coarse material that has not yet been ennobled by their touch and that requires fashioning by them. But life is never material or substance. Life itself, if you want to know, is a constantly self-renewing, eternally self-transforming first principle; it is eternally remaking itself and realizing itself; it is far beyond the reach of our stupid theories."

Thus the transformation of life is not necessary and the theories that inspire such transformation are stupid!

Behind the beautiful words about the renewing and transforming principle of life itself is concealed an embittered cry: "Leave me alone! Give me back what I had before—that is what is most important to me; I spit on all the rest!" A page later Zhivago says this in so many words:

"I admit that you are Russia's liberators, her shining lights—that without you she would be lost, sunk in poverty and ignorance. But for all that I have no use for you, I spit on you; I do not like you and say the hell with the lot of you."

It is hard to imagine a renegade position more base than this: Perhaps what you are doing for Russia is actually good, but I spit on it!

At one point in the book, Doctor Zhivago leaves the partisan detachment into which he had been impressed because there was no one to treat its wounded—and with which he had fired on the Whites though he sympathized with them and had treated the Reds though he felt revulsion for them—and returns to Yuryatin; he sees new decrees posted about the town, which has been occupied by the Reds. And he recalls the first decrees of the revolution, as his father-in-law had recalled them when they were leaving Moscow.

" 'What decrees are these,' he thinks, looking at them. 'Last year's? Year before last's?' Once in his life he had been carried away by the uncompromising nature of this language and the straightforwardness of this thought. Would he, in fact, have to pay for this moment of rash enthusiasm the rest of his life by seeing nothing but these clamorous cries and demands that, unchanging for years on end, become as time passes increasingly lifeless, unintelligible and impossible of fulfillment? Could it be that in a moment of expansive sympathy he had allowed himself to be enslaved forever?"

The thought that the revolution is winning is so oppressive to Zhivago that he is ready to curse himself—not, however, for anything he has done for the revolution, because he has done nothing, but merely for a single moment of enthusiasm for the first decrees of the Soviet regime!

Such is the philosophy of your novel's chief protagonist, a man who could no more be removed from it than a soul could be removed from a body. Such is the progression of his thoughts about the revolution; such is his prosecutor's tone; such is the strength of his hatred for the revolution.

One could cite many other passages from the novel where the same views are expressed under different circumstances and in different variations, but doubtless that would be superfluous; the general course of Doctor Zhivago's case against the revolution is clear enough without it.

One can say without hesitation that he conducts an unjust trial; moreover, the maliciousness of the injustice to which Zhivago resorts in his arguments about the revolution is compounded by his realization that he is powerless to impede its progress. Doctor Zhivago has ambivalent feelings: There is enough hatred of the revolution in him for two Denikins, but because at the same time he considers his own ego to be the most valuable thing in the world, he is unwilling to risk the safety of this ego by committing any outright counterrevolutionary action and, while long since committed to that side in spirit, he continues to stand between the two camps in body. The fourth chapter of book two of your novel is particularly indicative of this.

We have already made passing reference to this chapter, but in order to fully define the gulf that separates our view of Doctor Zhivago as you have limned him in the novel and your own attitude toward him as author, we feel that it is necessary to return to this chapter. It is not a long one; let us read it together in its entirety.

"The International Convention on the Red Cross forbids military doctors and orderlies to take armed part in the military operations of the belligerents. But on one occasion the Doctor was forced to break this rule. He was in the field when the action began, and he had to share the fate of the combatants and return the fire.

"The partisans the Doctor was with when the firing began held a position along the edge of a woods; he dropped to the ground beside the detachment's signalman. Behind the partisans lay the taiga; before them lay an open field, a bare, unprotected stretch across which the Whites were advancing.

"They kept advancing, and now they were quite close. The Doctor could see them clearly, make out their faces. They were boys and young men, civilians from the capital; and there were older men mobilized from the reserves. But it was the former—the young men, first-year university students and eighth-grade schoolboys who were recent volunteers—who set the pace.

"The Doctor knew none of them, but half their faces seemed familiar, as though he had seen them somewhere before. They reminded him of his old schoolmates. Perhaps they were their younger brothers? He felt as though he had met others in theater or street crowds in times past. Their expressive, fine-looking faces seemed near to him, as if these were his own people.

"Their call to duty as they understood it had instilled in them an overly zealous bravado, unnecessary, defiant. They advanced in a sparse, scattered formation, walking fully erect, surpassing in their bearing even the permanent members of the guards regiments, and scorning the danger, they made no effort to advance in short sprints from cover to cover, even though the field was uneven and dotted with hillocks and outcroppings behind which they could have shielded themselves. The partisans' bullets cut them down almost to a man.

"In the middle of the broad, bare field across which the Whites were advancing there stood a dead, charred tree. It might have been struck by lightning or scorched by the flames of a campfire or splintered and singed in earlier battles. Each of the advancing rifle volunteers cast a glance at it, fighting back the desire to duck behind it to get better aim and a safer shot, but disdained the temptation and continued to advance.

"The partisans were short of cartridges, and had to use them sparingly. There was an order, supported by general consent, to fire only at short range and only from as many rifles as there were targets.

"The Doctor lay in the grass without a weapon and watched the battle's progress. All his sympathies were on the side of the heroically dying youngsters. With all his heart he wished them success. They were the sons of families that were doubtless close to him in spirit, families with his education, his moral fiber and his mentality.

"It occurred to him to run out to the middle of the field and surrender and thus find deliverance. But such a step would be risky, dangerous.

"In the time it would take him to run to the center of the field with his hands up, he could be cut down from either front or back; by his own men as punishment for betrayal, or by the others through a failure to divine his intentions. He had been in similar situations several times before, had thought over all the possibilities and had long since rejected all these plans to save himself. So, resigning himself to his ambivalent feelings, the Doctor remained on his belly, facing the field, and watched, unarmed, the progress of the battle.

"But to remain a passive onlooker with a fight to the death raging around him was unthinkable and more than a man could stand. It was not a matter of loyalty to the camp that had drafted him against his will, not a matter of self-preservation, but a matter of conforming to the order of events, of submitting to the laws of what was happening in front of and around him. It was against the rules to remain indifferent to it. One had to do the same thing everyone else was doing. A battle was in progress. He and his comrades were being fired at. One had to return the fire.

"So when the signalman beside him in the line jerked convulsively and then lay still, stretched out and frozen motionless, Yury Andreyevich crawled over to him, took his rifle and cartridge pouch, crawled back and began to fire round after round.

"Pity prevented him from aiming at the young men he had been admiring and with whom he sympathized. But to shoot idly into the air would be too stupid, a waste of time and contrary to his intentions. So, waiting until no attackers were between him and his target, he began shooting at the charred tree. He had his own way of doing this.

"Sighting and gradually improving his aim, imperceptibly increasing his pressure on the trigger without pulling it full home—as though not even intending to shoot—until the fall of the firing pin and the shot followed of their own accord and as if contrary to expectations, the Doctor began with his customary precision to knock off the dry lower branches, scattering them around the dead tree.

"But—oh horror! Careful as the Doctor was not to hit anyone, first one, then another of the attackers stepped at the critical moment between him and the tree, crossing the line of sight just as the rifle went off. He grazed two of them, but the third, poor devil, paid with his life; he fell not far from the tree.

"Finally the White commanders, convinced of the uselessness of the attempt, gave the order to retreat.

"The partisans were few in number. Part of their main force was on the march and part had engaged a larger enemy force and moved off. The detachment, to avoid revealing how weak were its numbers, did not pursue the retreating enemy.

"Feldsher Angelyar brought two orderlies with a stretcher onto the field. The Doctor ordered them to see to the wounded and went over to where the signalman lay motionless. He vaguely hoped that the man might still be breathing and could be saved. But the signalman was dead. To make absolutely sure, Yury Andreyevich unbuttoned his shirt and listened to his heart. It was not beating.

"There was a small pouch hanging around the dead man's neck on a string. Yury Andreyevich removed it. Sewn in the scrap of cloth he found a small sheet of paper, rotted and crumbling at the folds. The Doctor spread it out.

"The paper contained excerpts from the 90th Psalm, with such changes and corruptions as creep into popular prayers from repetition to repetition, causing them to deviate increasingly from the original. The passages of the Church Slavonic text had been rewritten into everyday Russian.

"The psalm reads: 'The quick that dwelleth in the help of the Almighty.' A corrupt abridgement of this appeared at the top of the scrap of paper, 'Quick help.' The verse of the psalm that reads 'Thou shalt not fear * * * the arrow that flieth by day' had been changed to 'Thou shalt not fear * * * the flying arrow of war.' The psalm reads 'Because he hath known my name,' while the paper said 'It is late for my name.' 'I will be with him in tribulation; I will deliver him' had become 'Soon he will be delivered into winter.'

"The text of the psalm was believed to be miraculous, to be a protection against bullets. Soldiers had worn it as a talisman even in the last imperialist war. Decades later, prisoners would sew it in their clothing and would repeat it to themselves over and over when they were summoned in the night for interrogation by investigators.

"Yury Andreyevich left the signalman's body and went out onto the field, to the body of the young White Guard he had killed. The young man's handsome face bore the stamp of innocence and all-forgiving suffering. 'Why did I kill him?' the Doctor thought.

"He unbuttoned the dead man's tunic and opened it wide. 'Seryozha Rantsevich,' the dead man's name, had been embroidered in the lining in a careful and loving hand—his mother's, no doubt.

"A small cross, a medallion and some sort of flat gold case or snuffbox, its lid dented as if punched in by a nail, hung out of his shirt on a fine chain. The case was halfway open, and a folded piece of paper fell out of it. The Doctor opened it and could not believe his eyes. It was the very same 90th Psalm, only printed and in the full, original Slavonic text.

"Just then Seryozha groaned and stirred. He was alive and had, as it turned out, only been stunned by slight internal injuries. A spent bullet had struck the lid of this amulet from his mother; this had saved his life. But what was to be done with the unconscious boy?

"By this time the savagery of the combatants had attained its peak. Prisoners did not reach their destination alive, and enemy wounded were finished off with bayonets where they lay.

"Given the fluid state of the forest militia, with new volunteers constantly arriving and old partisans deserting to the enemy, it might be possible, if the secret were closely guarded, to pass Rantsevich off as a new, recently enlisted ally.

"Yury Andreyevich removed the signalman's outer garments and with the help of Angelyar, to whom he had divulged his plans, put them on the unconscious boy.

"He and the feldsher nursed the boy back to health. When Rantsevich was fully recovered, they let him go, even though he had not concealed from his saviors that he intended to return to Kolchak's forces and continue to fight the Reds."

After we had read the entire novel, our thoughts returned again and again to this chapter, because it contains the key to a great deal. We feel there can be no disputing the fact that the viewpoint of this entire chapter is one of the author's complete sympathy with Doctor Zhivago and of whole-hearted vindication of his thoughts and actions.

But what sort of thoughts, what sort of actions are these? Whom is it that you, as author, are sympathizing with, and what is it you are vindicating?

Let us recapitulate. The Doctor, mobilized against his will, is forced to serve with the partisans. Doctor Zhivago is, as you put it, forced to violate the International Convention on the Red Cross and to take part in the action. In the Doctor's eyes, the men attacking the partisan group are splendid, admirable and heroic. All his sympathies are on their side. They are close to him in spirit and in moral fiber; he wishes them success with all his heart; in other words, it would be no exaggeration to say that he is, in spirit, totally on their side. One wonders, then, what it is that keeps him from, as you put it, finding deliverance, from going over to their side physically as well. Nothing but the fact that this would endanger his life. That is the only reason! And you, apparently, feel quite seriously that this explanation suffices full well not only to explain but also to justify your hero's double-dealing. You call this by the more genteel term "ambivalence of feeling," but surely "ambivalence of feeling" is a somewhat mild term to apply to a man who, fighting alongside those he hates, shoots down those he loves merely to save his own skin.

And the entire following episode in which the Doctor shoots at the charred tree and, though not wanting to hit anyone, nevertheless cuts down three people who, as you so delicately put it, "crossed his line of sight just as the rifle went off"—all this smacks of Jesuitry, of the same Jesuitry that Doctor Zhivago himself is ready to accuse others of so frequently and so falsely. Here your Doctor Zhivago reminds us of the hypocritical monk who observes the fast by crossing the meat and calling it fish, the difference being that what is at stake here is not meat or fish but human blood and human lives.

Thus within a brief span of time your hero traverses a complex path of repeated treachery: He sympathizes with the Whites to the point of wanting to desert to them, but, lacking the resolve to do so, he at first begins simply shooting and ends up shooting at these very same Whites he sympathizes with. Then he feels pity not for the Whites but for the Red signalman the Whites have killed. After this he sympathizes with the

young White Guard he has killed and asks himself, "Why did I kill him?"
And when it turns out that the White soldier is not dead but has only
suffered slight internal injuries, he hides him and passes him off as a
partisan and, while remaining with the Reds himself, releases the young
man, who has told him that he will return to Kolchak's army and fight
against the Reds.

Such are the actions of your Doctor Zhivago, whose threefold, if not
fourfold, treachery can only arouse a feeling of outright revulsion in any
man who is even the slightest bit healthy spiritually or, setting aside for
the moment even differences in political views, in any subjectively honest
man who has ever, if only once in his life, valued his conscience above his
skin!

Yet you strive with the full force of your talents to find emotional
justification for Zhivago in this scene, and in doing so you are ultimately
brought to writing an apology for treachery.

What brings you to this apology? In our opinion it is that very same
individualism, hypertrophied to unbelievable proportions. In your eyes,
Zhivago the individual is a superior value. The spiritual world of Doctor
Zhivago is a superior level of spiritual development, and all crimes are
permitted in order to preserve this superior spiritual achievement and his
life as well, it being the vessel that contains this value.

However, what, ultimately, is the content of the superior spiritual
value of Doctor Zhivago, what is this individualism that he protects at such
a terrible price?

The content of his individualism is the self-glorification of his own
psychic essence, raised to a point of equating it with some sort of prophetic
mission.

Zhivago is not merely a doctor, he is a poet. And to convince the
reader that his poetry has true significance for mankind, which is how he
understands it himself, you end your novel with a collection of your hero's
poetry. In so doing you sacrifice the better part of your own poetic
talent to this character you have created in order to exalt him in the reader's eyes and, at the same time, to identify him as closely with yourself as
possible.

Doctor Zhivago has drunk his cup of earthly sorrow to the dregs; here,
then, is his notebook, his bequest to the future. What do we find in it? In
addition to the poems that have already been published, the poems about
Christ's path to the cross are particularly important for understanding the
philosophy of the novel. In these poems one hears a direct echo of the
hero's spiritual anguish as depicted in the prose part of the novel. The
parallels are made extremely clear; the author places a physically palpable
key to them in the hand of the reader.

The last of Zhivago's poems in the novel tells of the New Testament
"prayer of the cup" in the garden of Gethsemane. Christ's words to his
apostles include the phrase:

> "God has granted you
> To live in my time * * *"

Is this not, in fact, simply a repetition of the words the Doctor has already spoken about his "friends," the intellectuals who chose a course

different from his own: "The only bright and living thing about you is that you have lived in my time and known me"?

Zhivago's entire path is consistently likened to the passion of Christ, and the Doctor's notebook-testament in verse ends with the words of Christ:

> "Like a caravan of barges the centuries will float
> Toward me out of the darkness and I will judge them."

The novel ends with these words. As if repeating Christ's path to the cross on Golgotha, the hero of the novel, like Christ, prophesies, in his final words to the reader, the future recognition of the work he has done on earth to cleanse it of sin.

Does not Zhivago's "Road to Calvary" actually consist in the fact that the doctor-poet, in prophesying his "second coming" and sitting in judgment on man, has actually disdained living man and placed himself on a pedestal beyond the reach of ordinary mortals? Does not the true calling of this intellectual messiah consist in killing, betraying and hating mankind in order to save his own "soul," and feigning compassion for men only to elevate himself above them to the point of self-deification?

This is, in fact, the entire content of the superior spiritual value of Doctor Zhivago, his hypertrophied individualism. He does essentially nothing to realize his pretensions to a messianic mission because he distorts rather than repeats the path of the evangelical prophet he deifies: There is not the slightest hint of Christianity about Doctor Zhivago's dismal path because he is concerned least of all about mankind and most of all about himself.

Thus under cover of an outward sensitivity and morality there arises the figure of a man who is essentially immoral, who acknowledges no responsibility to the people, claiming only rights, including the right—allegedly permitted to supermen—of betrayal with impunity.

Your Doctor Zhivago, having steered a successful course between Scylla and Charybdis during the Civil War, dies at the end of the 1920's, after having lost his loved ones, entered into a strange sort of marriage and gone pretty much to seed. Not long before his death he has a conversation with Dudorov and Gordon (whom you have chosen to represent the members of the old intelligentsia who took the course of cooperation with the Soviet regime) in which, through them, he rewards this category of the intelligentsia with the vicious outpouring of a dying man's sputum.

And what a poor recommendation you give these unfortunate interlocutors of your Doctor Zhivago, how you condemn them for not having taken the stand of the superman, for having instead cast their lot with the revolutionary people and shared all their misfortunes and trials! They "lack the necessary means of expression," they are "ungifted in speech" and "to make up for their impoverished vocabulary they repeat the same thing over and over again." They suffer from "the misfortune of having average taste, which is worse than having no taste at all" and they are notable for their "inability to think freely or to conduct a conversation according to their own lights;" they are "enamored of their own stereotyped argument;" they "mistake the imitativeness of their copybook feelings for something universal;" they are also "hypocrites" and "unfree people idealizing their lack of freedom" and so on and so forth.

And, listening to them speak, your Doctor Zhivago, who, as you write, "could not stand the political mysticism of the Soviet intelligentsia, though it was the thing they regarded as their highest achievement or, as they would have said at that time, 'the spiritual ceiling of the era,'" arrogantly thinks of his friends who have chosen to serve the Soviet regime: "Yes, my friends, oh, how hopelessly commonplace you are—you and your circle, the brilliance and art of the names and authorities you quote. The only bright and living thing about you is that you have lived in my time and known me."

We advise you to read over carefully these words that you have written in your novel. The fact that they are ridiculously arrogant is bad enough, but surely you must realize that there is baseness in them as well as arrogance! Truth rarely accompanies bitterness; no doubt that is why there is so little truth in the part of your book in which your Doctor Zhivago dies and in the epilogue that follows, which we feel was written by an embittered and overly hasty hand, a hand in such haste from bitterness that it is difficult to regard these pages as literature.

You are no stranger to symbolism, and the death, or rather the passing, of Doctor Zhivago in the late 1920's is for you, we feel, a symbol of the death of the Russian intelligentsia, destroyed by the revolution. Yes, it must be admitted that for the Doctor Zhivago you depicted in the novel the climate of the revolution is deadly. And our disagreement with you is not over this but, as we have already mentioned, over something quite different.

To you, Doctor Zhivago is the peak of the spirit of the Russian intelligentsia.

To us, he is its swamp.

To you, the members of the Russian intelligentsia who took a different path from the one Doctor Zhivago took and who chose the course of serving the people betrayed their true calling, committed spiritual suicide and created nothing of value.

To us they found their true calling on precisely that path and continued to serve the people and to do for the people precisely the things that had been done for them—in laying the groundwork for the revolution—by the best segment of the Russian intelligentsia, which was then, and is today, infinitely remote from that conscious break with the people and ideological renegacy of which your Doctor Zhivago is the bearer.

To all that we have said there remains for us to add, with bitter regret, only a few words about how the people are depicted in your novel during the years of the revolution. This depiction, given mainly through Doctor Zhivago's eyes but at times in the form of direct narrative, is extremely characteristic of the antipopular spirit of your novel and profoundly contradicts the whole tradition of Russian literature which, while never fawning over the people, was, nonetheless, capable of seeing their beauty, their strength and their spiritual richness. But the people as depicted in your novel are divided into the good-hearted wanderers who cling to Doctor Zhivago and those close to him, and the creatures, half man, half beast, who personify the elemental forces of the revolution—or rather, as you see it, of the insurrection, the riot.

In order that this claim not go unsubstantiated, here are a few quotations in support of what has been said. We present them this time without commentary, one after another, to make our point clearer.

"At the beginning of the revolution, it was feared, on the strength of what had happened in 1905, that this revolution would also be a short-lived event in the history of the educated upper classes and would not touch the lower strata of society, would sink no roots in it, and every effort was made to propagandize the people, to spread revolution among them, to stir them up, muddle and enrage them."

"During those first days, people like the soldier Pamfil Palykh who, with no goading whatsoever, hated intellectuals, the gentry and officers with a fierce, brutal hatred were considered by the fervid leftist intellectuals to be rare finds and were very highly valued. Their inhumanity seemed a marvel of class consciousness, their barbarism a model of proletarian firmness and revolutionary instinct. Such was the fame that had accrued to Pamfil. He was held in the highest esteem by partisan chiefs and Party leaders."

"Chairs were set out for the honored guests; they were occupied by three or four workers who had taken part in the first revolution, including Tiverzin, morose and changed, and old Antipov, his constant friend and yes-man. Numbered among the divine hierarchy at whose feet the revolution had laid all its gifts and victims, they sat like silent and stern idols in whom everything living and human had been extinguished by political arrogance."

"It was a time that bore out the old saying: Man is a wolf to man. Travelers gave one another a wide berth, passers-by killed one another in order not to be killed themselves. There were isolated cases of cannibalism. The human laws of civilization no longer held. The law of the jungle prevailed. Man dreamed the prehistoric dreams of the cave-man era."

Many more such quotations could be cited, but those given above are sufficiently characteristic to show how the people, or at any rate those from among the people who participated actively in the revolution, are depicted in your novel. It is for precisely this participation that your heroes —and you along with them—are angry with them.

As yet we have hardly touched on the literary aspect of your novel. On this score it should be noted that because the novel is disjointed— even incoherent—in plot and composition, the impressions one gains from the various pages of the novel never cohere into a single, over-all picture but remain isolated.

The novel contains many pages of first-class writing, particularly in those places where your perceptions and impressions of Russian nature are recorded with amazing accuracy and poetry.

It also contains many clearly inferior pages, pages devoid of life and disfigured by didacticism. Such pages are particularly numerous in the second half of the novel.

However, we do not wish to dwell at any great length on this aspect of the matter, as we have already pointed out at the beginning of our letter: The crux of our argument with you has nothing to do with esthetic wrangling. You have written a novel that is distinctly and primarily a political sermon. You designed it as a work openly and completely placed at the service of specific political aims. And since that was the most important thing for you, it naturally became the principal object of our attention as well.

As unpleasant as it has been for us, we have had to call things by their proper names in our letter to you. We feel that your novel is profoundly unjust, that it lacks objectivity in its depiction of the revolution, the Civil War and the postrevolutionary years, that it is profoundly antidemocratic and alien to any conceivable understanding of the interests of the people. All this, by and large, stems from your position as a man who strives to show in his novel not only that the October Socialist Revolution had no positive importance in the history of our people and of mankind but that, on the contrary, it brought nothing but evil and misfortune.

As people whose position is diametrically opposed to yours, we naturally feel that publication of your novel in the magazine *Novyi Mir* is out of the question.

As concerns the bitterness with which you wrote your novel—leaving aside, for a moment, your ideological position as such—we would, recalling that in the past you have written things that differ greatly from the views you now express, like to remind you in the words that your own heroine addresses to Doctor Zhivago: "You have changed. You used to judge the revolution less harshly, without bitterness."

But the main thing, of course, is not the bitterness, because this is merely an accompaniment to ideas that have been refuted by history, bankrupt ideas that are doomed to perish. If you are still capable of thinking seriously about this, then give it some thought. In spite of everything, that is what we would like.

We are returning your manuscript of the novel *Doctor Zhivago*.

> B. Agapov
> B. Lavrenev
> K. Fedin
> K. Simonov
> A. Krivitsky

September 1956.

Selective Glossary

Apparatchiki: a derisive Russian term for members of the "establishment"; the equivalent of "organization men."

Azev: a leader of the Socialist Revolutionary Party who turned out to have been a police agent.

The Bell (Kolokol): an émigré journal published by Alexander Herzen in London 1857-1867; it served as an organ of liberal and socialist opinion.

Bolshevik: a member of Lenin's faction of the Russian Social-Democratic Labor Party which in 1919 was renamed the Communist Party.

Boyars: members of the ancient Russian aristocracy, distinguished from the servitor gentry *(dvoriane).*

Decembrists: participants in the abortive attempt at revolution in December 1825.

Duma: the lower house of the bicameral Russian parliament (1906-1917), consisting of elected representatives and endowed with extensive legislative powers.

Dvorianstvo (dvoriane): the Russian landed gentry.

The Great Reforms: the reforms carried out by the government of Alexander II, principally in the 1860's, including the abolition of serfdom and the introduction of local self-government in the cities and in the countryside (see *zemstvo).*

Kadets (Constitutional Democrats): members of Russia's principal liberal party, founded in 1905.

Kolkhoz: a collective farm.

Komsomol: the Communist Youth League, an organization for Soviet youths that serves as a preparatory training ground for membership in the Communist Party.

Menshevik: a member of that faction of the Russian Social Democratic Labor Party which emphasized the need for democratic procedures and was suppressed by Lenin shortly after he came to power.

Meshchanstvo: the Russian equivalent of "bourgeoisie."

NEP (New Economic Policy): the policy of granting peasants and traders a certain measure of private initiative; it was introduced by Lenin in 1921; in 1928 it was replaced with the program of planned economy and forced industrialization.

Obshchestvenniki: men active in public life in the USSR.

Obshchina (mir): the Russian peasant commune, much idealized by the Slavophiles and the Populists.

October Revolution: the coup that the Bolsheviks engineered in October 1917 against the Provisional Government and that led to the establishment of the Soviet government.

Octobrists: members of the Octobrist Party, a conservative party founded at the close of the 1905 revolution.

OGPU: the Soviet secret police 1924-1934.

People's Will *(Narodnaia Volia):* a terrorist organization that emerged within Populism in 1879 and eventually succeeded in assassinating Alexander II (1881).

Populism: a revolutionary movement, particularly active in the 1870's, whose adherents believed Russia could avoid going through the capitalist phase of development and build socialism on indigenous bases, of which the Russian commune *(obshchina)* was the most important.

Pugachev: the leader of the great peasant rebellion that took place in the eastern provinces of Russia in the reign of Catherine II (1773-1775).

Rabfaki: workers' high schools in the Soviet Union.

Revolution of 1905: disturbances throughout Russia that terminated with the granting of a constitution (1905-1906).

Shock-brigaders (Stakhanovites): members of labor unions who in the 1930's pledged themselves to exceed the working norms set by the government.

Slavophiles: adherents of the Slavophile doctrine formulated in the 1840's and 1850's; it held that Russia's culture and social order were qualitatively different from and superior to those of the West.

Social Democrats: members of the Russian Socialist-Democratic Labor Party, a Marxist party founded in 1898 that later split into the Menshevik and Bolshevik factions.

Socialist Realism: the official Soviet aesthetic doctrine, which among other things rejects modern art forms.

Socialist Revolutionaries: members of the Socialist-Revolutionary Party, a neo-Populist terrorist party founded at the turn of the century.

Sovkhoz: a collective farm operated directly by organs of the Soviet government.

Sovnarkhozy (Sovety Narodnogo Khoziaistva): institutions of local economic administration established by Khrushchev in an effort to decentralize the economic apparatus.

"Superfluous man": a term coined by Turgenev in the 1850's to describe enlightened Russians who found no outlet in society for their talents.

Tekhnikumy: intermediate professional schools in Soviet Russia.

Third Section: the department of the Imperial Chancery under Nicholas I (1825-1855) that was concerned with state security and censorship.

Vekhi: a symposium published in 1909 on the initiative of M. O. Gershenzon; it contained a strong condemnation of the political, intellectual, and moral qualities of the contemporary Russian intelligentsia (see pp. 29-30, 42).

Vuzy (Vyshshye uchebnye zavedeniia): all institutions of higher learning in the Soviet Union.

Westerners: the opponents of the Slavophiles; they upheld the view that Russia's path was essentially identical with that of the West.

Zemstvo: organs of local self-rule founded by the government in 1864.

Notes on Authors

DAVID BURG, born in Moscow in 1933, is at present a research student at King's College, Cambridge, where he is engaged on work in Russian literature. As a student of both English and Russian universities, he is especially interested in current developments in Soviet intellectual life. He has contributed articles in this field to various periodicals here and abroad, under his present pseudonym.

BORIS ELKIN, born in Kiev, Russia, in 1887, became a member of the St. Petersburg bar upon graduating from the University of St. Petersburg. Subsequently he served on the editorial board of the weekly law journal, *Pravo*. In 1919 he left Russia, going first to Berlin, then to Paris; for the last twenty years he has lived in London.

LEOPOLD H. HAIMSON, born in Brussels, 1927, is professor of Russian history at the University of Chicago and director of the project on the history of the Menshevik movement in Russia. A graduate of Harvard University, he has held academic posts at Columbia University and at Harvard. His publications include *The Russian Marxist and the Origins of Bolshevism*.

MAX HAYWARD, born in London in 1924, is a Fellow of St. Antony's College at Oxford University. From 1947 to 1949 he was attached to the British Embassy in Moscow. From 1949 to 1951 he was lecturer in Russian at Oxford, and from 1951 to 1955 head of the department of Russian language and literature at the University of Leeds. With Manya Harari, he prepared the English translation of Boris Pasternak's *Dr. Zhivago*.

DAVID JORAVSKY, born in Chicago in 1925, is professor of history at Brown University. After graduating from the University of Pennsylvania, he received his doctoral degree from Columbia University. His major interest is the intellectual history of modern Russia. Aided by grants from the Social Research Council and the American Academy of Arts and Sciences, he has prepared *Soviet Marxism and Natural Science, 1917-1932* (in press). His article in this volume is based on a chapter from that book.

LEOPOLD LABEDZ, born in Simbirsk in 1920, was educated first in Warsaw, and then at the universities of Paris and Bologna. In 1953 he graduated from the London School of Economics and Political Science, where he has since been engaged in research, especially in the field of Soviet ideology and social structure. An editor of the journal *Soviet Survey*, he also writes a monthly column, "From the Other Shore," in *Encounter*, and contributes to numerous other periodicals.

MARTIN MALIA, born in Springfield, Massachusetts, in 1924, received his doctoral degree at Harvard University, and is presently professor of Russian history at the University of California at Berkeley. Among his contributions to Slavic studies, he has edited (with Hugh McLean and George Fischer) *Russian Thought and Politics* (Harvard Slavic Studies, 4), and is the author of *Alexander Herzen and the Birth of Russian Socialism, 1812-1855* (in press).

229

Julián Marías, born in Valladolid, Spain, in 1914, was a cofounder, with Ortega y Gasset, of the Instituto de Humanidades, and has made a special study of the latter's philosophical system. Professor Marías has taught at Wellesley College, Harvard University, and the University of California (Los Angeles), Yale University, and (as research professor) at the University of Puerto Rico. Among his books are: *Historia de la Filosofía; Introducción a la Filosofía* (translated as *Reason and Life*); *Miguel de Unamuno; La Estructura Social;* and *Los Estados Unidos en Filosofía;* four of the six volumes of his Obras have already appeared.

Richard Pipes, born in Cieszyn, Poland, in 1923, is professor of history at Harvard University. His principal interest is in modern Russian history, particularly that of political thought and institutions, and imperial policy. Among his publications are *The Formation of the Soviet Union,* and *Karamzin's Memoir on Ancient and Modern Russia.*

Leonard Schapiro, born in Glasgow in 1908, spent his childhood in Russia. He was educated at the University of London, and in 1932 he began practice at the bar. During World War II he served as an officer of the General Staff. Thereafter he returned to legal practice, but in 1955 joined the staff of the London School of Economics and Political Science, where he is now reader in Russian government and politics. His publications include *The Origin of the Communist Autocracy,* and *The Communist Party of the Soviet Union.* At present he is engaged on the history of the Russian Social Democratic Party.

Benjamin I. Schwartz, born in Boston in 1916, is professor of history and government in the area of East Asian studies at Harvard University. Modern China is his particular interest, and he is the author of *Chinese Communism and the Rise of Mao.* At present he is engaged on a study of the intellectual development of China in the twentieth century.

Gustav A. Wetter, S.J., born at Mödling, Austria, in 1911, is professor of the history of Russian philosophy at the Pontificio Istituto Orientale at Rome. His principal publication is *Il materialismo dialettico sovietico,* which has appeared in English as *Dialectical Materialism: A History and Systematic Survey of Philosophy in the Soviet Union.*

Index

Academy of Sciences, Russian, "renovation" of, 124 ff.
Afinogenov, Alexander, *Fear,* cited, 128
Aksakov, Konstantin, quoted, 19-20
Alexander II, reforms of, 21-22
Aleksandrov, A. D., 145, 146, 147, 148-49, 198; "The Philosophical Content and Significance of the Theory of Relativity," 195-96
All-Union Conference on the Philosophic Problems of Modern Natural Science, 142
Ambartsumian, V. A., 150, `"Some Methodological Problems of Cosmogony," 197-98
Annenkov, P. V., quoted, 26
Anokhin, P. K., discussion of paper, 199
Apparatchiki, 88-89

Bakh, A. N., 123
Bakunin, Mikhail, 168, quoted, 79
Belinskii, Vissarion, 168
Bell, The, 25, 29
Berdiaev, Nikolai, view of the intelligentsia, 5; cited, 141
Biology, Russian views on, 150-58, 200-6
Blochintsev, D. I., 145-46; discussion of paper, 200
Bohm, David, 145, 200
Bohr, Niels, 143, 144, 146, 147, 196, 199; *Atomic Physics and Human Knowledge,* 147, 196-97
Bolsheviks, 36-42 *passim,* 46
Born, Max, 194, 199
Boyars, 52-53
Broglie, Louis de, 145, 197, 199, 200

Chaadaev, Peter, *Philosophical Letters,* 20-21
Ch'en Tu-hsiu, 174
Chernov, Victor, quoted, 40
Chiang Kai-shek, 173
Chicherin, B. N., 22, 24-27, 33; quoted, 25, 25-26
Child, Richard Washburn, *Potential Russia,* quoted, 63-64
China, Western influences in, 174-75, 176-77
Civil War, Spanish, 184-85
Conference on philosophical problems of science (October, 1958), 192 ff.

Confucian tradition, and Chinese intelligentsia, 171
Congress of Mathematicians, 132-33
Congress of Physiologists, 131-32
"Copenhagen school," 143-47, 196-97
Cosmogony, Russian views on, 197-98
Criqui, André, cited, 158
Cybernetics, 197

Dan, F., quoted, 34-35, 37, 40
Deborin, A. M., 125
Decembrists, 9-11
"Defensists," 43
Dewey, John, 174
Dubinin, Mikhail, 158
Dudintsev, Vladimir, 112, 115; *Not by Bread Alone,* 117, 119-20, cited, 60; quoted, 109, 120
Duma: first, 38-39; second, 39-40; third, 40-41; fourth, 40, 41, 43

Education, Russian, 13-14; *see also* Higher education, Russian; Mass education, Russian; Universities, Russian
Egorov, D. F., 132-33
Ehrenburg, Ilya, *The Second Day,* 118; *The Thaw,* 117, 119, quoted, 116
Einstein, Albert, 148-50 *passim*
"Ends and Beginnings" (Herzen), 29
Engelgart, V. A., and G. M. Frank, "On the Role of Physics and Chemistry in the Investigation of Biological Problems," 200-1
Engels, F., *Die Dialektik der Natur,* quoted, 162
Evtushenko, Evgenii Aleksandrovich, 119; quoted, 100, 121

Fedoseev, P. N., 155, speech of, 207
Feng Yu-lan, 173
Feuerbachianism, 56
Fischer, George, *Russian Liberalism,* quoted, 79
Fok, V. A., 145, 146-47, 148, 199; "On the Interpretation of Quantum Mechanics," 196-97
Fonvizin, Denis, quoted, 19
France, Fonvizin's view of, 19
Frank, G. M., *see* Engelgart, V. A.
Frank, Philipp, quoted, 193
Frank, S., quoted, 38
Friche, V. M., 125

Date Due

JUL 7 '81		
AUG 1 8 '81		
FEB 2 '62		
MAR 6 '64		
FEB 2 6 '65		
OCT 3 1 1970		
OCT 3 1 1970		
NOV 2 6 1975		
DE 28 '77		